The Abrahamic Encounter

The Abrahamic Encounter

Local Initiatives, Large Implications

Edited by Mazhar Jalil, Norman Hosansky, and Paul D. Numrich

Foreword by Robert P. Sellers

WIPF & STOCK · Eugene, Oregon

THE ABRAHAMIC ENCOUNTER
Local Initiatives, Large Implications

Copyright © 2016 Wipf and Stock Publishers. All rights reserved. Except for brief quotations in critical publications or reviews, no part of this book may be reproduced in any manner without prior written permission from the publisher. Write: Permissions, Wipf and Stock Publishers, 199 W. 8th Ave., Suite 3, Eugene, OR 97401.

Wipf & Stock
An Imprint of Wipf and Stock Publishers
199 W. 8th Ave., Suite 3
Eugene, OR 97401

www.wipfandstock.com

PAPERBACK ISBN: 978-1-4982-3461-0
HARDCOVER ISBN: 978-1-4982-8664-0
EBOOK ISBN: 978-1-4982-7600-9

Manufactured in the U.S.A.   SEPTEMBER 20, 2016

Chapters that appeared originally in *Muslims and Christians, Muslims and Jews: A Common Past, A Hopeful Future*, edited by Marilyn Robinson Waldman (Columbus: Islamic Foundation of Central Ohio, 1992), and *Muslims and Jews: Building a Hopeful Future*, edited by Norman Hosansky and Mazhar Jalil (Columbus: Islamic Foundation of Central Ohio, 2003), are used by permission.

From all three editors: To all of the children of Abraham who want to live as friends and neighbors.

From Mazhar Jalil: For my wife Betty, who is sunshine to me in winter, coolness and shade in summer, and who loves reading stories of Prophet Abraham to our children.

From Norman Hosansky: For the memory of my wife Gladys, a child of Abraham who welcomed all with open arms.

From Paul Numrich: For my wife Christine, who visited Abraham's tomb in Hebron with me.

Contents

Foreword by Robert P. Sellers | ix

Acknowledgements | xiii

Abbreviations | xiv

Contributors | xv

Introduction by Paul D. Numrich | xix

Part I: Local Initiatives, Large Implications | 1

    1: The Central Ohio Abrahamic Encounter | 3
        Paul D. Numrich

Part II: Circles of Scripture, Community, and Interpretation | 41

    2: Scripture and Community | 43
        Tamar Frank

    3: On Scripture and Its Exegesis: The Abraham-Ishmael Stories in the Torah and the Qur'an | 53
        Reuven Firestone

    4: Mary, Mother of Jesus, in Christian and Islamic Traditions | 64
        R. Marston Speight

    5: Jesus in the Qur'an: Some Similarities and Differences with the New Testament | 78
        Muzammil H. Siddiqi

    6: People of the Book: Potential Uniting Themes and Barriers to Unifying Dialogue | 90
        Jamal A. Badawi

Contents

Part III: The Past Is Never Dead | 103

    7: Historical Perspectives on Christian-Muslim Relations | 105
        Marilyn Robinson Waldman

    8: Historical Perspectives on Jewish-Muslim Relations | 114
        Marilyn Robinson Waldman

    9: A Historical Perspective on Jewish-Muslim Relations | 124
        Reuven Firestone

    10: Muslims and Jews in America | 132
        Sayyid M. Syeed

    11: Jewish and Muslim Perspectives on Intermarriage and Gender Roles | 139
        Nancy Heiden, Fatima Agha Al-Hayani, Batya Steinlauf, and Asma Mobin-Uddin

    12: The Moral Obligation of Muslim-Jewish Relations | 154
        Walter Ruby

    13: Christians as a Majority in the United States | 163
        Thomas Templeton Taylor

    14: American Christians and Their Abrahamic Neighbors | 172
        Paul D. Numrich

Foreword

Robert P. Sellers

INTERRELIGIOUS RELATIONSHIP-BUILDING, WHICH LEADS to mutual understanding and acceptance, constructive dialogue, and meaningful cooperation to address common global dilemmas, is the passion of my life. No other path, it seems, can lead us away from the dangerous precipice that threatens to undo the Human Family. Failing to connect positively will only further our stereotypes and misunderstandings, fear and rejection of the Other, arrogant and self-promoting monologues, and disruptive or even deadly confrontations.

That is why, as someone committed unequivocally to the interfaith movement, I am so impressed with the work of the Central Ohio Abrahamic Encounter and with this collection of informative, stimulating essays. While the history and contemporary associations between groups of Baha'is, Buddhists, Confucians, Hindus, Jains, Pagans, Sikhs, Taoists, Zoroastrians, and followers of Indigenous Religions, New Thought, Shinto, or Yoruba certainly fascinate me, I have been an active Christian since childhood and thus am particularly interested in the intersection of the three major Abrahamic religions—Judaism, Christianity, and Islam.

I was a small boy in Pensacola, Florida, where "religious diversity" largely signaled the presence and influence of Protestant and Catholic Christians, although interestingly Temple Beth-El in the town center was the oldest Jewish house of worship in the state. Moving to the larger city of Tampa as a seventh grader, however, I soon became friends with Tommy, a Jewish classmate—and attending his bar mitzvah was the first opportunity I had to experience a religious service somewhere other than in my Baptist church. Going to the synagogue on Shabbat and hearing my friend chant the blessings and read a portion of the Torah from the large scroll on the pulpit whetted my curiosity as a rather sheltered thirteen-year old. Today, more than fifty years after our high school graduation, Tom and I have re-established our friendship and serve as fellow trustees of the Parliament of the World's Religions.

The majority of my adult life has been spent internationally, primarily in Indonesia, the nation with the largest Muslim population in the world. For almost a quarter century, my wife, children, and I lived in Muslim neighborhoods where we enjoyed the gracious and kind people who were our friends and acquaintances. During those years, I gradually became aware of the high standards of personal morality and interpersonal respect that guided the lives of most Indonesian Muslims whom we encountered.

More recently, as a scholar-activist participating in local, national, and international organizations, it has been my privilege to develop friendships and to work with fascinating people who are committed to the interfaith movement. We have conducted our deliberations and launched projects from different starting points. The particularities of our belief systems have produced diverse opinions about complicated issues like solutions to climate change or the end of conflict in the Middle East, or about more practical matters such as governance or scheduling, yet we have worked through these alternative perspectives by intentionally treating one another as valued colleagues and genuine friends. What we have gained—far beyond consensus on controversial public statements or agreement on mundane programming decisions—has been the lasting enrichment of our very lives.

It seems to me that my experience of personal growth and interpersonal engagement with followers of other faiths is not unlike what has been experienced by the authors of this volume. Whether through entering one another's sacred spaces to increase understanding and appreciation for both similarities and differences in worship; sharing life together as individuals or families in homes, across meal tables, or on backyard patios; offering scholarly seminars and conferences to dispel popular myths and provide accurate information; standing in solidarity with mosques, synagogues, or churches damaged by natural disasters or vandalism; or working together on peace projects with elementary school children or teenagers—the Jews, Muslims, and Christians referenced here have given us a model for healing our increasingly xenophobic and fractured society.

Foreword

This book should be treasured as a valuable resource for the interfaith movement. Its account in Part I of promising multi-religious activities in Central Ohio can be inspiring for grassroots organizations everywhere. The essays in Part II provide helpful and perhaps unfamiliar information concerning textual foundations for these three "Peoples of the Book." The examination in Part III of the interfaith relations among these Abrahamic religions—in their historical, contemporary, global, and local manifestations—demonstrates a way forward.

I commend this fine work to your careful reading. *The Abrahamic Encounter* is not just about Ohio. It is about all of us—and not simply American Jews, Christians, or Muslims. The lessons of interfaith relationships herein hold an important key for building a more productive future for the whole world—a world that, in the mission statement of the Parliament of the World's Religions, will one day be more "just, peaceful, and sustainable." To that end, may we all commit ourselves anew.

Acknowledgements

MANY MORE PEOPLE HAVE participated in the Central Ohio Abrahamic encounter than appear in this volume. Omissions have been practical or unintentional, for which we beg forgiveness. We are indebted to all the interviewees who informed the story told in chapter 1; the following consented to be named: Rev. Timothy C. Ahrens, Dr. Tarunjit Singh Butalia, Rabbi Harold Berman, Jack Chomsky, Rev. Ward Cornett III, Robert C. Harrod, Norman Hosansky, Mazhar Jalil, Shani Kadis, Dr. John Kashubeck, Jeri Milburn, Dr. Asma Mobin-Uddin, Msgr. Stephan J. Moloney, Dr. Alam Payind, Richard C. Pfeiffer Jr., Rev. Leslie E. Stansbery, Rabbi Michael N. Ungar, and Rabbi Misha Zinkow. Special thanks go to Tariq Jalil for his advice and support, to Tarunjit Butalia for his wise counsel, to the staff at Wipf and Stock Publishers, especially Brian Palmer and Matthew Wimer, for their helpful professionalism, and to Tim Van Meter of Methodist Theological School in Ohio (MTSO) for recommending Wipf and Stock to us. Our interview procedures were approved by the human subjects research committees of MTSO and Trinity Lutheran Seminary and conducted by seminarians Sam Byrd, Jess Peacock, and Rina Shere of MTSO, and Stephen Zeller of Trinity. Ray Olson, Trinity's Hamma Library Director, and Trinity seminarian Ben Sloss provided valuable expertise on the digital interview files. Trinity seminarians Rick Catrone and Alexandria Long served as research assistants during this project. Alex deserves special commendation for her indispensable contributions to the preparation of this volume.

Abbreviations

Ali—Abdullah Yusuf Ali, *The Meaning of the Holy Qur'an*, 11th ed. (Beltsville, MD: Amana, 2004).

NIV—New International Version translation of the Bible (Zondervan).

NJPS—*Tanakh: The Holy Scriptures: The New JPS Translation according to the Traditional Hebrew Text* (Philadelphia: Jewish Publication Society, 1985).

RSV—Revised Standard Version of the Bible, copyright 1952 [2nd edition, 1971] by the Division of Christian Education of the National Council of the Churches of Christ in the United States of America. Used by permission. All rights reserved.

Contributors

Fatima Agha Al-Hayani was an instructor in Honors French and Honors English with the Swanton Board of Education in Swanton, Ohio at the time of the original publication of her contribution to this volume. She received a Master degree from the University of Toledo and both Master and PhD degrees from the University of Michigan. She is the author of the articles "Arabs and the American Legal System: Cultural and Political Ramifications" (1999) and "Islam and Science: Contradiction or Concordance" (2005).

Jamal A. Badawi is Emeritus Professor at Saint Mary's University, Halifax. In 2008, Saint Mary's granted him an Honorary Doctorate of Civil Law in recognition of his contributions to "civil society around the world." His publications include *Gender Equity in Islam* (1995) and *Leadership: An Islamic Perspective* (co-authored with Beekun Rafiq Issa, 1999). He is a member of the Islamic Juridical Council of North America, the European Council of Fatwa and Research, and the International Union of Islamic Scholars. He received his PhD in personnel management and labor economics from Indiana University in 1970.

Reuven Firestone received his PhD in Near Eastern languages and literatures from New York University in 1988 and his Rabbinic Ordination from Hebrew Union College in 1982. He is Regenstein Professor in Medieval Judaism and Islam at Hebrew Union College and a Senior Fellow at the Center for Religion and Civic Culture (CRCC) and the University of Southern California. He founded the Center for Muslim-Jewish Engagement, a joint program of the CRCC, Hebrew Union College, and the Omar Ibn Al-Khattab Foundation. His publications include *An Introduction to Islam for Jews* (2008) and *Who Are the Real Chosen People?* (2008).

Tamar Frank was Program Consultant to the Maurice Amado Foundation Sephardic Education Project in Cincinnati, Ohio at the time of the original publication of her contribution to this volume. She received her PhD in medieval studies from Yale University in 1975. She went on to teach at Solomon Schechter Day School in West Orange, New Jersey.

Nancy Heiden worked with interfaith couples in which one partner is Jewish in her position as Project Director of GATEWAYS at the Jewish Community Center of Columbus at the time of the original publication of her contribution to this volume. Previous to that, she taught in the adult education program at Congregation Tifereth Israel in Columbus.

Norman Hosansky received his PhD in organic chemistry from Rutgers University in 1953 and is retired from Chemical Abstracts Service, Columbus, after twenty-six years of service. He is a lay leader of Congregation Tifereth Israel in Columbus and co-edited (with Mazhar Jalil) *Muslims and Jews: Building a Hopeful Future* (2003). He received the Living Faith Award from the Metropolitan Area Church Council in 2006.

Mazhar Jalil received his PhD in biology from the University of Waterloo, Canada in 1967 and an "Alumni of Honour" award on the University's fiftieth anniversary in 2007. He is retired from the Ohio Department of Health, serves as a trustee of Islamic Foundation of Central Ohio in Columbus, and has been a longstanding member of the Interfaith Association of Central Ohio. In 2004, Ohio Governor Bob Taft presented him with the prestigious Martin Luther King Holiday Commission's Community Building Award for his interfaith work.

Asma Mobin-Uddin is a pediatrician in Central Ohio and a graduate of Ohio State University. She is the author of *My Name Is Bilal* (2005), *The Best Eid Ever* (2007), and *A Party in Ramadan* (2009), and is a member of the Society of Children's Book Writers and Illustrators. She has served as President of the Ohio chapter of the Council on American-Islamic Relations and on the Education Committee of the Interfaith Association of Central Ohio.

Paul D. Numrich received his PhD in religion from Northwestern University in 1992 and serves as Professor in the Snowden Chair for the Study of Religion and Interreligious Relations at Methodist Theological School in Ohio and Professor of World Religions and Interreligious Relations at Trinity Lutheran Seminary. His publications include the book *The Faith Next Door: American Christians and Their New Religious Neighbors* (2009) and the article "Christian Sensitivity in Interreligious Relations" in *The Asbury Journal* (2012).

CONTRIBUTORS

Walter Ruby is Muslim Jewish Program Director for the Foundation for Ethnic Understanding. He organized the Foundation's first national summit of imams and rabbis in New York City in 2007. He has served as a correspondent for the *Jerusalem Post* and *The Forward* as well as a contributor to *New York Jewish Week* and *New York Daily News*.

Robert P. Sellers, a lifelong Christian and Baptist who received his PhD in theological ethics and world religions from The Southern Baptist Theological Seminary in 1993, recently retired as professor of theology at Logsdon Seminary of Hardin-Simmons University. For almost twenty-five years he worked in Indonesia, where he grew to appreciate diverse cultures and ancient religions. Since 2000 he has been committed to the interfaith movement through his membership on commissions of the National Council of Churches, the Baptist World Alliance, and the Parliament of the World's Religions, which he currently serves as Chair.

Muzammil H. Siddiqi was Director of the Islamic Society of Orange County, California at the time of the original publication of his contribution to this volume. He is a graduate of Islamic University in Medina (Saudi Arabia) and Darul Uloom Nadwatul Ulama in Lucknow (India). He received his PhD in comparative religion from Harvard University in 1978.

The late **R. Marston Speight** was Director of the Office on Christian-Muslim Relations of the National Council of Churches of Christ in the U.S.A. and an adjunct faculty member of Hartford Seminary at the time of the original publication of his contribution to this volume. He was ordained in the United Methodist Church in 1963 and received his PhD in the history of religions from Hartford Seminary Foundation in 1970.

Batya Steinlauf is President of both the InterFaith Conference of Metropolitan Washington and the Montgomery County (Maryland) Executive's Faith Community Advisory Group. She also serves as Director of Social Justice Initiatives and Inter-group Relations for the Jewish Community Relations Council of Greater Washington. She is a graduate of Jewish Theological Seminary.

Sayyid M. Syeed is National Director of the Office of Interfaith and Community Alliances, Islamic Society of North America (ISNA). He served as President of the Muslim Students Association of U.S.A. and Canada from 1980 to 1983, where he was instrumental in its transition into ISNA. He has also served as Secretary General of the International Islamic Federation of Student Organizations, as General Secretary of the Association of Muslim Social Scientists, and as a founder and Editor-in-Chief of the *American*

Journal of Islamic Social Sciences. He received his PhD in sociolinguistics from Indiana University in 1984.

Thomas Templeton Taylor was Assistant Professor of History at Wittenberg University in Springfield, Ohio at the time of the original publication of his contribution to this volume. He received his PhD in history from the University of Illinois in 1988. He is the author of *The Spirit of the Awakening: The Pneumatology of New England's Great Awakening in Historical and Theological Context* (1990).

The late **Marilyn Robinson Waldman** was Professor of History and Comparative Studies at Ohio State University at the time of the original publication of her contributions to this volume. She received her PhD in history from the University of Chicago in 1974. She was the author of *Toward a Theory of Historical Narrative: A Case Study in Perso-Islamicate Historiography* (1980) and *Prophecy and Power: Muhammad and the Qur'an in the Light of Comparison* (posthumously, 2012).

Introduction

Paul D. Numrich

THE STATE OF OHIO has gained national notoriety in the contentious politics of recent decades. In 2010, three Ohio universities started The Ohio Civility Project in order to address the "lack of civility in public discourse in the United States." Ohio was chosen "because it is a bellwether state in national elections."[1]

During these same decades, the central part of the state, around the capital city of Columbus, has quietly modeled positive interfaith relations, especially among the Abrahamic faiths. "Everything is local," the saying goes. The story told in this volume is local, but the editors— a Muslim, a Jew, and a Christian—believe that an Abrahamic encounter in the American heartland has national implications. Here is a local story that can inform—even inspire—other communities across the country.

About This Volume

This volume will appeal to the growing audience for interfaith resources, particularly regarding the major Abrahamic faiths (Judaism, Christianity, and Islam). Books on Abrahamic relations are plentiful but few derive from local initiatives. The inclusion of several essays by noted religious scholars and leaders, chosen for their significance to the Central Ohio Abrahamic agenda, sets this volume apart from other publications on local initiatives. It is well-suited for individual or group study in churches, synagogues,

---

1. "Ohio Civility Project," 1.

INTRODUCTION

mosques, and interfaith organizations, and can also be assigned for undergraduate and seminary courses on Abrahamic relations or interfaith relations generally.

In Part I, "Local Initiatives, Large Implications," chapter 1 chronicles "The Central Ohio Abrahamic Encounter" and explores its larger implications as a model for other communities across the United States. In the chapter, I identify the three goals of the Central Ohio Abrahamic encounter (enhancing mutual understanding and relationships, disseminating accurate information about the three major Abrahamic traditions, and contributing to the general betterment of society), trace the history of Abrahamic relations in Central Ohio through two time periods (Jewish-Christian relations from the late 1800s to the 1970s and Jewish-Christian-Muslim relations since the 1980s), identify key strategies and challenges of the Central Ohio Abrahamic encounter, and assess the Central Ohio case as a model of Abrahamic relations. Chapter 1 also describes a series of local public conferences from which several chapters in parts II and III derive. These conferences provide insights into how Central Ohio Abrahamic leaders have determined their own agenda, drawing upon the resources they deem most relevant to their time, context, and faith commitments.

There is good reason for the Islamic designation for Jews and Christians as People of the Book since all three faiths draw deeply from their respective sacred texts for identity and guidance. The five chapters of part II, "Circles of Scripture, Community, and Interpretation," explore how these faith communities have been formed by their scriptures and how they interpret scripture vis-à-vis each other.

Chapter 2, "Scripture and Community" by Tamar Frank, provides a theoretical framework for part II in examining how a religious community's "circle of scripture and traditional interpretation" interacts with other circles. Frank exemplifies this interaction by focusing on three "reference points" in Judaism and Islam (prophecy, scripture, and authoritative interpretation), concluding with the hope that "whatever direction our communities take in the future, they will remain open to dialogues and to cooperation for the public benefit."

Reuven Firestone's "On Scripture and Its Exegesis: The Abraham-Ishmael Stories in the Torah and the Qur'an" (chapter 3) analyzes stories surrounding Abraham in Jewish and Islamic scriptures in order to highlight common practices used by communities in reading each other's texts, such as "older scripture is interpreted through the lenses of newer

Introduction

scripture" and "newer claims for sacred scripture can never be acceptable to older traditions if the new claims were made after the canonization of the earlier scripture." Firestone spotlights the variations between Jewish and Muslim versions of the Abraham-Ishmael story, concluding that "We must overcome the need to figure out 'who was right,' and move on to more important issues."

In chapter 4, "Mary, Mother of Jesus, in Christian and Islamic Traditions," R. Marston Speight focuses on the treatments of Mary in the New Testament and the Qur'an, suggesting that it is this "Scriptural figure of Mary that draws Muslims and Christians together." "Perhaps in mutual contemplation of this holy woman," Speight hopes, "we shall together learn to deal more adequately with our religious disagreements."

Chapter 5, "Jesus in the Qur'an: Some Similarities and Differences with the New Testament" by Muzammil H. Siddiqi, moves the reader from the scriptural figure of Mary to that of Jesus. Siddiqi squarely addresses both similarities and differences between New Testament and qur'anic portrayals of Jesus, as well as key doctrinal disagreements between the two religions. "Instead of shying away from discussion," Siddiqi concludes, "we should talk about these issues in an atmosphere of friendship and frankness."

Jamal A. Badawi turns our attention to "People of the Book: Potential Uniting Themes and Barriers to Unifying Dialogue" in chapter 6. Surveying themes found in both Judaism and Islam (such as perspectives on God, prophets, and morality) and barriers that have been erected between the two religions (including historical legacies and misuses of scriptures), Badawi ends by offering a plea to Muslims and Jews to work together for the common good through practical dialogues.

William Faulkner wrote, "The past is never dead. It's not even past." The eight chapters of part III, "The Past Is Never Dead," explore historical and contemporary relations among the Abrahamic faiths.

In chapters 7 and 8, Marilyn Robinson Waldman applies historical lessons to the contemporary American context. Chapter 7, "Historical Perspectives on Christian-Muslim Relations," alerts us to four "unfamiliar facts": the significance of Eastern Christianity's interaction with Islam, the long history of Christian-Muslim contact, the minority status of Christianity in most Muslim contexts, and the integral relationship between religion and nationality or ethnicity in areas of the world with large numbers of Christians and Muslims. Christian-Muslim relations in the United States represent a critical historical moment in which Muslims live as a minority in a society that claims to value religious diversity.

Chapter 8, "Historical Perspectives on Jewish-Muslim Relations," surveys the "changeable pattern of mutual influence" between Jews and Muslims using four historical case studies: the initial Muslim period in Arabia, the early Abbasid Empire, Al-Andalus (Muslim Spain), and the Ottoman Empire. Waldman again applies past lessons to the United States where Jews and Muslims live together as minorities in a society that claims to value religious diversity. She writes, "The history of Jewish-Muslim interaction provides us with enough resources to make the kind of creative adaptations so often required of Jews and Muslims in the past."

In chapter 9, "A Historical Perspective on Jewish-Muslim Relations," Reuven Firestone describes the realities of the so-called Golden Age of Jewish-Muslim relations in the Middle Ages, which included both positive and negative aspects and carries a legacy of deeply ingrained prejudices. Firestone advocates Jewish-Muslim cooperation for mutual benefit in the United States today.

Sayyid M. Syeed's "Muslims and Jews in America" (chapter 10) examines the Muslim community's position in contemporary America, drawing comparisons with the previous experiences of Catholics and Jews as well as highlighting key challenges in Muslim-Jewish relations in the United States, ranging from Middle East tensions to intermarriage.

The experiences of Jewish and Muslim women provide the focus for chapter 11, "Jewish and Muslim Perspectives on Intermarriage and Gender Roles" by Nancy Heiden, Fatima Agha Al-Hayani, Batya Steinlauf, and Asma Mobin-Uddin. The Jewish Heiden and the Muslim Al-Hayani explore the challenges for both religions posed by intermarriage trends in the American context, while the Jewish Steinlauf and the Muslim Mobin-Uddin consider "the struggle to find a balance between tradition and modernity" (as Steinlauf puts it) in women's roles in the United States.

Walter Ruby asserts "The Moral Obligation of Muslim-Jewish Relations" in chapter 12. He describes the Foundation for Ethnic Understanding's Weekend of Twinning program that pairs local synagogues and mosques for annual dialogues that can blossom into long-term cooperative relationships, contending that American Muslims and Jews have a moral imperative to model such relationships for the rest of the world.

In chapter 13, "Christians as a Majority in the United States," Thomas Templeton Taylor surveys demographic and theological shifts in the

Introduction

Christian population of the United States at the end of the twentieth century, concluding that "there is not one Christian majority in America." "There are serious implications here for Muslims," writes Taylor, including different approaches to Islam by evangelical and liberal Christians. "As a nation, we face fundamental questions about the role of religion in the public sphere; the answers to these questions will be as important to Muslims as they are to Christians."

The volume concludes with my own "American Christians and Their Abrahamic Neighbors" (chapter 14), which updates the national snapshot of Taylor's chapter and surveys various Christian approaches to neighbors of other faiths. I offer a deep Christian foundation for civil discourse and gracious relations with Jews, Muslims, and others regardless of one's Christian theological perspective or denominational identity.

Chapters 2, 3, 4, 5, 7, 8, 11, and 13 appeared originally in *Muslims and Christians, Muslims and Jews: A Common Past, A Hopeful Future*, edited by Marilyn Robinson Waldman (Columbus: Islamic Foundation of Central Ohio, 1992), and *Muslims and Jews: Building a Hopeful Future*, edited by Norman Hosansky and Mazhar Jalil (Columbus: Islamic Foundation of Central Ohio, 2003). These chapters have been edited to correct minor errors and to conform to the publisher's style requirements, such as rendering pronouns for God in lower case when in the author's voice (upper case is retained in scriptural quotations). Occasional editorial comments are inserted and indicated by brackets, thusly: [Ed.:] or [ed.:]. Qur'an quotations from Abdullah Yusuf Ali's translation have been standardized according to *The Meaning of the Holy Qur'an*, 11th ed. (Beltsville, MD: Amana, 2004).

Chapters 6, 9, 10, and 12 were first presented at the Muslims and Jews: Yesterday, Today and Tomorrow Together conference on December 6, 2009 in Columbus, Ohio. The authors have revised their talks for publication in this volume.

This volume could not have come to fruition without Mazhar Jalil and Norman Hosansky, who not only co-edited it but have served as the primary exemplars of the Central Ohio Abrahamic encounter (see chapter 1). It has been my honor and joy to collaborate with them for the greater Abrahamic good.

I joined the Central Ohio Abrahamic encounter only recently (in 2004) but I quickly grasped its significance. Celebrating civility is important in uncivil times, but that is too weak a compliment for what I have witnessed. More than merely "civil" to each other as fellow citizens, the

Abrahamic participants engage one another from religious motivations as well. As the president of Islamic Foundation of Central Ohio has written: "We are all creatures of our Creator, be it God or Allah; we are all descendants of Abraham; we all wish to live in peace, prosperity, happiness, and security.... As Americans partaking of the fruits of our country, we have the opportunity to help others. It must start here with us."[2]

This volume is presented with the hope that wherever the Abrahamic encounter has begun or will begin, it will be enhanced by the Central Ohio model.

Bibliography

Khan, Sohail. "Greetings from the Sponsors." In *Muslims and Christians, Muslims and Jews: A Common Past, A Hopeful Future*, edited by Marilyn Robinson Waldman, 2. Columbus: Islamic Foundation of Central Ohio, 1992.

"The Ohio Civility Project: Report and Recommendations." http://www.uakron.edu/bliss/about-us/ohio-civility-project.dot?newsId=2328165.

2. S. Khan, "Greetings from the Sponsors."

PART I

Local Initiatives, Large Implications

1

The Central Ohio Abrahamic Encounter

Paul D. Numrich[1]

> "To see Hosansky and Jalil come together, or even Christian, Jewish, and Muslim youth come together and be visibly present together in a public space—a lot of folks think this can never happen."

THIS QUOTE FROM TARUNJIT Singh Butalia, past president of the Interfaith Association of Central Ohio, references the friendship of two elder statesmen of the Central Ohio Abrahamic encounter. Mazhar Jalil is a Muslim leader from Islamic Foundation of Central Ohio, Norman Hosansky a Jewish leader from Congregation Tifereth Israel—a mere three lots apart on East Broad Street in Columbus, Ohio. As a local university professor told us, "They walked across that short distance between their institutions on Broad Street and opened up a door."

The relationships between these two individuals and the mosque and synagogue they represent epitomize the story told in this volume: the ardent desire to cross the boundary lines of the three major Abrahamic traditions—Judaism, Islam, and Christianity—in order to open the door to enhanced mutual understanding and relationships, dissemination of accurate information about these traditions, and general betterment of society. At times the distance is less than a city block, at other times the three faiths

---

1. My thanks to Tarunjit Singh Butalia and Christina Butler, past presidents of the Interfaith Association of Central Ohio, for contributing information and text to this chapter.

seem worlds apart. Sometimes the door opens, sometimes it does not. And sometimes a door that once stood open closes. Butalia's mention of the youth points up a fervent hope of those involved in the local Abrahamic encounter: that its trajectory will continue into the future.

Before chronicling the Central Ohio Abrahamic encounter, allow me to identify a type of engagement that will not be considered in this chapter, namely, organized proselytizing (to use the generic, albeit loaded term). Not surprisingly given Jewish history, there is no organized Jewish proselytizing of non-Jews in Central Ohio.[2] Nationally, Islamic *da'wah* (literally "to call or invite") has two main purposes, one to support Muslim identity and practice, the other to present Islam to non-Muslims, typically through lifestyle witness and dissemination of accurate information about Islam. In Central Ohio, *da'wah* toward non-Muslims is largely informal and decentralized but it does motivate some of the Islamic efforts described in this essay.[3] In Christian circles, although many local churches self-identify as evangelical, few see Central Ohio Jews and Muslims as a mission field.[4]

History of the Central Ohio Abrahamic Encounter

The state of Ohio has been predominantly Christian since the advent of European-American settlement in the late 1700s. Jews began arriving in the early 1800s, first in Cincinnati and by 1838 in Columbus. The first Muslim presence in Ohio may have been some African Muslim slaves in the late 1700s, but the first Muslim community—immigrants from the Middle East—emerged in Toledo in the late 1800s. The Muslim presence in Columbus is post–World War II, comprising Ohio State University students, immigrant professionals, and African Americans, the last group establishing the first mosque in Columbus, Masjid Al-Islam / Muslim Community Center, in 1962. Although such estimates are speculative, by the early twenty-first century Jews in Central Ohio numbered 22,000 and Muslims

---

2. Cf. D. Berger, "Reflections on Conversion and Proselytizing."

3. On *da'wah* in the United States, see Poston, *Islamic Da'wah in the West*. For a typical articulation of lifestyle witness to non-Muslims, see "Dr. Houcine Chouat."

4. Exceptions would include two local congregations of the Messianic Jewish movement that seeks to convince Jews of the messiahship of Jesus Christ (Beth Messiah Congregation of Columbus, http://www.bethmessiah.org/, and Congregation Shabbat Yeshua in suburban Delaware, http://acts1728ministries.org/home.html), and churches that partner with World Relief Columbus (see chapter 14 in this volume).

20,000-35,000, the latter population swelled by large-scale resettlement of Somali refugees since the 1990s.[5]

Late 1800s to the 1970s: Jewish-Christian Relations

The chronology of the Central Ohio Abrahamic encounter generally mirrors the national interfaith movement that most observers see as beginning with the World's Parliament of Religions held in Chicago in 1893, whose President, John Henry Barrows, later served as President of Oberlin College in Ohio. Early milestones of this interfaith movement included the founding of the National Conference of Christians and Jews in 1927 (now called the National Conference for Community and Justice), the decision of the Wichita (Kansas) Council of Churches in the 1930s to expand beyond its Protestant constituency to include Jews, Roman Catholics, and Orthodox Christians (later called Inter-Faith Ministries), the establishment of the Temple of Understanding in New York City in 1960, and the formation of a national branch of the international organization, Religions for Peace, in the early 1970s. The 1980s was a watershed decade: one study listed only twenty-four interfaith councils in 1980, but a directory published a few years later had 125 groups plus an umbrella organization, North American Interfaith Network, that was established in 1988 following a gathering hosted by Inter-Faith Ministries of Wichita. At this writing, the directory of the Pluralism Project at Harvard University lists more than 1,000 interfaith organizations across the United States.[6]

Likewise in Central Ohio, at first only Jews and Christians engaged each other and broader Abrahamic relationships developed much later. Jewish-Christian interaction in Columbus actually predates the 1893 World's Parliament by two decades. Large numbers of Christians attended

---

5. Information in this paragraph is gleaned from Smith, "Muslim Columbus"; http://www.facebook.com/pages/Masjid-al-Islam-Columbus/207355192620815?id=207355192620815&sk=info; Butalia and Small, *Religion in Ohio*; Jewish Federation of Columbus, http://columbusjewishfederation.org/page.aspx?id=38432; Hoover, "Rising Voice"; Nelson, "Some Thoughts on the U.S. Muslim Population"; and "Guide to Somali Culture."

6. http://www.pluralism.org/directory/country:US/tag:8. Information in this paragraph is gleaned from "America's Interfaith Infrastructure"; Gray, "What Excites Me about Interfaith Work?"; Sussman, "'Toward Better Understanding'"; and McCarthy, *Interfaith Encounters in America*. Also, see the Websites of National Conference for Community and Justice (https://nccj.org/), Inter-Faith Ministries (http://www.interfaithwichita.org/), Temple of Understanding (http://templeofunderstanding.org), Religions for Peace (http://www.religionsforpeace.org/), and North American Interfaith Network (http://nain.org).

services at B'nai Israel, a Reform synagogue later renamed Temple Israel, during the tenure of its first rabbi, Judah Wechsler (served 1870–1873). Rabbi Wechsler also regularly invited Christian clergy to participate in worship services and confirmation class examinations. Subsequent rabbis at B'nai Israel continued to invest time and energy toward enhancing local Jewish-Christian relations. Rabbi Louis Weiss (served 1893–1896) believed that "[t]he task of Reform Judaism must be to unite Christians and Jews." Christians, he wrote, "today are our friends, our neighbors, our brothers." Rabbi Joseph Kornfeld (served 1906–1921) instituted Sunday morning "nondenominational" worship services designed for "Jews and Gentiles." Kornfeld's successor, Rabbi Jacob Tarshish (served 1922–1932), augmented the Sunday morning service with lectures broadcast on local radio that catapulted him to public celebrity status. By 1929 he added Sunday evening talks that drew audiences of both Jews and Christians. B'nai Israel's next rabbi, Samuel Gup (served 1932–1946), engaged in "a continual flurry" of Jewish-Christian activities, "which ranged from interfaith dinners, sharing temple facilities with churches recovering from fires or rebuilding, preaching at Protestant and Catholic churches, serving as vice-president of the Franklin County Ministerial Association, and sponsoring annual 'Institutes on Judaism for Christian Clergy and Educators.'"[7]

Into the 1970s, Jewish-Christian relations in Columbus were largely Reform-Christian relations. Orthodox synagogues tended to focus on their own constituents, with the notable exception of Agudas Achim which participated in interreligious services. Historian (and rabbi) Marc Lee Raphael observes that the Reform rabbis "got on splendidly with their Christian counterparts." Raphael's 1975 survey of Columbus Jews reflected great admiration for those rabbis who serve as a "messenger to the gentiles," "keeping the bridges of communication open between Jews and non-Jews."[8]

In 1978, Temple Beth Shalom (Reform), led by Rabbi Raphael, entered into a rental agreement with Eastminster Presbyterian Church on East Broad Street in Columbus, pastored by Rev. Robert Butz. During the Jewish worship services, a portable Torah ark was brought into the sanctuary and the Christian cross was covered with a banner of the Star of David. In the 1990s, led by Rabbi Howard Apothaker, Beth Shalom purchased land for a new building in the Columbus suburb of New Albany, requesting that

---

7. Raphael, *Jews and Judaism in a Midwestern Community*, 62-64, 189–92, 196–97, 273–75.

8. Ibid., 198, 380, 362.

the adjoining plot be sold to a mainline church. Beth Shalom today shares a common entrance and parking lot with All Saints Episcopal Church, and the two congregations hold a joint annual Thanksgiving prayer service.

1980s to the Present: Abrahamic Relations

Broad Street and Beyond

In the wake of the arrival of the first Muslim students and immigrant professionals in Columbus in the 1950s and 1960s, Islamic Foundation of Central Ohio was established in 1972 and acquired its current facility on East Broad Street in 1976.[9] In 1984, Mazhar Jalil led a delegation of Muslims to meet with State Senator Richard Pfeiffer to request support for an annual statewide Islamic Day. They brought letters of endorsement from leaders of the Jewish and Christian communities as well. Islamic Day in Ohio was proclaimed by Governor Richard Celeste in 1987 and reaffirmed by his successor George Voinovich. It is organized by the Islamic Council of Ohio and celebrated its twenty-eighth anniversary in 2015 at the Islamic Center of Cleveland.[10]

Jalil's next initiative marked the beginning of sustained Jewish-Muslim relations in Central Ohio. Jalil reminisces that in the mid-1980s, "Whenever I passed the synagogue [Congregation Tifereth Israel] on my way to prayers or study, I would wonder what went on in there and what the Jewish people who worshiped there were like."[11] So in January of 1985 he wrote a letter to the synagogue's Rabbi Harold Berman expressing concern about tensions between Muslims and Jews abroad and suggesting that they meet to discuss how the two communities in Columbus might get to know each other. Rabbi Berman accepted the invitation immediately, writing that his congregation shared the same concerns and hopes.[12]

But geographic proximity is not sufficient cause for a synagogue and a mosque to enter into an amicable institutional relationship. As noted, a Reform synagogue in Columbus may likely do so, an Orthodox synagogue much less likely. Tifereth Israel originated in 1901 as an Orthodox congregation but declared itself Conservative in 1922, a "modern Orthodox"

---

9. M. Khan, "Islam," 290.
10. The Website for the Islamic Council of Ohio is http://ic-ohio.org/.
11. Jalil, "Muslims and Jews."
12. Correspondence between Mazhar Jalil and Harold Berman, January 18 and 24, 1985.

synagogue in the words of its trustees.[13] Its progressive identity, along with Rabbi Berman's "very important formative experience" in an innovative interfaith program during his seminary years, made for receptivity to Jalil's overture in 1985.[14]

The two met at Tifereth Israel. "Dr. Jalil spoke of his desire to have more contact with the synagogue," Rabbi Berman reports, "and to be able to exchange views not only on religious questions and on common elements of our history, but also on practical issues of minority life in an American Christian society." A second meeting at Islamic Foundation included leaders from both congregations. "We discovered," Rabbi Berman continues, "a community of people with whom we have a lot in common and who also felt that they have a lot in common with us. We recognized that we could learn from each other."[15]

The rabbi enlisted Norman Hosansky to work on behalf of the synagogue with Jalil. This led to a deep personal friendship between Hosansky and Jalil as well as a durable institutional partnership between the synagogue and the mosque. One of the most treasured symbols of this relationship is also profoundly simple: the fact that Tifereth Israel makes its parking lot available to worshipers attending Jumah (midday Friday) prayers at Islamic Foundation.[16] Early joint activities of the two congregations included lectures on a variety of religious and practical issues (especially surrounding their shared minority status), social events, and reciprocal letter writing on topics of joy or concern. People met not only at the mosque and the synagogue but also in members' homes and even in a public park for a picnic.

The first of four major public conferences took place on March 19, 1989, titled Muslims and Jews: A Common Past, A Hopeful Future. As Rabbi Berman explains, "In order to avoid questions of bias or control, we did not use any Jewish community or any Muslim community sources of funding. We also did not meet in either of our buildings, but used a downtown hotel instead."[17] In addition to Islamic Foundation and Tifereth Israel, the conference was co-sponsored by three academic centers at Ohio State University and supported financially by the Ohio Humanities Council

---

13. Raphael, *Jews and Judaism in a Midwestern Community*, 182, 186.

14. "Interview with Rabbi Harold Berman."

15. Berman, "Jewish-Muslim Dialogue in Our Communities," 111.

16. On the importance of "parking lot friendships," see Kniss and Numrich, *Sacred Assemblies and Civic Engagement*, chapter 10.

17. Berman, "Jewish-Muslim Dialogue in Our Communities," 113.

and the National Endowment for the Humanities. A follow-up session was held at the Columbus Museum of Art; also, groups from the mosque and synagogue met several times for fellowship and study.

Mazhar Jalil next set his eyes on engaging local Christians in a deliberate fashion. A small effort had been made even before Islamic Foundation was established when Muslims rented space in an Episcopal church near Ohio State University for an Islamic Sunday school.[18] Now Jalil approached Bishop James Griffin of the Catholic Diocese of Columbus with the idea of "establishing a formal relationship to promote dialogue between Muslims and Christians." Bishop Griffin appointed Fr. Stephan Moloney, Vice-Chancellor of the diocese, to coordinate the effort with Jalil. Meeting at Islamic Foundation in September of 1989, a small group of local Christian and Muslim leaders signed an agreement that spelled out their intention to dialogue with each other:

> Dialogue presupposes that each side wishes to know the other, and wishes to increase and deepen its knowledge of the other. It constitutes a particularly suitable means of favoring a better mutual knowledge and of probing the riches of one's own tradition. Dialogue demands respect for the other as he is; above all for his faith and his religious convictions.[19]

These efforts led to a second major public conference on March 25, 1990, titled Muslims and Christians: Common Themes, Distinctive Identities, also held at a downtown hotel. This conference was co-sponsored by Islamic Foundation and the Diocese of Columbus, in cooperation with the Metropolitan Area Church Board under the leadership of Executive Director Rev. Robert Erickson. The conference received financial support from the Ohio Humanities Council, the National Endowment for the Humanities, and the Columbus Foundation. Follow-up Christian-Muslim dialogues were held in church and mosque venues on the topics of law and justice, interfaith marriage, the arts, charity and fasting, religious and moral resources for Middle East peace, religious women, holidays and traditions, conflict and peace through the centuries, and social service and social justice.

Proceedings from these first two conferences form the core of a 1992 book, *Muslims and Christians, Muslims and Jews: A Common Past, A Hopeful Future*, published by Islamic Foundation in association with the Catholic Diocese of Columbus and Congregation Tifereth Israel. The book's

---

18. Smith, "Muslim Columbus," 10.
19. Moloney, "On-Going Muslim-Christian Dialogue," 107; also, see 109.

PART I: LOCAL INITIATIVES, LARGE IMPLICATIONS

editor, Marilyn Waldman, Professor of History and Comparative Studies at Ohio State University, summarized the purposes of the conferences as well as the book: "[T]o inform the general community about the historical, religious, ethical, and social commonalities of American Christians, Jews, and Muslims; to lessen the ignorance that leads to intolerance, fear, and strife; and to inform the media in a way that would contribute to reasonable and balanced reporting and editorializing."[20] Islamic Foundation's president, Sohail Khan, expressed the hope that the future would carry forward the successes of the past: "This volume, and the years of cooperation that have made it possible, should be the springboard toward achieving greater understanding, tolerance, and acceptance of other religions, cultures, and traditions. I hope that we do not stop here."[21] According to now-Monsignor Moloney, the Vatican was so impressed with the book that it requested a copy for its files.

A third major public conference, Muslims and Jews: Exploring Our Future Together, was held on November 9, 1997. Like the first conference, it was co-sponsored by Islamic Foundation, Tifereth Israel, and the three Ohio State University academic centers. Also lending support this time were the Leo Yassenoff Foundation, Bank One, and the Kobacker Foundation. Proceedings from the first conference plus this third conference and two follow-up sessions form the core of the book *Muslims and Jews: Building a Hopeful Future*, published several years later by Islamic Foundation in association with Tifereth Israel.[22]

Note that the Abrahamic activity in Columbus described thus far occurred well before the events of September 11, 2001. The fruits of the accumulated goodwill became evident in the aftermath of an "incident [that] shocked this growing city, which . . . considers itself a paragon of tolerance in the Midwest," as *The Christian Science Monitor* put it.[23]

When worshipers arrived at Islamic Foundation for morning prayers on Sunday, December 30, 2001, they discovered that the mosque had been severely vandalized. Water and other damages were estimated at $100,000, while some evidence suggested possible anti-Muslim motives. Other

---

20. Waldman, "Preface."
21. S. Khan, "Greetings from the Sponsors."
22. Hosansky and Jalil, *Muslims and Jews*.
23. Ghose, "Tides of Support"; also, see "Nation Challenged." The following account is pieced together from these articles and our interviews.

mosques in Ohio had been vandalized in the weeks after September 11 and Islamic Foundation had recently received a threatening letter.

Rabbi Harold Berman and Cantor Jack Chomsky of Congregation Tifereth Israel heard about the incident after their own morning services. "We went right to their door," Cantor Chomsky recalls, "and said, 'What can we do?' We stood with them. We said, 'This is terrible, it shouldn't happen in our community.... And we said, 'If you need a place to pray, feel free to come here [to the synagogue].'" "They were the first people who came to our mosque in sympathy," says Mazhar Jalil with gratitude.

The media were already at the mosque when the two leaders from Tifereth Israel arrived. A photographer captured Rabbi Berman offering help and he soon began receiving newspaper clippings from acquaintances across the country. "I didn't mean to make a big deal out of it. I just meant to be a good neighbor," he says today. The upshot: it became well publicized that in Central Ohio, "Jews and Muslims were neighbors and wanted to help each other."

Others joined Tifereth Israel in offering help, including the Columbus Rotary Club. After 150 people braved the cold weather in a rally of support, a spokesperson for the mosque said, "We may have a few people doing bad things, but . . . we have an awful lot of people with good hearts." Nearby First Congregational Church (United Church of Christ) housed the Islamic school during the mosque's renovation. A media report carried a quip about Christian-Muslim commonalities from senior pastor Rev. Timothy Ahrens: "I stuck my head in one of the classes, and I said, 'Are you all happy to be back in school?' All the girls said yes, and all the boys said no. It was just like my school." Reflecting on the vandalism incident, Rev. Ahrens says today, "Relationship is formed when you stand together around something."

A renovated Islamic Foundation was dedicated on a Saturday in January of 2003. Tarunjit Butalia, one of the speakers at the event, recalls his surprise at seeing Rabbi Harold Berman and Cantor Jack Chomsky there on the Jewish Sabbath. Rabbi Berman explained to him, "There are many things prohibited on the Sabbath, but this isn't one of them. I needed to be here today with my friends at the dedication of their mosque."

The events of 9/11 prompted many small but much appreciated tokens of support for the local Muslim community. One Muslim leader recalls spontaneous warm regards, neighbors stopping by to chat or leaving flowers on the doorstep, even homemade brownies delivered to the Islamic school.

Part I: Local Initiatives, Large Implications

9/11 also prompted a flurry of local Abrahamic youth activity. Monthly or bi-monthly programs involved youth groups from Tifereth Israel, Islamic Foundation, and several churches. "The teens would teach the teens," says Tifereth Israel's long-time youth director, Shani Kadis, especially about debunking the religious stereotypes floating around in the cultural atmosphere of the time. These activities trailed off after a while, likely for the practical reasons that make any youth programming difficult to sustain.

On April 7, 2002, Islamic Foundation, Tifereth Israel, and the Diocese of Columbus co-sponsored the International Campaign for Religious Tolerance and Understanding Forum held at Ohio State University. Mazhar Jalil was instrumental in bringing the keynote speaker, Francis Cardinal Arinze, President of the Pontifical Council for Interreligious Dialogue, to Columbus from the Vatican.

In 2005, Jalil and Norman Hosansky joined Ohio State University's Professor Amy Horowitz and others in a project called Living Jerusalem—Living Columbus, which described itself with the following questions: "Living Jerusalem: How do people of different cultures share knowledge of their heritage and practices across the borders between ethnic spaces, especially in disputed territories? Living Columbus: If Columbus were to become the model for religious understanding among Jews, Muslims, and Christians, how would we get there and what would our model look like?" The local component of this project included tours of Columbus neighborhoods by youth from Tifereth Israel and Islamic Foundation, and the Salaam, Shalom, Peace Project involving elementary school children from Sunrise Academy (Islamic), Columbus Jewish Day School, and St. Joseph Montessori School (Catholic). According to Horowitz, the purpose of the latter project was "to have children at each school think about what is important to them about their schools. Once children meet each other, any fears or misunderstandings are dissipated at a very young age."[24]

Over a span of fourteen months in 2007–2008, a steering committee comprising Jalil, Hosansky, Rev. Leslie Stansbery, an ordained Presbyterian minister, and for a time Deacon Thomas Berg of the Diocese of Columbus organized an Interfaith Community Dinner that rotated locally: St. Andrew Catholic Church, Columbus (September 2007); a Muslim home in Marion, Ohio (November 2007); Church of the Resurrection (Catholic),

---

24. Quoted in Jarman, "Show and Tell for Peace." On the project, see http://mershoncenter.osu.edu/expertise/ideas/livingjerusalem.htm; http://outreach.osu.edu/2005EinEGrants.php.

New Albany, Ohio (December 2007); Congregation Tifereth Israel (February and November 2008); Covenant Presbyterian Church, Columbus (May 2008); Sunrise Academy (Muslim), Hilliard, Ohio (June 2008); and Noor Islamic Cultural Center, Dublin, Ohio (August 2008). These dinners included both a formal program and informal table talk. Socializing, or the "schmooze" factor as Norman Hosansky calls it, was an important part of these gatherings. Food has the potential to put people at ease, but it can also put people on edge. Despite some early concerns about the dietary requirements of Judaism (*kashrut*) and Islam (*halal*), "We found we could work with each other," reports Hosansky. Another Jewish interviewee points out the significance of Christians respecting Jewish and Muslim restrictions while preparing these dinners.

In 2008, Tifereth Israel and Islamic Foundation joined a national program called Weekend of Twinning sponsored by the New York-based Foundation for Ethnic Understanding. "[T]he Weekend of Twinning is an annual initiative based on synagogues, mosques and Muslim and Jewish student and young leadership groups forming partnerships and holding joint programs together with the goal of building ties of communication, reconciliation and cooperation between Muslims and Jews." Norman Hosansky summed up the reasons for the Columbus participation in the program: "It's a way for the two groups to realize their similarities. We've both experienced prejudice against our communities. We can support them, and they can support us."[25]

The fourth major public conference took place on December 6, 2009 at a hotel near the Ohio State University campus. Sponsored by Tifereth Israel and Islamic Foundation, it was billed as The Third Muslim-Jewish Conference, harkening back to the 1989 and 1997 conferences, with the specific title of Muslims and Jews: Yesterday, Today and Tomorrow Together.[26] In his remarks at the conference, Mazhar Jalil looked hopefully to the Jewish-Muslim future in America: "I am confident that our combined energies will help build a new world of respect, enlightenment, and peace, as existed, for the most part, during the so-called Golden Age in Spain."[27]

---

25. The Weekend of Twinning program is described at http://www.ffeu.org/twinning.html. The Hosansky quote is from "Jews, Muslims to Discuss Ways." Also, see chapter 12 in this volume.

26. A two-DVD set of the conference was produced by Hoberg Studios, Inc., 1953 Bluff Avenue, Columbus, OH 43212.

27. Jalil, "Muslims and Jews."

PART I: LOCAL INITIATIVES, LARGE IMPLICATIONS

The four major public conferences (1989, 1990, 1997, 2009) were all bilateral, pairing Muslims with either Jews (three of the four) or Christians, which Mazhar Jalil explains by saying that "Muslims are the new kids on the block" in America.

Several of the key figures mentioned above have received local honors for their positive contributions to the Abrahamic encounter and other interfaith activities. The Metropolitan Area Church Council (now the Spirituality Network) has presented Living Faith Awards to Richard Pfeiffer (2003), Norman Hosansky (2006), Rev. Leslie Stansbery (2006), Mazhar Jalil (2007), Cantor Jack Chomsky (2011), and Rev. Timothy Ahrens (2014).[28] In 2004, the Ohio Martin Luther King Holiday Commission gave its Community Building Award to Rabbi Harold Berman, Mazhar Jalil, and Monsignor Stephan Moloney for working together to promote interfaith unity. Jalil fondly recalls Ohio Governor Bob Taft personally presenting the awards to the three and their loved ones.

Other Local Abrahamic Relationships and Initiatives

The previous section described initiatives rippling out from the relationship between the Broad Street neighbors Islamic Foundation of Central Ohio and Congregation Tifereth Israel. There are other relationships and initiatives that enliven Central Ohio's Abrahamic encounter, sometimes overlapping with the above.

The Interfaith Association of Central Ohio (IACO) traces its origin to an interfaith prayer service in November of 1985 held at yet another place of worship on Broad Street in Columbus, Trinity Episcopal Church. Planning for the service was headed by Rev. Leslie Stansbery, Rabbi Howard Apothaker of Temple Beth Shalom, and Kas Mohammed of Islamic Foundation.[29] Rabbi Apothaker served as IACO's first president.

IACO's membership has always been wider than the Abrahamic faiths, initially five traditions (Buddhism, Christianity, Hinduism, Islam, and Judaism), today nine (adding Baha'i, Jainism, the Sikh Faith, and Unitarian Universalism).[30] Each faith has equal representation on the Interfaith Council, IACO's governing board. IACO is deliberate in representing

28. http://www.spiritualitynetwork.org/livingfaith.html.

29. The program for this service is available at http://iaco.org/wp-content/uploads/2011/02/1985-IACO-Prayer-Service.pdf.

30. Sandhu, "Brief History"; http://iaco.org/.

many faiths in its activities rather than breaking out subgroupings like the Abrahamic traditions, says Rev. Stansbery, one of IACO's founders. Yet the interfaith spirit animating IACO is consistent with the spirit of the Abrahamic encounter described thus far, namely, "trying to sustain relationships across faith lines," in Rev. Stansbery's words. In fact, IACO's signature annual program today, the Main Event, dating back to 1993, is a vestige of the local interfaith work organized through the Anti-Defamation League's A World of Difference Institute, which included an interfaith gathering called the Main Event and an interfaith concert featuring sacred music from six religious traditions (Colleen Marshall, a news anchor from NBC-TV Channel 4 in Columbus, served as program host for the concert).[31] Along with his specifically Abrahamic efforts, Mazhar Jalil worked with A World of Difference until it discontinued its Columbus connection in 1992, after which Jalil merged his larger interfaith initiatives with IACO's efforts. He continues to serve as the contact person for the Muslim electing authority within IACO.

In 2007, IACO sponsored an educational forum titled The Many Voices of Islam at the Ohio Statehouse that was dubbed "Hamas in the House" on the Central Ohioans Against Terrorism Web blog.[32] The event, which had the backing of the Ohio Humanities Council, the Ohio Council of Churches, and Muslim groups, came off without incident.

The BREAD (Building Responsibility Equality And Dignity) organization mobilizes its Abrahamic constituents for social action. Founded in 1996, BREAD's mission statement reads, "People of faith building power to 'do justice,'" referencing Micah 6:8 of the Hebrew Bible / Christian Old Testament. In 2013, BREAD represented more than fifty local congregations, the great majority of them Christian, with four synagogues and the recent addition of Noor Islamic Cultural Center. Notable social issues tackled by BREAD include exorbitant interest rates on payday loans, affordable housing, and school truancy.[33]

Some of our interviewees explained how BREAD's model for Abrahamic relations differs from other interfaith projects. Rabbi Misha Zinkow, the current rabbi of Temple Israel, identifies BREAD as the centerpiece of his synagogue's and his own personal Abrahamic involvement. The "kindred

---

31. On the ADL's A World of Difference Institute, see http://www.adl.org/education-outreach/anti-bias-education/c/a-world-of-difference.html.

32. Ludlow, "Talk of Terrorism Ties Discounted."

33. http://www.breadcolumbus.org/.

spirit" he senses among the participants, the common ground they share, is of a singular nature—the social justice imperative of faith. The respective theologies get the representatives of the three faiths "in the room" together for a unified purpose of becoming a powerful force for systemic change. The clergy network created through BREAD can spin off other activities as well, explains Rabbi Zinkow, such as the 2012 dialogue program titled Three Paths Up the Mountain: An Interreligious Encounter with Abraham, which he organized with the pastor of Trinity Episcopal Church and the imam of Noor Islamic Center.

Cantor Jack Chomsky of Tifereth Israel also identifies BREAD as his primary venue for interfaith work. He expresses little patience with mutual niceties that accomplish nothing. "The reason for us to come together is to find out what we have in common that we can address for the betterment of our communities through our understanding of how God has spoken to us in our own traditions." Cantor Chomsky notes that BREAD's leadership decided to follow the DART (Direct Action and Research Training) Center model of congregational organizing instead of the broader Gamaliel model of faith-based organizing. In both models, social activism drives interfaith relations.[34]

"My interfaith work is justice work with people of all faiths," says Rev. Timothy Ahrens, pastor of First Congregational Church and one of BREAD's founders, who marvels at how well organized the Jewish community's social justice efforts have been. "There is a clarity of purpose when you're fighting for your lives religiously," he explains with regard to the Jewish minority experience. In 2005–2006, Rev. Ahrens and others convened a network of religious leaders called We Believe Ohio in opposition to a group calling itself Patriot Pastors, whom Rev. Ahrens considers "Christocrats" trying to "take over the state of Ohio for Jesus." We Believe Ohio began with Christian pastors but soon sought out other leaders, particularly Jews and Muslims, to oppose demonization of non-Christians, support democracy, and lift up the concerns of the poor, according to Ahrens.[35]

An important relationship emerged in the 1990s between the local Jewish community and Trinity Lutheran Seminary, a graduate school of theology of the Evangelical Lutheran Church in America (ELCA) located in the Columbus suburb of Bexley. A twenty-seven-foot Holocaust memorial

---

34. http://www.thedartcenter.org/; http://www.gamaliel.org/.

35. See the interview of Ahrens by the Internet site Faithfully Liberal, http://www.faithfullyliberal.com/?p=673.

sculpture titled Promise for Life, conceived and sculpted by Holocaust survivor Alfred Tibor and supported by a Jewish-Christian committee, was dedicated on the seminary campus in May of 1999. The stretch of College Avenue in front of the sculpture was designated Remembrance Way by the cities of Bexley and Columbus.[36]

Rev. Ward "Skip" Cornett, an ordained ELCA minister, began working with the local Jewish community around this time (he served as Trinity's Director of Continuing Education from 1994 to 2011). Lutherans have enjoyed a generally good reputation among American Jews, Rev. Cornett reports, particularly since the ELCA's 1994 repudiation of Martin Luther's anti-Jewish writings and their influence on later anti-Semitism.[37] A number of local Jewish-Christian collaborations have taken place over the years co-sponsored by Trinity Seminary, Jewish Federation of Columbus, and other organizations. For instance, a 2004 series titled A Jewish-Christian Forum: *Passion of the Christ* focused on the Mel Gibson movie, while a 2005 series, Yours, Mine or Ours? Looking at the Bible through Christian and Jewish Eyes, examined perspectives on scripture from the two faith traditions.

Certainly the most important topic is the Holocaust. The Jewish Federation's Holocaust Education Committee offers numerous resources, including a video database of survivor testimonies compiled with the help of Trinity Seminary students.[38] For long-time member of the Holocaust Education Committee Rev. Cornett, it is crucial to educate Christians about the importance of the Holocaust for Jews today, as well as about the Church's complicity in the Holocaust and the broader anti-Semitism that has been a part of Christian history. To that end, for instance, Trinity Seminary sponsored a 2007 lecture series titled Theologians under Hitler: Lessons from a Bad Experience? Also, an annual Kristallnacht Commemoration is held on Trinity's campus, which in 2012 was co-sponsored by the Jewish Federation and the Interfaith Association of Central Ohio.

IACO's participation in the Kristallnacht event is indicative of efforts to expand the parameters of these Jewish-Christian initiatives. In 2008, a traveling exhibit sponsored state-wide by the Ohio Humanities Council titled Children of Abraham was brought to Central Ohio by IACO and rotated among Jewish, Christian, and Muslim places of worship and other

---

36. "Promise for Life."
37. "Declaration of ELCA."
38. http://holocausteducationcolumbus.org/; http://www.holocausteducationvideo.com/.

venues.[39] On September 11, the exhibit was transferred from Congregation Tifereth Israel to Noor Islamic Cultural Center as a gesture of goodwill and friendship. A 2013 forum, Sharing Pain, Sharing Hope, Partnership for Peace, featuring testimonials from members of The Parents Circle-Families Forum, an Israeli-Palestinian organization of families who have lost loved ones, was co-sponsored by the Jewish Federation, Trinity Seminary, Congregation Tifereth Israel, and Noor Islamic Cultural Center.

Noor was established in 1998 and opened an impressive new facility in a northwest suburb of Columbus in 2006. It took some time for its diverse immigrant constituency to see the value of outreach and interfaith activities, explains one of Noor's leaders. As in most immigrant communities, other pressing matters took early precedence but relations with the larger community have steadily expanded in recent years. Noor is the only Islamic participant of the BREAD organization and regularly hosts or co-sponsors Abrahamic activities. In 2009–2010, for instance, Noor's Imam Hany Saqr joined Congregation Tifereth Israel's Rabbi Michael Ungar and First Congregational Church's Rev. Timothy Ahrens to team-teach an adult class on the biblical book of Genesis that rotated among the three houses of worship over several months. Recent initiatives include the Shalom/Salaam Project, a cooperative venture with Jewish Federation of Columbus that facilitated dialogue and relationship-building between young Muslim and Jewish professionals, and SAIL (Safe Alliances of Interfaith Leaders), an organization that seeks to strengthen families and neighborhoods in the northwest suburbs.[40]

In a memorable encounter, U.S. Army reservists from the Columbus-based 412th Civil Affairs Battalion visited Noor in 2012 in order to "learn more about a cultural environment that they may encounter if they should deploy again," to quote the report posted on the Army's official Internet homepage. One reservist expressed surprise at what he learned about the beliefs of Christianity and Islam: "I left the mosque shocked with how similar we are." According to Jeri Milburn, Noor's Director of Outreach when she was interviewed, this is the most common response of non-Muslim visitors to the mosque.[41]

39. "Panel Discusses the 'Children of Abraham' Exhibit."

40. http://www.noorohio.org/; http://columbusjcrc.org/page.aspx?id=248573; http://sail-ohio.org/.

41. D. Johnson, "Soldiers Visit with Islamic Center's Members"; also, see the local coverage, Jarman, "Soldiers Visit with Islamic Center's Members." Noor's Web site is http://www.noorohio.org/.

Local members of the Roman Catholic ecclesial movement Focolare have quietly engaged in "dialogues of love" since 1991. This group, which today claims a presence in 182 countries, began in Italy during World War II out of the vision of Chiara Lubich (d. 2008) and a small group of fellow Catholics who sought to embody the prayer of Jesus for his followers to be united in love (John 17). In the 1970s, Lubich enlarged the movement's vision of unity to include adherents of other faiths and "agnostics, atheists and people indifferent towards religion."[42]

Four *focolarini* women today live in the Focolare "house" in Columbus, which serves as a center for the movement's activities in Ohio and nearby states. Most remarkable is the longstanding relationship between the Focolare and the African American Muslim followers of Imam Warith Deen Mohammed (d. 2008), who established a mainstream Sunni group out of the Nation of Islam founded by his father, the Honorable Elijah Muhammad. Close friendships have developed between the *focolarini* women and some African American *muslimah*s (Muslim women) in the Columbus area.[43]

In the early 2000s, a new Abrahamic voice emerged in Central Ohio. Founded in 2003 as Scioto Educational Foundation and informed by the Gulen movement in Turkey, Niagara Foundation Ohio (as it is called today) seeks "to promote understanding and respect between the diverse groups of Central Ohio by creating peaceful settings for interaction . . . through education, dialogue, and community service."[44] Its wide-ranging programming includes a specifically Abrahamic component, highlighted by its annual Abrahamic Traditions Dinner. The 2013 dinner addressed the topic "Perspectives on Abrahamic Traditions: Prophet Abraham (PBUH)," with presentations by Rev. Timothy Ahrens, a representative of Jewish Community Center of Greater Columbus, and a local imam. The master of ceremonies introduced the evening by noting that the emphasis would be on commonalities rather than differences among the Abrahamic traditions.

Central Ohio's Abrahamic encounter has featured many other initiatives over the years. John Kashubeck, a Muslim physician who was raised Lutheran, organized local Muslim participation in the 1996 commemoration

---

42. http://www.focolare.org/en/in-dialogo/persone-di-convinzioni-non-religiose/. On the Focolare in Chicago and the movement generally, see Numrich, *Faith Next Door*, chapter 8.

43. I know this personally, but also see Puet, "Focolare Movement."

44. "Mission." Niagara Foundation Ohio has a close relationship with Turkish American Society of Ohio (http://tasocolumbus.org/). On the Gulen movement, see http://www.fgulen.org/.

of the 3,000th anniversary of Jerusalem's founding. He recalls a memorable talk by a Palestinian Muslim at one of the public high schools during which he could sense the audience beginning to think about others "as *people*, and not as caricatures on the screen or something 'other' or less than human, but to humanize them." Shortly after September 11, 2001, Kashubeck participated in an event at another public high school, making the point that evil was the real enemy of 9/11: in that instance evil dressed as a Muslim, but sometimes it dresses as a Jew or a Christian.

In 2011, an organization called I AM Youth (Interfaith Action Movement of Youth, formerly Columbus Interfaith Youth Group) held a major conference commemorating the tenth anniversary of 9/11. Called Better Together: Path to Peace and Justice, the conference was hosted by Congregation Tifereth Israel's youth group and co-sponsored by several local Christian and Muslim organizations, and drew nearly five hundred people.[45]

In 2012, the Columbus Faith Coalition Against Violence was organized by the Dominican Sisters of Peace, whose Motherhouse is adjacent to Ohio Dominican University in Columbus. This group of mostly Christians, Jews, and Muslims meets for monthly prayer services focusing on all forms of violence, such as gun violence, human trafficking, and violence against women. First Congregational Church's pastor, Rev. Timothy Ahrens, one of the group's founders, said about it, "When you pray together, you begin to connect at the most basic root of your relationship, and so it begins to change things. . . . If all of us get connected in a meaningful way, we will begin to influence legislators and we will begin to go to the Statehouse."[46]

One lost opportunity, in the opinion of a local Jewish leader, deserves mention. Many of the early Somalis who came to Columbus were resettled by Jewish Family Services as an extension of its century-long immigrant resettlement work. It is important for Jews to be involved in this work, the leader explained. "Jews are a classic immigrant community. The thing that the Torah says more than anything else is, remember you were strangers in the land of Egypt, and to respect the stranger, to care for the stranger."

Jewish Family Services discontinued its resettlement services in 2005. The gap was partially filled by a mutual assistance agency called US Together, which receives funding from New York City-based HIAS (Hebrew

---

45. http://zerqaabid.blogspot.com/2011/09/i-am-youth-call-for-better-together-on.html.

46. On the Columbus Faith Coalition Against Violence, see the notice posted November 24, 2012 at http://iaco.org/2012/11/24/columbus-faith-coalition-against-violence/.

Immigrant Aid Society).[47] But the Jewish connection on the ground is not as obvious as when Jewish Family Services was involved. Says the Jewish leader, "It was great that the Muslims coming to town knew that the ones who helped them most and helped them first were the Jews."

Strategies and Challenges

As noted earlier, participants in the Central Ohio Abrahamic encounter seek to enhance mutual understanding and relationships, disseminate accurate information about the three Abrahamic traditions, and contribute to the general betterment of society. We can identify key strategies and challenges in pursuing these goals.

Meeting Face-to-Face

From large public conferences to small groups, face-to-face contact is integral to the Abrahamic encounter. In one sense, the encounter is not as much about religious traditions broadly construed as it is about individual adherents of those traditions engaging their Abrahamic counterparts.

In a time when face-to-face relationships have become increasingly difficult to sustain due to mobility patterns, lifestyle choices, and online social networking, participants in the Central Ohio Abrahamic encounter emphasize the importance of gathering together in the same physical space. It is especially critical to engage real people rather than the stereotypes of public discourse, or even to rely on relatively accurate and objective information available in the information age. Says Tifereth Israel's Rabbi Michael Ungar, "It's very easy to paint things in big brush strokes, but when you get to know individuals, that's very different." He finds it more compelling to learn about a tradition from people who live it than "getting it from the Learning Channel or online." Drawing an analogy to the scientific method, Alam Payind, Director of the Middle East Studies Center at Ohio State University, explains this as a process of discovering what others believe and experience.

Mutual respect is as important as mutual understanding in face-to-face encounters. These are times for listening, says Temple Israel's Rabbi Misha Zinkow, for opening one's mind and expanding one's awareness

---

47. http://ustogether.us/, http://www.hias.org/.

of others. Mutual respect and understanding are the highest priorities in Abrahamic relations, according to Jeri Milburn of Noor Islamic Cultural Center. She does not consider Judaism, Christianity, and Islam to be three separate faiths, but rather three periods in the history of the same prophetic lineage. For her, the fact that Islam is the latest Abrahamic iteration requires its adherents to respect the earlier ones: "When you're Muslim, you have to be Jewish and Christian too, in a sense."

Fond acquaintanceships and even close friendships emerge from and are renewed at Abrahamic activities. Cantor Jack Chomsky of Congregation Tifereth Israel emphasizes the importance of a "growing affection" between people, a basic and verifiable trust that the other person is interested in your welfare and not just in self-promotion. Bonding among young people is particularly heartening. Remarking about his experience with I AM Youth, a founding member says, "As I walked into the very first meeting, I immediately felt welcomed by the various faith backgrounds that were present."[48]

The close friendships that emerge from Abrahamic activities are treasured and sometimes offered as public models. The value of public friendships across religious boundaries should not be dismissed, particularly in this contentious time in American history. The public friendship of Mazhar Jalil and Norman Hosansky stands over against the incivility of culture wars and red/blue states. To see Muslims and Jews as friends breaks stereotypes, says Tarunjit Butalia of the Interfaith Association of Central Ohio.

Jalil and Hosansky have been asked to bring their model of friendship to bear on contentious situations. One university professor asked them to visit a class comprising Jewish and Muslim students as tensions elevated in the wake of a global conflict. That visit changed the tone and tenor of the class.

Strategic Leadership

"Before I came to the U.N.," observed Ambassador Juli Minoves-Triquell of Andorra, "I knew all about its structures. But actually working in it and being a part of its life has made me see how strong the personal factor is in all the U.N. does. Personalities matter. Bureaucracy is not king. The personal touch is vital in all U.N. negotiations."[49]

48. Palm-Houser, "Interfaith Action Movement of Youth."
49. Cited in Grey, *U.N. Jigsaw*, 38.

As it is in complex international organizations like the United Nations, so it is with local intergroup relations. Personalities matter. Individuals matter. Most importantly, intergroup relations strategically depend on the initiative, creativity, energy, and dedication of individual leaders.

Richard Pfeiffer is a longtime civic leader in Ohio. Recall that as a state senator he met with Mazhar Jalil and a Muslim delegation to discuss the possibility of an annual Islamic Day in Ohio. Since 2003, Pfeiffer has served as the City Attorney of Columbus. He stresses the importance of leaders in any interfaith endeavor: "Everything's about leadership. It all depends, in every community, on those who step forward and want to lead an effort to impact dialogue, to have conversations."

Robert "Chip" Harrod goes a step further. Formerly the Executive Director of the Cincinnati branch of the National Conference for Community and Justice and currently Vice President for Advancement at Wilmington College, a Quaker school in southwest Ohio, Harrod has been deeply involved in the Abrahamic encounter in Cincinnati. He asserts that individuals, not institutions, have always been the driving force of the interfaith movement. "The history of interfaith relations in this country has not been one of institutions initiating progress," says Harrod. In fact, he continues, "the 'organized church' has tended to resist interreligious ecumenism. Progress has always been driven by well-meaning individuals unencumbered by institutional politics. These individuals often do their interfaith work, at least initially, unsupported by their respective religious institutions."

The figures of Norman Hosansky and Mazhar Jalil stand out in the Central Ohio Abrahamic encounter, as we have seen. "Dr. Jalil is a very quiet, reserved guy," testifies Hosansky, "but if he has an idea in his head, we follow through." But what motivated Jalil to reach out to Jews and Christians in Central Ohio? Perhaps it goes back to his experience as a child in St. Mary Catholic Convent School in India. He fondly recalls the love and affection shown by the nuns of the school, especially how they woke up the children every morning with a song: "Rise and shine, it is a lovely day!"

What motivated Norman Hosansky to accept his rabbi's invitation to work with Jalil? He points to the influence of his father, who "from an early age was curious and even skeptical about everything religious." Norman remembers a story his father often told about performing a small task that nevertheless qualifies as work on a Sabbath at the age of four or five. "Nothing happened," his father said. "No angry words from God. No thunder. No lightning. No punishment."

That story profoundly affected Norman's view of religion. "It made me wonder from early childhood even until today why we humans create religious beliefs, create gods, question our beginnings and ends, rewards and punishments, heaven and hell." So when he was asked to work with Muslims, "I thought that this would be a good way to explore another religion, which I knew was closely related to Judaism, to find out how and why it arose, how it is practiced, why it is observed."

Jalil and Hosansky are lay leaders. Abrahamic relationships must be sustained by lay leadership across the three religious groups, particularly in organizing activities, maintaining momentum, and attracting new participants. Youth group directors from the three faith communities have worked together intently at times, for instance, though this has been difficult to sustain.

Clergy also play a part in the leadership of local Abrahamic activities. Rabbis, pastors, and imams allocate time and energy to interfaith work, sometimes developing close personal relationships thereby. Rabbi Misha Zinkow of Temple Israel has done so through his involvement in BREAD, as noted earlier. Rabbi Michael Ungar of Congregation Tifereth Israel points to the mutual trust that can be built up through cooperative ventures and speaks fondly of a dinner at a local Turkish restaurant shared by the three clergy who team-taught the study of Genesis mentioned earlier and their wives. Rev. Timothy Ahrens of First Congregational Church recalls arguing "nose-to-nose" with Imam Hany Saqr of Noor Islamic Cultural Center over interpreting a Genesis story at one of the class sessions. This publicly modeled the kind of honesty about faith differences that stems from a deep personal friendship, he explains. "That's what friendship does—you can be honest in that way with a friend." Rev. Ahrens nurtures such friendships by joining Muslims during Ramadan and regularly attending Shabbat services in local synagogues.

Interfaith clergy bonds can be invoked in times of public crisis or alarm. For instance, the mass shooting carried out by a Muslim U.S. Army officer at Fort Hood in Texas occurred during the Genesis study in November of 2009. Rabbi Ungar, Rev. Ahrens, and Imam Saqr joined military veterans from each faith for a public discussion of the shooting on Veterans Day.[50]

We know from the literature that a majority of American Christian clergy do not engage in interfaith work for a variety of reasons, from time constraints to theological reservations. The majority of American rabbis

---

50. Heagney, "Men of Faith Talk."

likewise do not engage in interfaith work given that such efforts are largely limited to the Reform branch of Judaism. Although a majority of the mosques in the United States engage in interfaith work, less than half of the mosques have full time imams and it is difficult to know how many of them take the lead in their mosque's interfaith activities. Due to their minority status in American society, Jewish and Muslim clergy face a particular strain, which Rabbi Harold Berman calls "outreach fatigue." Those who make themselves available to the larger community may soon find themselves overwhelmed with invitations.[51]

The clergy-lay relationship in Abrahamic work can be intriguing. Sometimes clergy take the lead, sometimes laity. And sometimes lay people keep their clergy in check, holding them accountable for extreme views about another group. As one of our interviewees put it, "Interreligious work also impacts intra-religious work." Another said bluntly, "Each side must muzzle its own fools."

Commonalities, Differences, and Elephants in the Room

Many of our interviewees emphasized the strategy of focusing on the commonalities of the Abrahamic traditions and communities. Mazhar Jalil likened the Abrahamic relationship to a marriage: spouses understand that they have differences but it would be counterproductive to brood over them. He also invoked the ubiquitous Central Ohio analogy, Ohio State University football: Monday morning water cooler conversations can either become contentious when Buckeye fans and fans of other teams square off against each other, or everyone can agree on their shared love of the game.

This focus on commonalities shaped the themes of the four major public conferences described earlier. Specific topics and speakers were chosen in order to highlight what unifies the Abrahamic communities—past, present, and future—as reflected in the conference titles: Muslims and Jews: A Common Past, A Hopeful Future (1989), Muslims and Christians: Common Themes, Distinctive Identities (1990), Muslims and Jews: Exploring Our Future Together (1997), and Muslims and Jews: Yesterday, Today and Tomorrow Together (2009). That three of the four conferences were bilateral gatherings of Jews and Muslims can be explained by the affinities of their experiences as immigrants and minorities in the United States.

---

51. On Christian clergy, see Wuthnow, *America and the Challenges of Religious Diversity*; Numrich, "Plan B." On imams, see Bagby, "American Mosque 2011."

Part I: Local Initiatives, Large Implications

One interviewee pointed out that many Muslims look to Jews as a model religious minority, another suggested that they must be advocates for each other's rights.

That Christians were the odd ones out of those conferences recognizes the fact that there are significant and meaningful differences among the Abrahamic faiths. The strategy of focusing on commonalities does not ignore the particularities of each group; rather, these are placed within a larger context of appreciation and solidarity. This approach contrasts to one that broods on differences, to invoke Mazhar Jalil's insight again, perhaps never transcending entrenched positions and polemical rhetoric. As one person told us, "If you keep digging into the negative, you can never do anything positive." "When you think of difference, you never see what you have in common," said another. "I would rather begin with the things we have in common."

But several of our interviewees expressed concern about the strategy of focusing on Abrahamic commonalities. This certainly attracts an audience sympathetic to the goals of the national interfaith movement mentioned earlier, particularly how it models an alternative to religiously motivated conflict.[52] But that audience is limited, which can result in the "preaching to the choir" syndrome. Or worse, as critics of certain kinds of interfaith activities put it, emphasizing commonalities can devolve into little more than merely singing "Kumbaya" or "We Are the World" together, making "feeling good about each other" the only goal. We should explore what we share in common, explained one interviewee, but we should not apologize for our differences.

Several interviewees acknowledged potential deal-breaker issues in the Abrahamic encounter, issues so sensitive that they can trump all commonalities and shut down communication. But there was a difference of opinion about how to negotiate these issues. Some advocate facing them head-on, even if only to dispense with them before moving quickly to commonalities. Others wish to avoid them altogether—as one interviewee put it, focusing on political topics may simply do more harm than good. Mazhar Jalil is adamant: "Keep the politics out."

"It's clear that there is an elephant in the room," says the Interfaith Association's Tarunjit Butalia of the most volatile deal breaker of Abrahamic relations. "What happens in the Middle East—what do you do with it?" Jalil

---

52. McCarthy, *Interfaith Encounters in America*, 20; also, see Duin, "Interfaith Movement Gains New Strength."

recalls a Middle Eastern Muslim in the Broad Street mosque calling him a traitor to the Palestinian cause when he began his dialogue with the Broad Street synagogue in the mid-1980s. Norman Hosansky tells the story of a dinner at a Toledo, Ohio mosque that derailed both before and after the meal: Muslims took offense at a table decoration featuring an Israeli flag that was brought by Jewish participants, Jews in turn took offense during the after-dinner tour of the mosque upon seeing maps of the Middle East with Israel crossed out. The snafu became so public that Hosansky was invited to speak to Toledo city officials about how Central Ohio avoids such incidents.

The Abrahamic encounter is further complicated by the kind of Christian who typically participates. Tarunjit Butalia observes that liberal Christians across the United States have shifted their energies away from conservative Christians and even ecumenical relations with other liberal Christians, and toward interfaith work. Liberal Christian views about the Middle East, particularly the Israeli-Palestinian issue, sometimes make both Jews and Muslims reluctant to include them in dialogue, according to Butalia.

Tensions between certain Christian denominations and Jewish supporters of Israel have reverberated in Central Ohio. For instance, an October 5, 2012 letter from several church leaders called upon the U.S. Congress to investigate possible human rights violations and misuses of American aid by the government of Israel that might be jeopardizing a peaceful solution to the Israeli-Palestinian conflict. Several national Jewish organizations responded by canceling the upcoming meeting of the Christian-Jewish Roundtable, a venue created in 2004 to improve deteriorating Christian-Jewish relations, and calling for a summit of leaders on both sides to address the breach created by the letter. Some in the Columbus Jewish community suggested breaking off relations with Trinity Lutheran Seminary since the ELCA's presiding bishop was a signatory of the letter.[53]

Elephants in a room can be ignored but it takes a great deal of effort because they are so large. Tifereth Israel's Rabbi Harold Berman deals with the Middle Eastern elephant by acknowledging its presence from the start

53. Goodstein, "Church Appeal on Israel." The letter to Congress is available at several Internet sites (e.g., http://blogs.elca.org/peacenotwalls/files/2012/10/12oct5letterabou taid.pdf); the national Jewish protest is documented on the October 17, 2012 blog of the Jewish Council for Public Affairs (http://engage.jewishpublicaffairs.org/blog/comments.jsp?blog_entry_KEY=6599). On October 25, 2012, the ELCA's presiding bishop and his assistant in charge of ecumenical and inter-religious relations wrote a letter to Jewish participants in the Christian-Jewish Roundtable expressing hope for resumption of the dialogue. The Roundtable did not resume meeting until March of 2014; see "Dialogue between U.S. Christian, Jewish Leaders Resumes."

with the intention of bracketing it out of the conversation. At the Muslims and Jews: Yesterday, Today and Tomorrow Together conference in 2009, he spoke frankly:

> I think it would be less than honest if I didn't say that the Jewish community that's represented here today is a very strongly Zionist community and has very strong and passionate feelings about the State of Israel and the right of Jews to live in the State of Israel and to defend themselves in the State of Israel. That may be a point of contention and it may be a point of contention that should be the subject of some discussion further, but probably not today.[54]

Similarly, at the 2012 Weekend of Twinning event, Rabbi Berman noted, "We generally do not come together to talk about politics, which is a good thing." But he continued, alluding to a conflict that had erupted in Gaza just days before, "I think it would be inappropriate *not* to acknowledge that it is a time of deep concern, a time when there is fighting going on, and all of our hearts are concerned for people right now in the Middle East at a time of danger for many." He then placed Jewish-Muslim relations into a context of prayer "that people will, all over the world, find a way to come together as brothers and sisters and see their way to a kind of peace that may, please God, embrace us all."

Tarunjit Butalia points out the realism of this approach to the Middle East elephant in the room: "It is too big for us to handle so why don't we do what we can here and try to become friends with each other, and the rest will follow as we go." Significantly, according to Butalia, those Central Ohio Jews and Muslims who engage each other in formal dialogue and other joint activities recognize the pain that the Palestinian-Israeli conflict has inflicted on both sides. Thus the elephant is not ignored; rather it is acknowledged and then set aside in order to pursue "more understanding of the 'other' on issues that are not related to conflict," "a common ground" upon which to build respectful relationships.

This approach succeeds, according to one of our Jewish interviewees, because participants paradoxically suspend their own political pain that would create barriers to understanding while at the same time

---

54. In his unpublished review of this conference commissioned by one of the organizers, Rev. Skip Cornett notes the intentional bracketing of the Israeli-Palestinian conflict. He writes, "It was addressed at one point by one of the presenters in a rather blunt and discomforting fashion in a question-answer session. But, otherwise, it was referenced only in passing at a couple of points."

acknowledging the political realities that created their pain. The interviewee pointed out that this is not political activism, but rather another kind of activism that has larger implications than whatever religious topic happens to be on the agenda since the encounter with the "other" can impact the whole being of the individuals involved.

Another palpable elephant in the room of Abrahamic relations is 9/11. During one Jewish-Muslim meeting at Islamic Foundation, a young Muslim tossed his backpack down in the hallway outside of the room and ran off. Some in the room immediately became very anxious. It turned out that the youth was simply running late for the daily prayers being held in another part of the mosque. At such times, the elephant of violence perpetrated in the name of Islam makes itself known in the room.

Asma Mobin-Uddin, a Muslim physician, author, and community activist, noted the watershed of 9/11 in terms of local public discourse about the Abrahamic faiths: whereas it was general and varied before 9/11, since 9/11 it has often directly addressed perceptions and suspicions about Islam. But even when other topics are featured, the 9/11 elephant nearly always emerges. Once, several years after 9/11, while attending a scholarly interfaith presentation about education of girls in Afghanistan, Mobin-Uddin was accosted by the man in the next seat with questions like why most terrorists are Muslims. Since then, she has been on guard against such accusations and does not feel "safe" even in interfaith settings until getting to know and trust the participants, usually after extended interaction with them.

Other Muslim leaders agreed that 9/11 created a heightened awareness of the need to educate the larger public about Islam. John Kashubeck, the physician, seeks to dispel the myths about violence in Islam, both in interfaith circles and among fellow Muslims who may not understand Islam's teachings about justifiable and unjustifiable uses of force. Jeri Milburn from Noor Islamic Cultural Center says that "you can't let the bad guys speak for you." She recalls a question from one visitor after she had given her standard "Islam 101" presentation to a group: "Where do you do your training for jihad?" Noor must spend a great deal of time and effort on what could be called 9/11 damage control. "We feel horrible for what's been done by Muslims who say they are doing it in the name of Islam," says Milburn. "They not only hijacked planes, they hijacked our faith." She is grateful for the many visitors to Noor who thank her for changing their negative opinions about Islam.

A more subtle elephant in the room of Abrahamic relations is what one interviewee called a sense of superiority of one group over others. This can involve "evangelism under the table," in the words of another interviewee, that is, making offhanded remarks about one's own religious perspective being the best. This can also occur in more deliberate and confrontational ways, as when a Messianic Jewish group challenged the Christian speaker's interpretation of the Bible at a Jewish-Christian conference.

Jeri Milburn was once contacted by a Christian who had developed an interest in Islam from conversations with a Muslim co-worker. He wanted his congregation to establish a relationship with Noor so that they could learn about each other's faiths. Milburn met with the man and three pastors from the church over lunch. As she tells the story, the senior pastor said to her immediately, "I don't understand the point of this. You're going to try to convert us and we're going to try to convert you." She assured him that Noor had no interest in proselytizing the members of his church. He assured her that there was no reason for the church to establish a relationship with Noor if the Muslims would not convert to Christianity.

Conversion can be a sensitive topic in Abrahamic circles, given both historical patterns of proselytization and contemporary social contexts. When First Congregational's Rev. Timothy Ahrens visited Egypt, many Muslims sought to convert him to Islam. This did not offend him, he explains, because he knew it was motivated by a compassionate concern for his eternal salvation, not out of spite or hatred. If done with the proper attitude of love, he says, attempts to convert others are acceptable.

This is sage advice for Christians who constitute the numerical and cultural majority in American society. The differential power relationship can make Jews and Muslims hypersensitive, even to the most benign Christian advances. This, plus the disgraceful history of Christian treatment of Jews, explains the stance taken by some Jews that "Even if proselytizing other groups is appropriate, proselytizing Jews is arguably not."[55]

Assessing the Central Ohio Abrahamic Encounter

Recall the self-description of the Living Jerusalem—Living Columbus project mentioned earlier: "If Columbus were to become the model for

---

55. D. Berger, "Reflections on Conversion and Proselytizing," 7. On the proper Christian attitude toward adherents of other faiths, whether one seeks their conversion or not, see Numrich, *Faith Next Door*, conclusion.

religious understanding among Jews, Muslims, and Christians, how would we get there and what would our model look like?" This begs two questions about the Central Ohio Abrahamic encounter: Is it a model of Abrahamic relations? If so, is it a viable model for the rest of the country?

A Model of Abrahamic Relations?

The Three Goals of the Central Ohio Abrahamic Encounter

Has the Central Ohio Abrahamic encounter met its three goals of enhancing mutual understanding and relationships, disseminating accurate information about the Abrahamic traditions, and contributing to the general betterment of society?

As we would expect, the participants themselves answer yes to this question. Typical of interfaith initiatives across the country, this yes comes with qualifications, however. "No one doing community-based interfaith work that I spoke with was completely satisfied with what his or her group had achieved," reports Kate McCarthy in her study, *Interfaith Encounters in America*. She adds quickly, "But modest successes are enough to sustain them."[56] Tarunjit Butalia of the Interfaith Association of Central Ohio elaborates: "Interfaith engagement is a journey not a destination. We learn from the religious other as we engage and then, if possible, work for the common good."

Our interviewees reported many modest successes. In fact, when asked to describe one or two memorable occasions or incidents in local Abrahamic relations, positive or negative, the positive examples significantly outnumbered the negative. Each example may be small—a one-to-one conversation, a study group, a shared meal, a public conference—but the cumulative effect makes a case that the Central Ohio Abrahamic encounter has met its goals.

Consider the all-too-common scenario of a religiously inspired act of violence somewhere in the world. If a person in Central Ohio has established a positive relationship with someone from that religious group and gained some accurate knowledge of that religious tradition, he or she would be less likely to make negative generalizations. People's stereotypes and misconceptions are changed by the Abrahamic encounter, says Noor's Jeri Milburn. Says John Kashubeck, the Muslim physician, "If you can see the supposed enemies

---

56. McCarthy, *Interfaith Encounters in America*, 124.

sitting around the table and having a discussion together, that's a great example for anybody to look at and follow." This is the seemingly small work that makes a large contribution toward a better society.

Consider the positive effects on neighborhoods and communities. Rabbi Harold Berman thinks that the neighborhood shared by Congregation Tifereth Israel and Islamic Foundation of Central Ohio is a better place today because of their relationship. First Congregational Church's Rev. Timothy Ahrens explains how relationships formed during times of crisis, like the vandalism at Islamic Foundation, become the means for mobilizing a response to the next crisis: "A call comes to a cell phone, not to an empty line somewhere in a building that has been destroyed: 'What do you need? We're here for you.'" Tarunjit Butalia points out that in years past there was a reluctance to visit one another's places of worship, but that has softened. Organizations like the Interfaith Association of Central Ohio, BREAD (Building Responsibility Equality And Dignity), and SAIL (Safe Alliances of Interfaith Leaders) make measurable improvements in community life.

Consider the significance of Christian participation in the Abrahamic encounter. As members of the majority religion in American society, Christians can easily invoke their privileged status and opt out of meaningful interaction with Jews and Muslims. Even those Christians who participate in the Abrahamic encounter could stand on privilege and resist the constraints imposed by a relationship with Jews and Muslims, for instance being asked to prepare meals that conform to *kashrut* and *halal* guidelines. The fact that any Christians are willing to engage Jews and Muslims with these conditions is an accomplishment that should not be discounted.

The Four Rules of Successful Interfaith Work

In *Interfaith Encounters in America*, McCarthy lists four rules "that seem naturally to evolve in the most successful interfaith ventures": "(1) Be quiet and listen. (2) Find a point of connection, but not too many—allow the other to remain other. (3) Enter deeply into your own religious identity, with all its difficulties and ambiguities. (4) Don't just talk; find something to do."[57]

On the basis of these four rules, the Central Ohio Abrahamic encounter can also be judged an overall success. Rule (1) is fundamental: we have seen the ardent desire to enhance mutual understanding and relationships, which requires both the willingness and the ability to discern when to

---

57. Ibid., 210.

listen to others and when to share of oneself. As Tarunjit Butalia remarks, "Over the last several decades our Christian, Jewish, and Muslim friends here have done a good job of listening more than talking." If the Central Ohio Abrahamic encounter had been characterized by more diatribe and discord than dialogue and concord, the preceding narrative would have been much different. Rules (2), (3), and (4) are more complicated, however, and deserve fuller consideration.

Rule (2) reads: "Find a point of connection, but not too many—allow the other to remain other." What are the points of connection in the Central Ohio Abrahamic encounter, and how many points become too many?

The most obvious points of connection are the commonalities of the Abrahamic traditions and communities. This involves placing the particularities of each religion within a larger context of appreciation and solidarity instead of "brooding" on differences. As we have seen, not all agree on the best calculus of commonalities vis-à-vis differences, but many share the view articulated by Rev. Timothy Ahrens of First Congregational Church: "The things that divide us and separate us are minimal compared to the things that unite us." Drawing upon the Islamic tradition, one Muslim leader suggested that our differences are God-given in order to impel us to learn about each other (see Qur'an 49:13).

But how wide should the circle of commonalities be drawn? We have seen affinity groupings within the Central Ohio Abrahamic encounter, particularly between Jews and Muslims. There has been a clear intentionality to limit the circle to Jews, Christians, and Muslims in order to maintain focus, yet as Tifereth Israel's youth director Shani Kadis observed, involving all three Abrahamic groups in one event or activity is still a lot of ground to cover. Some suggest that the circle should be expanded even further to include other religions that might wish to claim the Abrahamic label (such as Baha'is, Unitarian Universalists, and Mormons), non-Abrahamic religions, and the so-called "nones" demographic, that is, those who claim no institutional religious affiliation or have a non-religious worldview.[58]

Such new partnerships would significantly alter the Central Ohio Abrahamic encounter. To take one example, consider addressing the topic of authoritative texts, a favorite over the years. The commonality of texts (not to mention their interpretations) decreases dramatically as one moves from Judaism and Christianity which share the Hebrew scriptures, to Islam

---

58. On the "nones," who may number twenty percent of the American population, see Kosmin et al., "American Nones"; "'Nones' on the Rise."

which adds the Qur'an and only provisionally recognizes the authority of the extant biblical texts, to Mormons who add a third Testament to the Christian canon, to Baha'is who see the Kitab-i-Ahd and the Will and Testament of 'Abdu'l-Baha as continuations of the biblical covenant, to other religions that adhere to sacred texts unrelated to the Abrahamic corpus, to "nones" who might consider the Humanist Manifesto authoritative. The focus on commonalities would shift from an overlapping set of authoritative texts among the Abrahamic faiths to a more broadly construed concept of religious authority or shared ethical values. For some participants, this might be an exciting expansion; for others, it might feel like a loss of focus or settling for the lowest common denominator.

Rule (3) asks interfaith participants to "Enter deeply into your own religious identity, with all its difficulties and ambiguities." The conventional wisdom of the interfaith movement has it that one's own faith deepens through serious consideration of the faiths of others. As Diana Eck of Harvard University's Pluralism Project puts it, "each of us will begin to understand our own traditions afresh in light of what we have learned from the other."[59] Recall the agreement signed by local Christian and Muslim leaders in 1989 quoted earlier: "Dialogue presupposes that each side wishes to know the other, and wishes to increase and deepen its knowledge of the other. It constitutes a particularly suitable means of favoring a better mutual knowledge and of probing the riches of one's own tradition."

We have noted how probing the riches of the respective traditions can uncover commonalities and enhance positive relationships. But such probing can also reveal the internal difficulties and ambiguities of the respective traditions that negatively affect Abrahamic relationships, rough edges that scrape against each other rather than come together in perfect harmony, elephants in the room that threaten to shut down communication. One mark of the success of the Central Ohio Abrahamic encounter has been its longevity despite all the real and potential derailments that come with the relational territory.

Rule (4) is "Don't just talk; find something to do." Of course, this begs the questions: Do what? And to what end? Some of our interviewees expressed impatience with activities that have no political or social justice agenda. The support for the BREAD organization stems at least in part from such impatience. "I'm not a big conference guy when it comes to interfaith stuff," said one local leader when asked about the major public conferences

---

59. Eck, *Encountering God*, 187.

described earlier. "I believe we need to do the work of justice together," a case in point being the interfaith advocacy that helped to influence Ohio Governor John Kasich's support of Medicaid expansion.[60]

Kate McCarthy sees this as a "basic split" in the interfaith movement "between a focus on interfaith relations and a focus on community service work," "a perennial issue for interfaith groups: Do they come together to achieve a common goal, or is coming together itself the goal?"[61] McCarthy's research lends support to those who eschew politics and social justice, suggesting a less dramatic but no less important accomplishment, one that ironically transcends the dialogue at the heart of the interfaith movement: "It may be, in fact, that the greatest value of these [interfaith] organizations does not lie in interreligious dialogue, or even in the community programs and activism that absorb so much of their energy. Rather, it may lie simply in people of different religious identities being present to one another." McCarthy goes on to say that creating "communities of trust across potentially divisive religious lines" does not depend on "structured dialogue," but rather on the principle that "just being together is enough."[62] Whatever else has been accomplished by the Central Ohio Abrahamic encounter, it has brought many people together over decades.

A Viable Model for the Rest of the Country?

Since everything is local, as the saying goes, we must ask whether the Central Ohio Abrahamic model is adaptable to other parts of the country. If an Abrahamic encounter emerges in a particular place, local dynamics will determine which aspects of the Central Ohio experience might be replicated and which not.

We have evidence that others see the Central Ohio model as somehow instructive. Rabbi Harold Berman has been asked to speak to national Jewish groups about his on-the-ground Abrahamic relationships. Recall the city officials in Toledo who sought Norman Hosansky's advice about the snafu at a local Jewish-Muslim dinner. The Cincinnati group that Chip Harrod of Wilmington College has been involved with once invited Hosansky and Mazhar Jalil to share their approach to Abrahamic relations. The upshot of that exchange was that, although some of the Abrahamic

60. See Viviano, "Religious Groups Push."
61. McCarthy, *Interfaith Encounters in America*, 86.
62. Ibid., 124–25.

dynamics are similar in Columbus and Cincinnati, the Cincinnati group, composed of seven Jewish and Muslim couples, was more intentional in their discussions of Middle Eastern politics.

This points up the two most important factors in any local Abrahamic encounter, the leaders and the people involved. These are more important even than a critical mass of religious diversity, which is a necessary but not sufficient factor for the emergence of an Abrahamic encounter. A neighborhood, city, or region might have many Jews, Muslims, and/or Christians but they could remain in their respective enclaves or their relationships could be characterized by tension and hostility. As we have seen, it takes strategic leadership and organized effort to move from indifference or antagonism to an ardent desire to traverse the distances between Judaism, Christianity, and Islam in order to enhance mutual understanding and relationships, disseminate accurate information about the three Abrahamic traditions, and contribute to the general betterment of society.

Serendipity plays a role in this as well. One wonders what Abrahamic relations in Central Ohio would have been like had Islamic Foundation of Central Ohio not located on East Broad Street, had Congregation Tifereth Israel's Rabbi Harold Berman not responded to Mazhar Jalil's letter, had First Congregational Church not offered space for the Islamic school after the mosque was vandalized. The participants of the Central Ohio Abrahamic encounter would likely attribute this to more than serendipity.

The Abrahamic Future

As our interviewees pondered the future of the Central Ohio Abrahamic encounter, their aspirations and concerns coalesced under two related categories, audience and activities.

Reflecting on his long-time coverage of the local Abrahamic encounter for the *Columbus Dispatch*, Felix Hoover observed, "Reaching out to the larger community seems to be an ongoing challenge." The "preaching to the choir" syndrome mentioned earlier is a common lament in religious circles. There is a kind of catch-22 quality to all religious claims of universal significance since they can never garner universal support. Thus, even the laudable goals of the Central Ohio Abrahamic encounter will attract a finite audience. As Mazhar Jalil points out, only open-minded people will become involved.

The question then becomes how to increase the share of this finite audience. This is more complex than it appears on first glance. Continuing with activities that have worked well in the past is an obvious strategy, as is learning from what has not worked well. This will keep the regulars in the fold and probably result in an incremental growth in the number of participants through word of mouth and other forms of recruitment. As one leader argued, it is increasingly important in a shrinking world to make the case for the crucial topics of today, even if we repeat ourselves.

The complexity emerges when new strategies or topics are considered. For example, a more deliberate focus on Abrahamic differences and controversial elephants in the room may both draw in new people and turn away current participants who prefer focusing on commonalities. We have already considered the basic split between those who prefer simply spending time together and those who see time together as a means to another end.

One relatively untapped audience is uncontroversial and can be cultivated without making a philosophical shift, namely, youth. This goes beyond the simple recognition that youth participation in the local Abrahamic encounter has been irregular. Concern for this generation involves more than the usual platitudes about the children being our future. For Jews and Muslims, this is part of a larger concern that future generations will assimilate into the mainstream culture and lose their distinctive religious identities. For Jews, Muslims, and Christians alike, complacency cannot counter the strong cultural forces of today, as one leader explained with understandable hyperbole: "Perfectly wonderful, open-minded, non-prejudiced parents are giving birth to a generation of really hateful kids. Parents are saying, 'Where did my kids pick this up because I'm not like this.'" Two of our interviewees suggested that the values and experiences of the local Abrahamic encounter should be taken into the public schools.

Kate McCarthy speculates that "some of the most interesting new interfaith encounters will be among young people." Her optimism is based on this age group's high level of tolerance, broad exposure to religious diversity, and deep interest in personal spirituality, if not organized religion. "Among young Americans, then," McCarthy concludes, "'interfaith' is an increasingly plausible religious identity."[63]

When pondering the future of the Abrahamic encounter in Central Ohio and the nation at large, Mazhar Jalil's perspective is instructive. This work takes time, he says, quoting Ralph Waldo Emerson's line about "slow

---

63. Ibid., 207.

but constant progress."[64] Appealing to a higher authority, Jalil says we can rest assured that God sees our good intentions and helps us in our efforts to create a better world. Thus providence, not serendipity, is at work.

Bibliography

"America's Interfaith Infrastructure: A Pilot Study." http://www.pluralism.org/interfaith/.

Bagby, Ihsan. "The American Mosque 2011: Report Number 2 from the US Mosque Study 2011." Islamic Society of North America, 2012. http://www.hartfordinstitute.org/The-American-Mosque-Report-2.pdf.

Berger, David. "Reflections on Conversion and Proselytizing in Judaism and Christianity." *Studies in Christian-Jewish Relations* 3 (2008) 1–7.

Berman, Harold J. "Jewish-Muslim Dialogue in Our Communities: An Idea and an Opportunity Whose Time Has Come." In *Muslims and Christians, Muslims and Jews: A Common Past, A Hopeful Future*, edited by Marilyn Robinson Waldman, 111–14. Columbus: Islamic Foundation of Central Ohio, 1992.

Butalia, Tarunjit Singh, and Dianne P. Small, eds. *Religion in Ohio: Profiles of Faith Communities*. Athens, OH: Ohio University Press, 2004.

"Declaration of ELCA to Jewish Community." http://www.elca.org/Who-We-Are/Our-Three-Expressions/Churchwide-Organization/Office-of-the-Presiding-Bishop/Ecumenical-and-Inter-Religious-Relations/Inter-Religious-Relations/Christian-Jewish-Relations/Declaration-of-ELCA-to-Jewish-Community.aspx.

"Dialogue between U.S. Christian, Jewish Leaders Resumes." http://www.elca.org/News-and-Events/7656.

"Dr. Houcine Chouat—Principles of Dawah Methodology." Presented at Masjid Omar Ibn El-khattab, Columbus, Ohio, posted March 17, 2012. http://www.youtube.com/watch?v=BnF5qNF8t48 (Part 1); http://www.youtube.com/watch?v=mMyTrJBBTAE (Part 2).

Duin, Julia. "Interfaith Movement Gains New Strength." *The Washington Times* (April 5, 2010). http://www.washingtontimes.com/news/2010/apr/5/interfaith-movement-gains-new-strength/?page=all.

Eck, Diana L. *Encountering God: A Spiritual Journey from Bozeman to Banaras*. Boston: Beacon, 1993.

Ghose, Dave. "Tides of Support Buoy a City's Displaced Muslims." *The Christian Science Monitor* (January 15, 2002). http://www.csmonitor.com/2002/0115/p2s2-ussc.html.

Goodstein, Laurie. "Church Appeal on Israel Angers Jewish Groups." *New York Times* (October 20, 2012). http://www.nytimes.com/2012/10/21/us/church-appeal-on-israel-angers-jewish-groups.html?_r=0.

Gray, Bettina. "What Excites Me about Interfaith Work?" *The Interfaith Observer* (December 5, 2011). http://theinterfaithobserver.org/journal-articles/2011/12/5/what-excites-me-about-interfaith-work.html.

Grey, Wilfrid. *U.N. Jigsaw*. New York: Vantage, 2000.

---

64. Emerson was referring to the history of the town of Concord, Massachusetts, in his talk, "Historical Discourse" (1835).

"A Guide to Somali Culture: An Educational Initiative from the Community Engagement Office." Ohio Department of Public Safety. HLS 0075 5/10.

Heagney, Meredith. "Men of Faith Talk about Fort Hood Shootings." *Columbus Dispatch* (November 12, 2009) 4A.

Hoover, Felix. "Rising Voice: With 35,000 Followers, Islam Has Become Region's Second-Largest Major Faith." *Columbus Dispatch* (February 11, 2005) 1E.

Hosansky, Norman, and Mazhar Jalil, eds. *Muslims and Jews: Building a Hopeful Future*. Columbus: Islamic Foundation of Central Ohio, 2003.

"Interview with Rabbi Harold Berman." The Columbus Jewish Historical Society. http://www.columbusjewishhistory.org/oral_histories/Interviews/HTML/berman_rabbi_harold.htm.

Jalil, Mazhar. "Muslims and Jews: Hope for a New Golden Age in America." Remarks prepared for the Muslims and Jews: Yesterday, Today and Tomorrow Together conference, December 6, 2009, Columbus, Ohio.

Jarman, Josh. "Show and Tell for Peace—Students Play Host to Peers from Other Faith-Based Schools." *Columbus Dispatch* (May 18, 2007) 1B.

———. "Soldiers Visit with Islamic Center's Members as Cultural Lesson in How to Be Special-Operations Liaisons between Troops, Public Overseas." *Columbus Dispatch* (February 27, 2012) 1B.

"Jews, Muslims to Discuss Ways that They're Alike." *Columbus Dispatch* (November 21, 2008) 4B.

Johnson, Dave. "Soldiers Visit with Islamic Center's Members as Cultural Lesson" (March 5, 2012). http://www.army.mil/article/75054/Soldiers_visit_with_Islamic_center_s_members_as_cultural_lesson/.

Khan, Meena. "Islam." In *Religion in Ohio: Profiles of Faith Communities*, edited by Tarunjit Singh Butalia and Dianne P. Small, 286–303. Athens, OH: Ohio University Press, 2004.

Khan, Sohail. "Greetings from the Sponsors." In *Muslims and Christians, Muslims and Jews: A Common Past, A Hopeful Future*, edited by Marilyn Robinson Waldman, 2. Columbus: Islamic Foundation of Central Ohio, 1992.

Kniss, Fred, and Paul D. Numrich. *Sacred Assemblies and Civic Engagement: How Religion Matters for America's Newest Immigrants*. New Brunswick, NJ: Rutgers University Press, 2007.

Kosmin, Barry A., et al. "American Nones: The Profile of the No Religion Population." Hartford, CT: Program on Public Values, Trinity College, 2009.

Ludlow, Randy. "Talk of Terrorism Ties Discounted." *Columbus Dispatch* (October 19, 2007).

McCarthy, Kate. *Interfaith Encounters in America*. New Brunswick, NJ: Rutgers University Press, 2007.

"Mission." http://www.niagarafoundation.org/ohio/?page_id=5.

Moloney, Stephan J. "On-Going Muslim-Christian Dialogue." In *Muslims and Christians, Muslims and Jews: A Common Past, A Hopeful Future*, edited by Marilyn Robinson Waldman, 107–109. Columbus: Islamic Foundation of Central Ohio, 1992.

"A Nation Challenged: American Muslims; Community Lends Its Support after Vandals Strike Mosque." *The New York Times* (January 3, 2002). http://www.nytimes.com/2002/01/03/us/nation-challenged-american-muslims-community-lends-its-support-after-vandals.html.

Part I: Local Initiatives, Large Implications

Nelson, Tariq. "Some Thoughts on the U.S. Muslim Population." http://muslimmatters.org/2007/05/23/some-thoughts-on-the-us-muslim-population/.

"'Nones' on the Rise: One-in-Five Adults Have No Religious Affiliation." Washington, DC: Pew Research Center's Forum on Religion & Public Life, 2012.

Numrich, Paul D. *The Faith Next Door: American Christians and Their New Religious Neighbors.* New York: Oxford University Press, 2009.

———. "Plan B in the Pluralist-Dialogue Approach to Religious Diversity in America." *Journal of Ecumenical Studies* 43 (2008) 453–75.

Palm-Houser, Steve. "Interfaith Action Movement of Youth Will Host 'Better Together' Event on 9/11." http://www.examiner.com/article/interfaith-action-movement-of-youth-will-host-better-together-event-on-9-11.

"A Panel Discusses the 'Children of Abraham' Exhibit." http://columbusjcrc.org/page.aspx?id=184262.

Poston, Larry. *Islamic Da'wah in the West: Muslim Missionary Activity and the Dynamics of Conversion to Islam.* New York: Oxford University Press, 1992.

"Promise for Life: History of Promise for Life Sculpture." http://www.tlsohio.edu/about-trinity/introduction/promise-for-life.

Puet, Tim. "Focolare Movement." *Catholic Times: A Journal of Catholic Life in Ohio* 64.29 (April 26, 2015) 10–11.

Raphael, Marc Lee. *Jews and Judaism in a Midwestern Community: Columbus, Ohio, 1840–1975.* Columbus: Ohio Historical Society, 1979.

Sandhu, Ranbir S. "A Brief History of the Interfaith Association of Central Ohio." http://iaco.org/history/.

Smith, Marcus. "Muslim Columbus: Unity and Diversity in an American Religious Community." MA thesis, University of Cincinnati, 2013.

Sussman, Lance J. "'Toward Better Understanding': The Rise of the Interfaith Movement in America and the Role of Rabbi Isaac Landman." *American Jewish Archives* 34 (April 1982) 35–51.

Viviano, JoAnne. "Religious Groups Push for Kasich's Medicaid Expansion." *Columbus Dispatch* (March 4, 2013) 4B.

Waldman, Marilyn Robinson. "Preface." In *Muslims and Christians, Muslims and Jews: A Common Past, A Hopeful Future*, edited by Marilyn Robinson Waldman, 1. Columbus: Islamic Foundation of Central Ohio, 1992.

Wuthnow, Robert. *America and the Challenges of Religious Diversity.* Princeton: Princeton University Press, 2005.

PART II

Circles of Scripture, Community, and Interpretation

2

Scripture and Community

Tamar Frank

DIALOGUE IS ALWAYS A tricky affair. From trivial exchanges about everyday matters to the proverbially difficult areas of religion and politics, even the most sensitive and self-aware must constantly remember to listen, to understand the other viewpoint, to re-evaluate ideas held as axiomatic. The staged debates of the medieval period, when scholars of different faiths were invited to a court to present arguments for the superiority of different points of view, are hardly a model for interfaith discourse today. Yet how many of us allow assumptions about the way "we" do things or what "they" believe to go unchallenged? Perhaps greater understanding is the most that we can expect from interfaith dialogue; to me it seems like a great deal. Certainly, an understanding of similarities and differences among religious traditions, an increased knowledge of shared or diverse traditions, can only enhance the possibility of future dialogue.

It is perhaps a commonplace that the Jewish and Islamic traditions have many points of similarity. Let us consider a process of evolution and development that appears similar in these two communities. This parallel process will also show that both communities are similar in the things they hold important and in the ways they respond to new problems and ideas. Please read the word "similar" carefully: I am not implying the influence of one tradition upon the other, nor do I mean "identical." I mean, rather, that the similarities discussed here between the two traditions are so striking as to enhance future possibilities for dialogue and reflection.

Part II: Circles of Scripture, Community, and Interpretation

We know that Judaism and Islam are "religions of the Book": each of these sister faiths has its origin in a revelation that was codified in scripture. We know, too, that each of these faiths has a normative interpretation of that scripture, or perhaps, an authoritative mechanism by which scripture can be interpreted. Let us look, then, at three reference points to see what they indicate about the growth of these traditions. They are prophecy, scripture, and authoritative interpretation.

Prophecy

The revelations which gave the impetus to Islam came over a short period of time, some twenty years, to a single person, the Prophet Muhammad. The various texts which compose the Hebrew Bible cover a time span of perhaps a thousand years and the experiences of many individuals. Despite this difference, however, there are some remarkable similarities in prophetic message and experience.

One prominent theme in both cases, for example, is the divine call for social justice. Look for example at Amos' injunction to "let justice well up like water" (5:24) and at his indictment of those who have become wealthy at the expense of the poor and downtrodden. Jeremiah, too, speaks of "wicked men" whose "houses are full of guile"; they "pass beyond the bounds of wickedness" for "they will not judge the case of the orphan, nor give a hearing to the plea of the needy" (5:26–28) [ed.: NJPS].

Muhammad, too, from early in his prophetic mission, brings a message of divine retribution against those who mistreat the poor and defenseless. The Qur'an's Sura (chapter) 107, the Sura "Charity," warns "Woe . . . to those who make display and refuse charity," that is, those "who repulse the orphan and urge not the feeding of the needy" [ed.: we have not been able to identify the translation used here]. The people singled out for protection in the qur'anic message, as in the Bible, are those with no "protection network" or power of their own in traditional Middle Eastern societies: women, orphans, the poor, sometimes strangers. In fact, the social message of the Qur'an was concretized by the extension of the idea of kinship group to the *umma*, the community of faith. This new entity, a revolutionary social change for sixth-century Arabia, was intended to become a "family" of believers whose members would be responsible for one another.

In addition to the social message brought by both Old Testament prophets [ed.: "Old Testament" is the Christian designation for the Hebrew Bible]

and Muhammad, we discover similarities in other aspects of their messages. An emphasis on the generosity of God, on his willingness to accept those who hear him, and the moving use of natural imagery (God's generosity to humankind in its most visible form) are found in both revelations.

Finally, the persona of prophet has many shared aspects. The prophet himself is reluctant to receive his call: Isaiah, for example, protests that his "lips [are] unclean" (6:5); Jeremiah tries to refuse his call with the words, "I am still a boy" (1:6). Muhammad, too, reacts in this way to his first revelation—with a refusal, or an inability to repeat the word "Recite!" which the angel Gabriel finally shakes out of him. His biography, or *sira,* preserves a story of his fear that his revelation might not be a true one. (See, for example, Suras 96, 74, and traditions concerning the first revelations.)

The old proverb about a "prophet without honor in his own country" applies, again, both to our Hebrew prophets and to Muhammad. Amos was accused by Amaziah, the priest, of conspiring against the king, and told not to prophesy in the "king's sanctuary" (7:12–13); Jeremiah, of course, was imprisoned, and the revealed messages which he dictated to his scribe were destroyed at the king's command. Muhammad's revelations, at least initially, were greeted with hostility and derision by many of his kinsmen and other citizens of Mecca. Even after he had gathered a group of followers and they had established themselves in Medina, he had to lead military campaigns to win both territory and the right to make a pilgrimage to the Meccan sanctuary.

Another point of similarity is the notion of revealed law, and of the prophet as lawgiver. This is not the place for an examination either of biblical or of qur'anic law, but we can make the point that, in each case, what the community of the faithful receives on the prophet's authority is a core of revealed legal material that will be elaborated by the community through commentary, analogy, and other authorized means. We will look at some of these methods a bit later.

We should also acknowledge here the idea of the prophet himself as a leader of his community and even as a judge during his own lifetime. Moses as lawgiver and leader, Joshua as military commander, and the Israelite judges are biblical examples; Muhammad, of course, ruled his community of Muslims and led them in battle during his lifetime.

In both message and circumstances, then, we can see some similarities in the prophetic impulse behind our two "daughters of Abraham." Let us turn next to the scripture that grew from these prophetic impulses.

Part II: Circles of Scripture, Community, and Interpretation

Scripture

The canonization of the Hebrew scriptures was a lengthy process, taking works from many different periods and of many different types and combining them into a book that could be thought of as a unified whole. The Qur'an was redacted in less than a generation and consists of materials revealed in a single prophetic voice. Nevertheless, each text functions for its community in a similar way: it is the ultimate validation of the community's experience. Put in a simpler way, without a Book, there is no Community, no sense of a group bound together by a God-given message. Both traditions are very conscious of the centrality of the written message. In fact, the Qur'an is full of references to scriptural revelation, to the Book itself, to the Preserved Tablet, some of which probably date from a time when Muhammad's revelations were first orally preserved.

Now it is easy to see that a community with a living prophetic voice is vital and growing. So, too, a community in the process of editing, arranging, sorting, and compiling the records of such voices. But how have these two communities remained dynamic throughout the long period following the closing of scripture? What mechanism have they for "hearing" the divine, following the right path, and doing the proper thing in the absence of living prophetic guidance?

Authoritative Interpretation

The answer to these questions, of course, is "interpretation," but this is an answer we must qualify. Surely, any interpretation will not do; there must be a way to determine a course of action that can be sanctioned within the community. And here both of our communities, the Jewish and Muslim, have a remarkably similar way of dealing with new questions, new situations, and new movements. Let us consider the concepts of "Torah" and "Sunna" and the way in which they function in their respective communities.

The word Torah, of course, is used to designate the Pentateuch, the Five Books of Moses. Let us look at the word itself, and how it came to mean these things and much more. Originally, the word *torah* was a legal term, and meant a specific decision in a specific legal case. By extension, it came to mean the general principle by which that decision was made, that is, a law. By further extension, it came to mean the general principle that such principles—or laws—exist, that is, the notion of Law itself. Hence, it came to mean a teaching or a tradition. So it was applied to the Pentateuch, that part of the Bible that contains the laws God gave to Moses.

It came to mean more still. When God tells Isaiah to "Bind up the message, seal the instruction [that is, *torah*] with My disciples" (8:16), the reference is to the whole of God's plan for the world, to the totality of revelation and experience. Prophecy, then, is Torah—so is the whole of the biblical canon. Torah is the total of authoritative teachings, teachings whose authority and formulation precede their use by the tradition. But as we can easily see, authoritative teachings must include both the law and its interpretation. Even the clearest-seeming of laws can admit problems; what about laws that do not seem clear at all?

A biblical example is the problematic divorce law in Deuteronomy 24:1–4, which would pose serious practical problems without some kind of interpretation. Readers familiar with qur'anic law might think of the inheritance laws, and of the generations of children who have had to work out trigonometry and sums by trying to divide a man's field among his heirs. Yes, the communities must try to live by the laws God gave them, but they must have some kind of guidelines, an interpretation that is somehow sanctioned, in order to apply these laws to their own situations.

The idea of an authorized interpretation gave rise, among Jews, to the idea of the Oral Torah, that is, the traditional, community-authorized interpretation. Of course, this approach was not without problems. Which, of the many oral *torahs*, was the one to follow? The position of the teacher of the Law began to take on great importance: people would follow a particular interpretation because of a scholar's reputation for rectitude and knowledge, so that his practice might be followed even when his reasons for it were not known or had been lost with time.

A phenomenon arose that will seem very familiar to those who know about the *hadith* and the idea of *isnad*, that is, a chain of transmission. Interpretations were cited in the name of a particular scholar, and his whole scholarly lineage would be set out in authentication. The sage became the new figure of authority; no longer was it the hereditary priesthood that established the community norms, but the sages. The important connections were one's teachers, rather than one's family.

What we see is the gradual development of a kind of circle: Torah needs the Tradition for its continued life and authority; Torah (the fixed, the past) remains part of Tradition (the living, the present); finally, the living tradition becomes part of Torah. That is, the Written Torah, the Scriptures themselves, are not to be thought of in the absence of the Oral Torah, the commentaries and interpretations. And finally, the Oral Torah became a written collection itself, a text to be studied in its own right. So the legal directives, decisions, legends, homilies, commentaries of various kinds that had been passed on in the academies came to be collected as the Talmud, the subject of study by subsequent generations. An apt expression of this dynamic is the Sephardic saying that all Jewish literature is the interrelation between text, *hibbur,* and commentary, *perush*: the history of Jewish literature is the history of *perushim* becoming *hibburim.*

Of course, the process did not stop there. The tradition continued to grow and change, to meet challenges, and finally, to incorporate ideas, trends, or movements that originated in opposition to it, but of this, more later.

I would like to turn now to the development of the concept of *sunna,* a process that is strikingly similar to the one we have just seen. After the death of Muhammad, the need was felt to collect the revelations from wherever they could be found: "whether written on palm leaves or flat stones or in the hearts of men," as the tradition tells us.

As in the case of the Hebrew Bible, where the establishment of the best possible text was the first step in the scholarly tradition (first century BCE to second century CE), the Islamic scholarly tradition began by assembling a Qur'an text that would be normative. The establishment of a definitive text, one that would be recognized and used by the entire community, was in itself a kind of interpretation, the first step in constituting and asserting an authoritative voice for the community.

It was in the formulation and development of the ideas of *hadith* and *sunna* that the community really found a voice. A *hadith* is a verbal communication, a bit of news or a news report; it has come to mean "a tradition," specifically, "a prophetic tradition," a report about something that the Prophet Muhammad did or said. Of course, a saying or an action of Muhammad would provide an example of appropriate behavior, whether the case might be the giving of charity, the repetition of a particular prayer, or even the use of a comb at certain times. These doings and sayings were recorded in two-part formulas, the *isnad,* or chain of transmission documenting the saying (and remember the Talmudic sages above), and the *matn,* the content of the tradition.

However, even these *hadith*s did not cover all cases or provide interpretations for all difficulties, and we come now to the concept *sunna*. Here, as in the case of the word and concept *torah,* the Muslim community was making use of an older term and idea. *Sunna* means a well-trodden path, that is, the way of older generations, the customary way of doing things. For the new Muslim community, it referred first to the Prophet's own *sunna*, to his way of doing things, then to the *sunna* of his Companions and the Successors; finally, it came to mean the *sunna*, the customary way, of the generations that followed, that is, the traditional way or the norm of the community. As in the case of the Talmud, the collections of traditions and legal materials came to be the objects of study in their own right; the commentaries themselves were commented upon and studied in schools, epitomes were gradually made, and these became the primary texts for study, and so on.

As the study of Islamic law, or *shari'a*, became formalized, the idea of the four roots of law took hold, especially as defined by al-Shafi'i (d. 820 CE). Using these "roots" or principles in sequence, or so the theory is, any legal problem can be solved. First, of course, comes the Qur'an, then the Sunna. If recourse to these sources will not solve a particular problem, a scholar may use *ijtihad*, personal effort at interpretation in the form of *qiyas* (a very strict kind of analogical reasoning).

Let us now examine the fourth, or last, root: *ijma'*, the consensus of the community. This notion concretizes a dynamic discussed above in connection with Judaism: the symbiosis between the community and its authorized interpreters. This relationship is not usually based on formal titles, certainly not on titles alone, but rather on the respect accorded to particular scholars, or to the scholarly establishment, and on the community's willingness to accept interpretations. Both of the communities we are considering—the Muslim and Jewish communities particularly during the medieval period—were more interested in accommodation than in exclusivity. That is, they wanted to keep believers within the fold, and, in general, the fold could be made to hold many different shades of opinion and practice. But of course, there were always checks on radical, self-serving, or partisan interpretations. In the long run, the mechanism of *ijma'*, of consensus, brought the extremes in toward the middle.

The idea of a new movement that gradually becomes the mainstream or establishment is a familiar one, and in the case of the Jewish and Islamic traditions, we see this process again. As the normative traditions grew more and more scholastic and legalistic, as the study of religion and religious texts became more and more a process of learning what commentators had written about previous commentaries on commentaries, both traditions saw the growth of movements concerned with spiritual renewal.

Part II: Circles of Scripture, Community, and Interpretation

At first, there were only individuals, then a few teachers with their disciples, who sought to recapture the immediacy of the prophetic experience, the initial impulse behind the words of the scriptures. While realizing, in the case of each of these two traditions, that prophecy was closed, that God would not choose a new human voice, these people sought an experiential, rather than a scholastic, knowledge of the divine: these people, of course, were the mystics.

However, in the Talmudic period—in fact, the Talmud itself contains texts that reflect mystical ideas and experiences—and into the medieval period, Jewish mysticism existed in a guarded and secretive way. Both because of the danger of mystical experimentation to the uninitiated, and because of the potential heterodoxy of the mystics' ideas, mysticism was frowned on and discouraged by the community authorities. Judaism saw the growth of a number of mystical movements: the *merkabah* mysticism of the early texts, the Zoharic *kabbalah* of the Spanish period, the Lurianic *kabbalah* of the sixteenth century, and the development of Hasidism in the seventeenth century.

The early movements began as esoteric ones, strictly for the initiates whose level of understanding was adequate to instruction in the mysteries of coded texts and mystical encounters; Hasidism, on the other hand, was more a movement of social revolution, since it invited the participation of worshippers who were not necessarily strong in "book-learning" but ready to praise God in any way they could, in song, dance, and story. Both types of movement reflect a dissatisfaction with what was perceived as a static and legalistic tradition, far removed from the divine voice that spoke through the words of Torah. Both types of movement, too, were met with intense hostility; the leaders were chastised for leading the faithful into error, and the followers were exhorted to mend their ways and return to the community.

However, the consensus mechanism of the community worked to normalize the extreme by inclusion. A few specific examples: some of the most famous (and beautiful) hymns and liturgical poems—now part of every mainstream Sabbath liturgy—are the product of these different mystical groups. The frequently used image of the Sabbath as a beautiful bride, again, is a legacy from the Lurianic kabbalists of sixteenth-century Palestine. And the Hasidim, some of whose songs are used by most congregations in North America, are hardly revolutionaries any more, but are rather seen as the arch-conservatives of Judaism.

Among Muslims, too, a mystical movement—or sequence of mystical movements—arose as early as the eighth century, associated with the label "Sufi." Led by pious figures who were already mourning the "golden age" of pure faith barely one hundred years before, a movement toward asceticism gradually took on mystical coloring. The ascetics were at least tolerated, and often respected, great figures like Hasan al-Basri (d. 728 CE) or Harith al-Muhasibi (d. 837 CE); but with the coming of a more ecstatic mysticism, the community, or what could be called the orthodox establishment, began to get uneasy. Abu Yazid al-Bistami's ecstatic utterances, the *ahikr* rituals of ecstasy-inducing dancing and chanting, and the antinomian (antilegalistic) tendencies of some of the other mystics created a climate of hostility and distrust on the part of the establishment that led, finally, to the execution of the most famous, and perhaps the most scandalous of the early mystics, al-Hallaj (d. 922 CE).

Surely, one might think, this kind of event would decide, once and for all, the community's consensus against mysticism. But once again, we see the wonderful dynamic of a religious community. The struggle among Muslims between intellectualized faith and mysticism was personified by the figure of al-Ghazali (d. 1111 CE), whose life both exemplified and guided the community's evolution. Having studied *falsafa* (which included Greek and Greek-influenced philosophy and the natural sciences) and the Islamic religious sciences, he felt that his life—and perhaps the life of the community—was at a standstill. The spiritual refreshment and renewal he found through a period spent in mystical retreat was also expressed in his great compendium, *Ihya' 'ulum al-din, The Revival of Religious Sciences*. In this guide, he showed how a reflective or meditative dimension can be introduced into all religious duties and obligations, and even into the most mundane aspects of life. His personal experience and recognition of the mystical way—together with an emphasis on "sober" mysticism and on meditative discipline—gave the definitive expression of legitimacy to a tendency or movement that was gaining ground within the community.

Conclusion

This all too hasty look at the development of the Islamic and Jewish traditions should have served at least one function, that of showing that a religious community cannot be a static entity. Living traditions, like living things, are characterized by organic growth, by changes that develop within the tradition. Even in responding to external challenges, these traditions use their own means, their own scriptures, their own *sunna* or *torah*, their own customary way of doing things. We have seen that through the circle of scripture and traditional interpretation, these communities have a great potential for evolution, and it will be interesting to see, too, how these communities change in the future.

In North America, where religious communities are close neighbors and interact more, perhaps, than in many other parts of the world, we have seen in the past tendencies toward liberalization and toleration, as well as an emphasis on civic virtues and on participation in the greater community. Let us hope that, whatever direction our communities take in the future, they will remain open to dialogues and to cooperation for the public benefit.

3

On Scripture and Its Exegesis

The Abraham-Ishmael Stories in the Torah and the Qur'an

Reuven Firestone

As BOTH A UNIVERSITY professor and a congregational rabbi, I find that I wear two different hats when approaching religious literature. At the university, I attempt to read religious texts from the standpoint of the objective scholar. I look at the Bible, for example, from a number of different angles, but I am always wary of reading it through the particularist lens of a religious tradition. My reference to the "particularist lens of a religious tradition" applies to the phenomenon in which religious dogma determines the manner in which sacred Scripture is read and interpreted.

A classic example of this phenomenon is the variance in Jewish and Christian readings of Isaiah 7:14–15 [ed.: NJPS]: "Assuredly, my Lord will give you a sign of His own accord! Look, the young woman is with child and about to give birth to a son. Let her name him Immanuel. (By the time he learns to reject the bad and choose the good, people will be feeding on curds and honey.)" Jewish tradition understands the text as a sign of God's unhappiness regarding a decision of the rulers of Israel, while Christian tradition reads it as God's sign of the future virgin birth of Jesus (see Matt 1:23).

One common practice found in religious exegesis, or interpretation, is that of assigning a new meaning to an old text. New interpretive meanings often become necessary as the ideas of the religion evolve and change. Sometimes, a new interpretive meaning may even be inserted awkwardly into a text which would not appear to provide that meaning. According to the standards of academic scholarship, which seeks to uncover what is assumed to have been the original intent of the text examined, religions tend to read their sacred texts subjectively, that is, through the shaping lens of religious dogma.

In contrast to my activities as an academic, however, I find that as a rabbi to my congregation, I read and interpret religious texts largely through the eyes and lenses of Jewish tradition. As a member of the Jewish clergy, I am an active participant in a long tradition of subjective religious interpretation. I delve deeply into the particularist Jewish styles of textual interpretation in order to derive moral or spiritual lessons, and I may even insert meaning into Scripture homiletically in order to derive a new lesson.

In an ecumenical and educational religious forum such as this collection of essays, neither the dry academic approach nor the subjective approach of any single religious tradition is satisfactory. To read a text only in one traditional religious mode—that is, for example, only through the lenses of Jewish tradition—is to withhold the respect due to other religious traditions such as Islam or Christianity. But to read a religious text only as an "objective" academic exercise also misses the point. That is, to reduce religion to nothing more than an instinctual universal human response to the unknown denies the unique spiritual reality of each and every individual tradition. A third approach must be considered which affirms the particularism of religious exegesis while at the same time transcends its tendency toward insularity or xenophobia. What follows represents an experiment in this enterprise, based on the divergent Jewish and Islamic readings of the story of Abraham and Ishmael.

Before beginning our examination of the topic at hand, however, I wish to stress an observation about monotheism. The "theism" of monotheism tends to be treated in great detail by all monotheistic religions, but the "mono," meaning "one," tends to have been taken for granted since the elimination of polytheism in the Middle East and in the West. That is to say, all expressions of monotheism agree in the existence of only one deity, however that deity may be understood and defined among the great variety of monotheistic theologies. The "mono" of monotheism, however, is invariably applied by each religious tradition as firmly to *itself* as it is to God. It is expressed by all monotheistic religions in the following way: "There is only one God, and God has affirmed for us that there is only one true religion—our religion."

Monotheism is, by definition, exclusivist. God is the exclusive object of worship. But the religious institutions professing monotheism are also exclusivist. Each claims that, just as there is only one God, God has chosen it to bring God's message to all humankind. In common speech, the message is that there is only one "true religion," and that is . . . "our religion." It should be noted that this sense of absolutism in self-definition is expressed within as well as among the three great monotheistic traditions. Each has its own internal bickering as to which expression of Judaism or Christianity or Islam is the "true" religion.

With this attribute of monotheistic exclusivism in mind, we realize that though there are many holy books in this world, monotheism demands that there be only one true Scripture. The logic of monotheism insists that one God could not have given three or more different and sometimes even contradictory scriptures. Only one scripture can be true Scripture. For Jews, it is the *Tanakh,* or Hebrew Bible, and most specifically that divinely revealed section known as the Torah, revealed to the people of God's covenant: the Jews. For Christians, it is the New Testament, the proof of the New Covenant obtaining between God and Christians: those who witness the reality of Jesus as the Messiah and the Salvation of humankind. For Muslims, it is the holy Qur'an, the final and perfect revelation given through the last and final prophet Muhammad, to the early Arab Muslims, and taught to the "true believers": the *umma,* or community of Islam.

All monotheistic religions approach other religions' holy books through lenses formed by their own Scripture and tradition. Two important considerations apply here. The first is that older scripture is interpreted through the lenses of newer scripture. Christians, for example, read the "Old Testament" through the hermeneutic of the New Testament. To use my now familiar metaphor, they read and interpret it through the particularist lenses of their own religious tradition. Similarly, Muslims see the *Tawrat* (Torah) and the *Injil* ("Evangelikon" or New Testament) through the lenses of religious tradition established by the Qur'an. No religion reads any scripture "objectively," without being profoundly influenced by the claims of its own religious tradition.

The second rule is that newer claims for sacred scripture can never be acceptable to older traditions if the new claims were made after the canonization of the earlier scripture. Once the boundaries are established, they cannot be broken. Christians, therefore, cannot accept the Qur'an as revelation. And Jews can accept neither the New Testament nor the Qur'an. Each of the monotheistic traditions agrees that there can be no God but

God, but each also insists that there can be no true or accurate revelation but the "real," that is . . . "our" revelation.

With all this in mind, we can begin to understand the natural difficulty that adherents of Western monotheistic religions have in truly respecting the sacred scripture of other religions. It is difficult for even the most open-minded to escape the feeling that s/he is observing in another Scripture a mistaken presumption, a misinterpretation of God's true design. It is, for this very reason, necessary to try as best we can to remove our particularist lenses if we wish to engage in a truly open and fruitful discussion across the exegetical boundaries of religious traditions. We shall try to do just that as we examine two recognizably similar but quite different tellings of the story of Abraham and Ishmael.

Many of us are familiar with the journeys and activities of Abraham found in the Hebrew Bible. He left Ur of the Chaldees with his father, and journeyed to Haran (in today's southern Turkey), where his father died. From Haran, he journeyed along with his wife Sarah and nephew Lot to a land known as *eretz kana'an*, the Land of the Canaanites, in response to God's command. Aside from a brief sojourn in Egypt, the Bible depicts Abraham thereafter living a nomadic life within the area known later in the Bible as *eretz yisra'el*, the Land of the Israelites. He never again leaves his new land, the land promised by God to him and his offspring. While in Egypt, however, according to Jewish tradition but not explicitly mentioned in the Bible, Hagar was given as a handmaid to Abraham's wife Sarah.

Abraham proceeds to have a number of adventures until we arrive at chapter 16 of Genesis. Now we must realize that any retelling of a story, whether translation or paraphrase, is an interpretation of that story. By our choice of words or even inflection, we emphasize or deemphasize various aspects, unconsciously as well as knowingly, whenever we re-tell a story. With that caveat in mind, we shall continue the narrative.

Sarah cannot become pregnant, so she gives her Egyptian handmaid, Hagar, to Abraham so that he will attain progeny through her. After Hagar becomes pregnant, a serious family conflict develops between the two women. Sarah, the woman with higher social status, treats Hagar so harshly that she flees into the desert, where she meets an angel of God. The angel commands Hagar to return to Sarah, and gives Hagar a somewhat enigmatic prophecy regarding her future son, Ishmael, whose offspring will be innumerable. Hagar returns and Ishmael is born.

In chapter 17, the covenant between Abraham and God is reaffirmed through the act of circumcision. Ishmael is circumcised along with Abraham's entire male household. God also promises Abraham a son through Sarah, and informs him that the covenant will be attained only through Isaac—not through Ishmael. But God also assures Abraham that Ishmael will father a great nation, begetting twelve princes.

Chapter 18 is the story of the three visitors to Abraham, who tell him in Sarah's presence of their future son who will be born the following year. The visitors then set out to destroy the cities of Sodom and Gemorah.

When the story returns to the occasion of Isaac's birth in chapter 21, we learn that Isaac is born and circumcised. At Isaac's weaning celebration a year or so later, however, the smoldering conflict between Sarah and Hagar bursts forth into a full-scale fight. Abraham is deeply saddened by this, but God instructs him to follow Sarah's wishes. Sarah thereupon decides to banish Hagar and Ishmael, so Abraham rises early and sends them off with provisions which are soon spent in the desert.

Hagar sets Ishmael down under a bush and walks far enough away so that she will not hear the cries of her son dying of thirst, for she cannot bear the pain. She sits down and cries. But God hears the voice of Ishmael and sends an angel who confirms God's promise that Ishmael will become a great nation. God provides a well for them and also continues to provide for the boy as he grows up in the desert of Paran.

This is essentially the end of Ishmael's story in the Bible. A brief comment can be found in Genesis 25:9, where Ishmael joins with Isaac in burying their father Abraham. The names of Ishmael's twelve sons are also listed there, along with the statement that Ishmael lived to the age of 137.

Nothing more can be found of Ishmael in the Hebrew Bible. A few references to him can be found in the New Testament, with one striking allegory found in Galatians 4:21–31. The New Testament references, however, provide no additional insight into Ishmael's life.

The Qur'an, however, provides important additional information about Abraham and Ishmael. Because the Qur'an is not organized by chronology as is most of the Hebrew Bible, no single section will provide a full accounting of their story. References to Abraham and Ishmael must therefore be collected from a variety of chapters and contexts.

Qur'an 14:37 mentions that Abraham caused some of his offspring to live in a desolate valley next to God's sacred House in order to establish regular prayer. While the location of that sacred place is not given here,

Qur'an 3:96 teaches that the first house of worship provided for humankind was at the blessed Bakka, a synonym, say the Muslim commentators, for the sacred city of Mecca (pronounced "Makka" in Arabic). The Qur'an continues in the following verse to tell us that the famous *maqam Ibrahim*—the station of Abraham—is located in that place. In Mecca today can be found a Station of Abraham within the Sacred Compound, in which lies the Ka'ba, the sacred ritual center of Islam. The Qur'an explains further that this is the place to which the Pilgrimage, the Hajj, is a religious obligation. In fact, Qur'an 2:124–129 depicts Abraham and Ishmael raising up the foundations of the Ka'ba and purifying it for the Pilgrimage and for prayer.

How did Abraham get to Mecca? The Qur'an does not tell us. It rather assumes that those hearing or reading the Qur'an already know the answer. And indeed, traditional Islamic exegesis recalls ancient legends explaining how Abraham came to Mecca. The following legend can be found in most of the authoritative Qur'an commentaries and is told on the authority of one of the most respected early Qur'an commentators, 'Abdallah ibn 'Abbas, known as the father of qur'anic exegesis.

Although no biblical verses are quoted, nor is the Bible ever referred to, the legend is immediately recognizable to those familiar with the biblical story of the tragic conflict between Sarah and Hagar. As in Genesis 21:14, Abraham gives Hagar provisions for her journey; but in the Islamic legend, Abraham leaves Sarah and the land of the Canaanites and personally brings Hagar and Ishmael to the desert location of the future holy city of Mecca. Abraham deposits them under a thorned tree next to the location of the future Ka'ba, reminiscent of Hagar's leaving Ishmael under the bush in Genesis 21:15. Abraham then begins his long journey home, but Hagar follows and asks to whom Abraham is entrusting them in such a desolate place. After a long silence, he answers, "to God." Abraham then recites this prayer found in Qur'an 14:37 [ed.: the author provides his own translation of qur'anic passages]: "O Lord! I have made some of my offspring live in an uncultivated valley by Your sacred house, in order, O Lord, that they establish regular prayer."

Ishmael is only an infant at the time, and when the water in Hagar's water skin is depleted, she becomes dehydrated and her milk stops flowing for her son. As Ishmael's thirst becomes unbearable, he begins writhing or having a seizure. Hagar cannot bear to see him die, so she leaves him under the bush and climbs a nearby hill looking for help. When none is to be found, she runs across to the opposite hill and looks from there, but sees nothing. She runs between the two hills seven times. Desperate, she finally hears a voice and runs back to her son, whom she sees is accompanied by an angel, often named in the text as Gabriel. He brings forth water from the ground for them and Hagar dams up the flow and scoops it into her water skin, thus saving the life of her son. The angel then tells Hagar that the boy and his father will one day build the House of God at that very spot.

According to Muslims, the well that the angel brought forth is called Zamzam, and is the very well within today's Sacred Precinct at Mecca, the well from which today's pilgrims drink when they make the Hajj to Mecca and its environs. The hills between which Hagar ran searching for help are the famous hills of Safa and Marwa in Mecca, and every Muslim pilgrim ritually re-enacts Hagar's running between them seven times even today when participating in the Hajj.

The story is not over, however, for after Hagar and Ishmael are established in Mecca, a group from the Arab tribe of Jurhum happens by and notices signs of life in what was thought to be a desolate and dry valley. They send a scout, who finds Hagar and Ishmael near the sacred well. The tribal leaders ask permission of Hagar to settle with them there, which is granted, and they then bring their families to Mecca. As Ishmael grows up, he learns the Arabic language and culture from the Jurhum tribe, and eventually marries one of the Jurhumite women.

This might be an appropriate ending to the legend as well, but in fact it continues, for Abraham is not satisfied that he left his oldest son alone with Hagar in the desert, despite the fact that he knows God will be with the boy (as in Gen 21:20). As a loving and responsible father who has not rejected his eldest son, he feels the need to check up on him, so he journeys to Mecca. Ishmael is away from home at the time, but Abraham meets Ishmael's wife. She is inhospitable, rude, and downright mean to Abraham (who represents the very epitome of hospitality in both Jewish and Islamic tradition). Abraham gives her a message for Ishmael: "divorce your wife," in a code she cannot understand. He then proceeds on his return journey homeward. Upon Ishmael's return, he immediately senses that his father was there, and asks his wife what has happened. She innocently tells him about a strange and ugly old man who came by, and Ishmael knows from the coded message that he must divorce her. He then marries another woman from the Jurhum tribe.

A while later, Abraham once again feels the need to check up on his son. Ishmael is again away when he arrives, but this time Abraham is received with wonderful hospitality and respect by Ishmael's new wife. Abraham then asks her to give Ishmael the coded message that his wife is the proper choice. They have children, and through a long genealogy not provided in this legend but connected to the legend by other Islamic sources, we come to realize that the ultimate result of this divinely sanctioned match (through the prophet Abraham) is the birth of Muhammad, the last and greatest of all prophets.

Abraham visits Mecca a third time. This time he finds Ishmael at home, trimming arrows in the shade of the same tree under which Abraham left him and his mother so many years before. Abraham informs Ishmael that God has given him a command. Ishmael replies that if God has commanded anything to Abraham, he is obligated to carry it out. Abraham then informs Ishmael of God's command to them both to build God's house, the sacred Ka'ba, as in Qur'an 2:127. They both follow the divine commandment, and Ishmael hands his father the stones as Abraham sets them in place on God's House. As they build, they pray the verse found in Qur'an 2:127: "Our Lord, accept [this] from us, for You are the All-Hearing, the All-Knowing."

We have in the Jewish and the Islamic tellings of the Abraham-Ishmael story two different, and in many respects contradictory versions, each based upon a different sacred scripture. According to the biblical view, God's covenant with Abraham is established with Isaac, not the rejected Ishmael. Isaac has a son named Jacob, who is subsequently renamed Israel by God's angel, and he fathers the twelve tribes who will make up the Israelite people. The covenant is established with Isaac—not Ishmael. Isaac is a willing Sacrifice to God on Mt. Moriah, the very location of the future Temple in Jerusalem—God's House. Abraham's progeny will include David, the greatest king of Israel, and the symbol for unity and salvation of the Jewish people. [Ed.: Though not named in the qur'anic telling of the story, Islamic tradition identifies Ishmael as the son willing to be sacrificed to God.]

But according to the qur'anic view, Abraham personally brings his oldest son Ishmael, never rejected, to the sacred site of Mecca. It is in Mecca that they will build the House of God. And Abraham is careful to see to it that Ishmael marries a proper woman who will be worthy of the status of matriarch, mothering the genealogical line that will result in Muhammad, the greatest prophet and the vehicle for God's greatest gift, the Qur'an.

According to Jewish tradition, Ishmael's history became irrelevant to the sacred history of God's people. God's sacred design in history rests in the line of Isaac. But according to Islamic tradition, Ishmael is the progenitor of God's greatest prophet who would one day lead his people to establish God's rule on earth. Sacred history rests in the line of Ishmael.

Now here is a classic case of two religious traditions telling different and even competing stories about the same paradigmatic characters. This observation is not new. Ever since ancient times, adherents of various religions knew that other religions perceived history and the path to salvation differently, and they often discussed, argued, disputed, and even committed violence over their disagreements.

Every monotheistic religious tradition has evolved its own exclusivist defense against the claims of others. Jewish tradition has tended to consider the Islamic claims to be mistakes or attempts to distort religious truth in the name of temporal power. Islamic tradition has tended to consider Jewish claims to be the result of tampering with the text of the Torah, which originally contained a clear prophecy telling of the coming of Muhammad and the rise of Islam. Both have considered their scripture coeval with Creation. Contradictory claims cannot be tolerated. There can only be one TRUTH. Somebody has got it right, and the others have got it wrong. And one knows who's who.

The classic academic approach would be to analyze the texts of both traditions and try to determine if one tradition may have "borrowed" from the other, or to try to determine if they both may have evolved out of a common tradition. It would break down and analyze each unit of each rendition of the legend to try to extract its secrets. This tendency toward reductivism among academic approaches has the effect of reducing the power of the legends to merely the sum of simple, even mediocre parts. It tends to ignore the unique literary qualities of the different versions and the truths that legends such as these provide.

A different approach to competing religious claims such as these is needed, but not one based on theological doctrine. I have heard religious thinkers, for example, devise intricate theological devices to solve mutually exclusive doctrinal problems such as the example discussed here. But these attempts tend to remain unsatisfactory to at least one, and often both parties to the conflict. I have also heard the common defeatist atheistic view that the contradictory claims do nothing more than demonstrate the arbitrariness of religion, showing that religion can only grasp at straws to explain human and natural phenomena.

An alternative approach to competing, even contradictory religious beliefs such as the example given here with Abraham, Isaac, and Ishmael might serve to stimulate some discussion about the process of interreligious dialogue. This approach would require, first of all, that we be willing to acknowledge that we will never determine the "original" text. Jews claim that the Torah is chronologically older than the Qur'an. The qur'anic stories of biblical characters therefore, must be variants (i.e., mistaken versions or distortions) of biblical stories. According to this view the Islamic telling of the Abraham story is a conscious distortion of the Bible in order to justify the later claim that Islam is God's favored religion.

Muslims, however, claim that the Qur'an was never created but actually preceded Creation. It existed before the giving of the Torah on Mt. Sinai. And since the "true" story once existed also in biblical revelation Jewish religious leaders once knew of Ishmael's chosen status but consciously distorted their scripture in order to justify the claim that Judaism is God's favored religion. Both claim the "original" and therefore "correct" story.

But modern studies in literary theory challenge both views. It has become evident that early stories on biblical themes have been found in a number of ancient civilizations, from Mesopotamia to Egypt, which predate the biblical tellings. It appears, in fact, that there never was an "original" telling of the Abraham story in the literary sense. The legends have existed in various forms since time immemorial. No religion can claim exclusive ownership or the right to an exclusive "truth" in this regard.

The answer to the question of which is the "original" text is simple: it is the wrong question. Arguments over "which came first" can never be resolved. They are counterproductive. They do not promote dialogue and understanding—only polemics and dispute. We must overcome the need to figure out "who was right," and move on to more important issues.

Second, we must be willing to respect the religious drives of those coming out of different paths to God. We all need the personal and religious confidence to stake our efforts on the assumption that something cherished by intelligent and sensitive people over many generations is at least unlikely to be trivial. More likely, it contains great truths from which we may also learn.

For me as a religious Jew having grown up believing in the reality of God's covenant with the Jewish people, the Islamic telling of the Abraham-Ishmael story presents a challenge—not to my beliefs, but to my smugness, to my general attitude toward other religions. Studying the Islamic approach does not cause me to abandon my beliefs. On the contrary, it opens my eyes to understand that Muslims, like Jews, see themselves in a special relationship with God in their acting-out of God's commandments. As I come to understand the depth of this relationship, I come to respect and value the spirituality and religious imperative of my Muslim colleagues, even though I am coming from a different place.

This is not to say that religious truth is only relative. God does not change. God is one and is eternal. But human perceptions and understandings of God differ, and our perceptions are affected by many things, including language, culture, technology, and history. Jews and Muslims act on what is believed to be God's demands upon them. As we learn to respect the religiosity and spirituality of each other's traditions at the same time that we affirm the depth and meaning of our own, we need no longer suffer the affront nor the anger when we note the differences between us.

In the case of the Abraham-Isaac-Ishmael story, Jews and Muslims cannot resolve the question of whether God's blessing to Abraham passed to Isaac or Ishmael. But that question is the wrong question. We must ask ourselves, rather, how to accept the fact that we have different, even sometimes contradictory assumptions and beliefs, and still work together for mutual benefit.

We need not try to convince each other to agree with each other's religious views. We need not seek converts. And we need not try to create a new hybrid religion of Judaism and Islam. We should rather note these differences at the same time that we affirm our commonalities. When Jews and Muslims work together and learn more about one another, even if for limited periods of time, we promote contact and discussion about interests that we do have in common, and we learn that some of the negative assumptions we have had about each other are not borne out in fact. We learn to eliminate many of the stereotypes and subsequently learn to deal with the important issues in a new and more constructive manner. Each group need only offer the respect that is due to ancient traditions and religious beliefs, and expect the same in return.

In this shrinking world with greater intermingling between religions and cultures, in an age when the term "global village" has become an accurate description of modern life, every group must learn to accept differences at the same time that it believes in its own way. Whether Abraham's blessing passed to Isaac or Ishmael is a question that cannot be reconciled by Jews and Muslims. The question is, can we accept the fact that we have different assumptions and beliefs and still live together? In the world of interreligious dialogue, the term "mutual respect" is the key. Not "right" or "wrong." With this in mind, the children of Ishmael and the children of Isaac, all the children of Abraham, will be able to work together here and abroad in order to build a future beneficial to all.

4

Mary, Mother of Jesus, in Christian and Islamic Traditions

R. Marston Speight

THE FIGURE OF MARY, the Mother of Jesus, as depicted in the Qur'an and the Bible, is one of the important meeting places for Muslims and Christians. When we talk about Mary together, at least in Scriptural terms, we have a fairly clear idea of what the other party is saying. Perhaps the reason for this is that in the Qur'an and Bible, Mary is always referring to someone else or to something else.[1] In the Qur'an, for example, even when Mary's mother holds her newborn girl-child before the Lord, making the infant the centerpiece of the scene, the mother says, "[I] commend her to Thee with her seed, to protect them from the accursed Satan" (Qur'an 3:36). Already the mighty seed of Mary is joined in thought with the emerging figure who exists for the purpose of nurturing that seed and bringing it to fruition.

When we leave the domain of Scripture, Christians and Muslims diverge widely in their interpretation of Mary, so widely that I have not chosen in this context to explore the avenues of rich development either of Mariology in Christian thought or of the veneration of Mary in Islam. I shall keep to the Scriptural material in this chapter for the most part.

---

1. A remark made regarding Mary in the Bible by Halkes, "Mary and Women," 68.

My approach to the Scriptural data calls for two other preliminary remarks:

1. I am interested in the cross-referencing of the two religious traditions, to use a term of Kenneth Cragg.[2] The Scripture of one religion is not set forth as the standard beside which the other Scripture is placed, to see how it measures up. Instead, the two Books interact with each other, with cross-referencing in both directions. The appendix to this chapter shows the biblical verses in the first column, and the qur'anic verses in the second, but this arrangement is chronological only. It does not indicate judgment of priority in importance or in truthfulness.

2. Such an approach requires that we not think of Islam (coming later than Christianity) as "borrowing" from Christianity in its elaboration of the figure of Mary, but rather that we consider both Islam and Christianity as drawing upon a common store of information and inspiration, a fund of material that goes beyond either what the Bible says or what the Qur'an says about Mary.

Looking at the printed texts arranged in parallel columns in the appendix, the qur'anic passages are taken from Arberry's translation[3] and the biblical passages are from the Revised Standard Version. The following parallels may be noted:

    a. The first heading (see appendix) is the "Family of Joseph" and the "Family of Mary," so we have a summary background of the legal parents of Jesus. In dealing with the family members of Mary and Joseph, serious difficulties have long been noted: Mary, as a member of the family of Imran (Qur'an 3:33–37), is called the sister of Aaron (Qur'an 19:28), suggesting a confusion of her identity with that of Miriam in the Hebrew Scriptures (Exod 15:20). Joseph's father is named Jacob in Matthew's account but Heli in Luke 3:23. So exegetes made a tremendous effort to clear up these discrepancies or differences. However, efforts to clear up these problems are not entirely adequate, at least not to everyone's satisfaction. The names given may represent a symbolic approach to the family background of Mary and Joseph, rather than a strictly genealogical approach.

2. Cragg, *Christ and the Faiths*.
3. Arberry, *Koran Interpreted*.

Part II: Circles of Scripture, Community, and Interpretation

b. Regarding the *dedication* of the infant Mary to God by her Mother, unnamed in the Qur'an, and named St. Anne in extra-biblical sources, this incident paves the way for the important stage in Mary's life, that is,

c. Her miraculous *purification*. Christians depend on the extra-biblical sources for their information about this event. But in the Qur'an it is clearly said that the child will be protected from the accursed Satan. See Qur'an 3:42 for another mention of the purification.

d. In the Bible Zechariah is not brought into direct touch with Mary, although he is an important figure, as the father of John the Baptist, in preparing the way for Jesus. On the other hand, the qur'anic story of Zechariah's *watching over the young Mary* and her testimony to the exuberant mercy of God (3:37) sets the tone for the lavish display of divine mercy soon to be described in the coming pivotal event of Mary's life, for Mary says, "Truly God provisions whomsoever He will without reckoning."

e. Without going into the details of the *announcement of Mary's conception*, we note the following parallels:

f. *Withdrawal* of Mary from human society to a place apart from the world. In the Qur'an this occurs before the appearance of the angel, whereas in the Bible Mary goes to the hill country of Judah after the announcement of the angel.

g. The *messenger* of God is Gabriel (Gospel), the divine Spirit in the form of a man (Qur'an), and a collective angelic announcement (Qur'an).

h. The Bible records the *salutation* of the angel to Mary, but the Qur'an simply states that the messenger presented himself to her.

i. Mary's surprise and troubled *state of mind* are noted in both the Qur'an and the Bible. In the Gospel it simply states that she was troubled and perplexed. But the Qur'an shows her perplexity and her troubled state of mind in her prayerful seeking of refuge in God and her appeal to the messenger's integrity (19:18).

j. The angel *reassures* Mary, and, in the same breath,

k. gives the *promise* of a child. The elaboration of the promise, found in Qur'an 3:45, is packed with information about Jesus. Sura (chapter) 3 of the Qur'an is a later revelation than Sura 19.

l. Mary's *perplexity* on hearing the promise of a child focuses on her virginity: "How shall this be," she says, "since I have no husband?" (Luke 1:34).

m. *Reassurance* comes as the messenger in the Gospel describes the holy, divine, miraculous birth, and adds confirmation by telling about Elizabeth (the kinswoman of Mary), who has conceived a child in her old age. The qur'anic word emphasizes the sovereign creative power of God (corresponding to Luke 1:37). Luke says, "For with God nothing will be impossible." The Qur'an says, "God creates what He will. When He decrees a thing He does but say to it 'Be,' and it is" (Qur'an 3:47).

Two other qur'anic passages speak of the mysterious divine action resulting in the virgin birth. Here it is a question of the "how" of the creative act. In the previously cited text, Sura 3, God simply says "be," and it is, whereas in Suras 21 and 66 there is a certain elaboration upon this, a statement very mysterious indeed, but an approach at least to the "how" of this divine creative act. Take Sura 66:12, which is astonishing indeed: "And Mary, Imran's daughter, who guarded her virginity, so We breathed into her of Our Spirit, and she confirmed the Words of her Lord and His Books, and became one of the obedient."

Arberry's translation of this verse (see the appendix) conceals the concrete meaning of the original Arabic. He translates the first part of the verse figuratively or idiomatically, "And Mary . . . guarded her virginity"; but the literal meaning of the Arabic brings the generative organs of the woman into the picture: *Wa Maryama ibnata 'Imran allati ahsanat farjaha* . . . ("And Mary, the daughter of Imran, who guarded her vulva . . ."). According to Arberry, the second part of the verse says that God breathed into *her* of his spirit, but grammatically the Arabic seems to say that God breathed into *it* (i.e., her vulva): *fa-nafakhna fihi min ruhina*. In this way divine power is said to have brought about pregnancy in Mary.

This striking figurative language in the Qur'an finds a parallel in the Gospel of Luke (1:35), where the angel says to the Virgin: "The Holy Spirit will come upon you, and the power of the Most High will overshadow you; therefore the child to be born will be called holy, the Son of God." The original Greek of this verse is as follows: *pneuma hagion epeleusetai epi se, kai dunamis hupsistou episkiasei soi. Dio kai to gennomenon hagion klethesetai huios theou.*

The divine spirit is the active force in both Scriptural statements. In Luke, the action is mysterious ("come upon, overshadow") and less concrete than in the Qur'an. However, the result is the same in both cases: pregnancy in the virgin womb. And the Gospel goes on to specify further the outcome of this divine intervention in Mary's life: a "holy" child, the "Son of God."

The Qur'an is silent as to Mary's response to this reassurance, but the Bible enlarges on her faithful response and her overflowing joy as the realization dawns that she is the object of extraordinary divine favor (Luke 1:38, 46–55). So we have the beautiful song of Mary which Christians sing and recite constantly in their services of worship, "My soul magnifies the Lord, and my spirit rejoices in God my Savior" (46–47), Mary's grateful response to the reassurance of the angel.

n. Telling of the *birth of Jesus,* the Gospel describes its taking place in a semi-public setting, amid the crowds in Bethlehem, in a busy inn-yard, with an audience of shepherds not long after. In contrast, the Qur'an tells of an absolutely private birth in the desert: "So she conceived him, and withdrew with him to a distant place. And the birthpangs surprised her by the trunk of the palm-tree" (Qur'an 19:22–23).

o. The Gospel discreetly notes the *people's lack of understanding* by giving Joseph's plan to divorce Mary when he found her pregnant. By contrast the Qur'an describes a sharp confrontation between Mary and her people, and a miraculous defense by the voice of the infant Jesus.

p. The Scriptures are concerned to show how Mary was strengthened in her faith and also challenged after bearing her son. Only the Qur'an records her momentary wavering as she gives birth in the desert. And we have a combined witness or testimony of shepherds, wise men, miraculously provided food and drink, an aged saint's inspired words, and a mysterious voice all joining to amaze and confound the humble virgin. Her response is to "ponder" these things in her heart (Gospel), and to vow a fast to God (Qur'an).

Mary has no title in the Scriptures of either Islam or

Christianity. However, in two Suras of the Qur'an (19 and 21), the accounts of her lifetransforming experiences are placed in a context of stories about the prophets. Therefore, there is justification for the statement, supported by many Muslims, that Mary was one of the prophets from God.

In what is said about Mary in Qur'an and Bible, we, who live in the aftermath of thirteen centuries of discussion, sense that we are only a step away from all of the stark and apparently irreducible divergence that exists between Islam and Christianity: the questions of the divine sonship of Jesus, of original sin, and of the incarnation. It has not been my purpose to develop the nature of this multiple divergence. Rather I have stressed the Scriptural figure of Mary that draws Muslims and Christians together. Perhaps in mutual contemplation of this holy woman, who with her child is "a sign unto all beings" (Qur'an 21:91), we shall together learn to deal more adequately with our religious disagreements, and even better, perhaps we can take steps together, Muslims and Christians, to share that superlative quality of Mary, mirrored by her words in the Gospel, "Let it be to me according to Your word" (Luke 1:38) and described in the Qur'an as "she became one of the obedient" (66:12).

Part II: Circles of Scripture, Community, and Interpretation

Appendix

Mary, Mother of Jesus, in Christian and Islamic Traditions

Bible	*Qur'an*
a. Family of Joseph	a. Family of Mary

Matt 1:1, 16
    The book of the genealogy of Jesus Christ, the son of David, the son of Abraham . . . and Jacob father of Joseph the husband of Mary, of whom Jesus was born, who is called Christ.
	3:33–37
	    God chose Adam and Noah and the House of Abraham and the House of Imran above all beings, the seed of one another; God hears, and knows.

	b. [Mary's mother dedicates her to God] When the wife of Imran said, "Lord, I have vowed to Thee, in dedication, what is within my womb. Receive Thou this from me; Thou hearest, and knowest." And when she gave birth to her she said, "Lord, I have given birth to her, a female." (And God knew very well what she had given birth to; the male is not as the female.) "And I have named her Mary, and commend her to Thee with her seed,

Mary, Mother of Jesus

    c. [Purification of Mary]
       to protect them
       from the accursed Satan."
       Her Lord received the child
       with gracious favour,
       and by His goodness
       she grew up comely,

    d. [Zachariah watches over Mary]
       Zachariah taking
       charge of her. Whenever
       Zachariah went in to her
       in the Sanctuary, he
       found her provisioned.
       "Mary," he said,
       "how comes this to thee?"
       "From God," she said.
       Truly God provisions
       whomsover He will
       without reckoning.

e. Announcement of Conception

Luke 1:26–56

g. In the sixth month the angel Gabriel was sent from God to a city of Galilee named Nazareth, to a virgin betrothed to a man whose name was Joseph, of the house of David; and the virgin's name was Mary.

h. And he came to her and said, "Hail, O favored one, the Lord is with you!" But

19:16–21

And mention in the Book Mary

f. when she withdrew from her people
   to an eastern place,
   and she took a veil apart from
   them;

g. then We sent unto her Our Spirit
   that presented himself to her

h. a man without fault.
   She said, "I take refuge in
   the All-merciful from Thee!
   If thou fearest God...."

i. she was greatly troubled at the saying, and considered in her mind what sort of greeting this might be. And the angel
j. said to her, "Do not be afraid, Mary, for
   you have found favor with God. And behold, you will conceive in your womb
k. and bear a son, and you shall call his name Jesus. He will be great, and will be called the Son of the Most High; and the Lord God will give to him the throne of his father David, and he will reign over the house of Jacob for ever; and of his kingdom there will be no end." And Mary
l. said to the angel, "How shall this be,
   since I have no husband?" And the angel
m. said to her, "The Holy Spirit will come upon you, and the power of the Most High will overshadow you; therefore the child to be born will be called holy, the Son of God. And behold, your kinswoman Elizabeth in her old age has also conceived a son; and this is the sixth month with her who was called barren. For with God nothing will be impossible." And Mary

j. He said, "I am but a messenger come from thy Lord, to give thee
k.   a boy most pure."
l. She said, "How shall I have a son whom no mortal has touched, neither
   have I been unchaste?"
He said, "Even so thy Lord has said: 'Easy is that for Me; and that We
m. may appoint him a sign unto men and a mercy from Us; it is a thing decreed.'"

3:42–47
And when the angels said,
g. "Mary, God has chosen thee, and purified
c. thee; He has chosen thee above all women. Mary, be obedient to thy Lord, prostrating

said, "Behold, I am the handmaid of the Lord; let it be to me according to your word." And the angel departed from her.

f. In those days Mary arose and went with haste into the hill country, to a city of Judah, and she entered the house of Zechariah and greeted Elizabeth. And when Elizabeth heard the greeting of Mary, the babe leaped in her womb; and Elizabeth was filled with the Holy Spirit and she exclaimed with a loud cry, "Blessed are you among women, and blessed is the fruit of your womb! And why is this granted to me, that the mother of my Lord should come to me? For behold, when the voice of your greeting came to my ears, the babe in my womb leaped for joy. And blessed is she who believed that there would be a fulfillment of what was spoken to her from the Lord." And Mary said, "My soul magnifies the Lord, and my spirit rejoices in God my Savior, for he has regarded the low estate of his handmaiden. For behold, henceforth all generations will call me blessed; for he who is mighty and has done great things for me, and holy is his name. And his mercy is on those who fear him from generation to generation. He has shown strength with his arm, he has scattered the proud in the imagination of their hearts, he has put down the mighty from their

and bowing before Him."
(That is of the tidings
of the Unseen, that We
reveal to thee; for thou
wast not with them,
when they were casting quills
which of them should have
charge of Mary; thou
wast not with them, when
they were disputing.)
When the angels said,

k. "Mary, God gives thee good
tidings of a Word from Him
whose name is Messiah
Jesus, son of Mary;
high honoured shall he be
in this world and the next
near stationed to God.
He shall speak to men
in the cradle, and of age,
and righteous he shall be."

l. "Lord," said Mary,
"how shall I have a son
seeing no mortal has
touched me?" "Even so,"

m. God said, "God
creates what He will.
When He decrees a thing
He does but say to it
'Be,' and it is."

thrones, and exalted those of low degree; he has filled the hungry with good things, and the rich he has sent empty away. He has helped his servant Israel, in remembrance of his mercy, as he spoke to our fathers, to Abraham and to his posterity forever." And Mary remained with her about three months, and returned to her home.

Birth of Jesus

Luke 2:4–7

n. And Joseph also went up from Galilee, from the city of Nazareth, to Judea, to the city of David, which is called Bethlehem, because he was of the house and lineage of David, to be enrolled with Mary, his betrothed, who was with child. And while they were there, the time came for her to be delivered. And she gave birth to her first-born son and wrapped him in swaddling clothes, and laid him in a manger, because there was no place for them in the inn.

Matt 1:18–25

Now the birth of Jesus Christ took place in this way. When his mother Mary had been betrothed to Joseph, before they came together she was found to be with child of the Holy Spirit;

21:91

m. And she who guarded her virginity, so We breathed into her of Our spirit
and appointed her and her son to be a
sign unto all beings.

66:12

And Mary, Imran's daughter, who guarded her virginity, so We breathed into her of Our Spirit, and she confirmed the Words of her Lord and His Books, and became one of the obedient.

19:22, 23a

So she conceived him, and withdrew with him to a distant place. And the

n. birthpangs surprised her by the trunk of the palm-tree.

o. The People's Lack of Understanding

and her husband Joseph, being a just man and unwilling to put her to shame, resolved to divorce her quietly. But as he considered this, behold, an angel of the Lord appeared to him in a dream, saying, "Joseph, son of David, do not fear to take Mary your wife, for that which is conceived in her is of the Holy Spirit; she will bear a son, and you shall call his name Jesus, for he will save his people from their sins." All this took place to fulfill what the Lord had spoken by the prophet: "Behold, a virgin shall conceive and bear a son, and his name shall be called Emmanuel" (which means, God with us). When Joseph woke from sleep, he did as the angel of the Lord commanded him; he took his wife, but knew her not until she had borne a son; and he called his name Jesus.

4:155, 156

God sealed them . . . for their unbelief, and their uttering against Mary a mighty calumny, ...

19:27–32

Then she brought the child to her folk
carrying him; and they said,
"Mary, thou hast surely committed
  a monstrous thing!
Sister of Aaron, thy father was not
a wicked man, nor was thy mother
  a woman unchaste."
Mary pointed to the child then;
but they said, "How shall we speak
to one who is still in the cradle,
  a little child?"
He said, "Lo, I am God's servant;
God has given me the Book, and
 made me a Prophet.
Blessed He has made me, wherever
I may be; and He has enjoined me
to pray, and to give the alms, so
  long as I live,
and likewise to cherish my mother."

Part II: Circles of Scripture, Community, and Interpretation

p. Confirmation and Comfort for Mary

Luke 2:16–19

> And they [the shepherds] went with haste, and found Mary and Joseph, and the babe lying in a manger. And when they saw it they made known the saying which had been told them concerning the child; and all who heard it wondered at what the shepherds told them. But Mary kept all these things, pondering them in her heart.

Matt 2:10–11

> When they [the wise men] saw the star, they rejoiced exceedingly with great joy; and going into the house they saw the child with Mary his mother, and they fell down and worshiped him. Then, opening their treasures, they offered him gifts, gold and frankincense and myrrh.

Luke 2:33–35

> And his father and his mother marveled at what was said about him; and Simeon blessed them and said to Mary his mother, "Behold, this child is set for the fall and rising of many in Israel, and for a sign that is spoken against (and a sword will pierce through your own soul also), that thoughts out of many hearts may be revealed."

19: 23b–26

> She said,
> "Would I had died ere this, and become
>   a thing forgotten!"
> But the one that was below her called to her, "Nay, do not sorrow; see, the Lord has set below thee
>   a rivulet.
> Shake also to thee the palm-trunk, and there shall come tumbling upon thee
>   dates fresh and ripe.
> Eat therefore, and drink, and be comforted; and if thou shouldest see
>   any mortal,
> say, 'I have vowed to the All-merciful a fast, and today I will not speak
>   to any man.'"

Bibliography

Arberry, Arthur J. *The Koran Interpreted*. New York: Macmillan, 1955.
Cragg, Kenneth. *The Christ and the Faiths: Theology in Cross-Reference*. Philadelphia: Westminster, 1986.
Halkes, Catharina. "Mary and Women." *Concilium* 168 (1983) 66–73.

5

Jesus in the Qur'an

Some Similarities and Differences with the New Testament

Muzammil H. Siddiqi

JESUS IS THE COMMON link between Islam and Christianity. Muslims believe in Jesus as they believe in Muhammad and other prophets of God. Prophet Muhammad is not the only prophet in Islam—he is only one of the many prophets of God. Before him came many prophets who preached the same message of submission to God, that is, Islam. The uniqueness of Muhammad, according to Muslim beliefs, is that he is the final prophet and messenger of God. Islam does not recognize any prophet after Muhammad.

Jesus is called *'Isa* in the Qur'an. He is also known as *al-Masih* (the Christ) and *Ibn Maryam* (Son of Mary). He has many other beautiful names and titles in the Qur'an. He is a highly respected religious figure. Outside the Christian church, there is no religious community that has given Jesus as much honor, respect, esteem, and love as Muslims have done.

The Qur'an and Bible as Sources for the Life of Jesus

The Qur'an and the New Testament are the two most important sacred texts that have spoken about Jesus. The nature of these two texts is, however, quite different. The central theme of the Qur'an is not Jesus, but God. The Qur'an mentions Jesus as one among the many great prophets of God. The Qur'an talks about God on every page and tells us about what he has done and continues to do for humankind, and what he wants from them. God's prophets came for this very purpose. They came to remind people about their relation with God and his creation. For the authors of the New Testament, Jesus is the main figure. He is the center and the focus of the New Testament story. They talk about his life, death, and resurrection. They focus on his teachings, his message, and the response of his contemporaries to him.

It is comparatively easy to present the Christology of the Qur'an. The Qur'an is one book, coming from one source. It was presented, memorized, and preserved within the life of Prophet Muhammad and shortly thereafter. Muslims believe that the Qur'an is the *ipsissima verba* of God. It is, literally, *the* word of God. God revealed the Qur'an to Prophet Muhammad over a period of twenty-three years of his prophetic career. For Muslims, it contains the most authoritative truth about all matters of importance. The New Testament is a collection of twenty-seven books, written by at least twelve different authors between fifty and two hundred years after Jesus [ed.: current scholarship would date the New Testament books between about twenty and one hundred years after Jesus' death; our thanks to Ryan Schellenberg of Methodist Theological School in Ohio]. These authors wrote in a language that Jesus never spoke and, probably, did not even know. These writers had no personal acquaintance with Jesus, nor did they ever meet him. It is for this reason that the New Testament lacks a personal and physical description of Jesus. Basic biographical information about Jesus is very minimal in the New Testament. Many Christians hold that the authors of the New Testament were inspired by the Holy Spirit. However, more critical readers of these texts, both among Catholics and Protestants, have found many inconsistencies. Many of them are increasingly inclined to believe that, instead of representing the Holy Spirit, these authors were representing a variety of views and theologies that were held by different individuals and groups in the Greco-Roman world in the early centers of Christianity. Thus, the task of the discovery of the "historical Jesus" and the reconstruction of a uniform New Testament Christology is extremely difficult, if not impossible.

Some Christians argue that the New Testament came centuries earlier than the Qur'an and is, chronologically, closer to the time of Jesus.[1] Thus, from a historical point of view, they claim, it is a more reliable source about Jesus than the Qur'an. Therefore, they contend that wherever the Qur'an

---

1. These and similar arguments are often made by Christian missionaries and polemicists in their debates with Muslims. See a study of this in Shafaat, *Missionary Christianity and Islam*. Also, see Robinson, *Christ in Islam and Christianity*, especially chapter 2.

and the New Testament differ concerning Jesus, such as on the question of crucifixion, the New Testament should be given preference to the Qur'an because of its historical antecedence. However, New Testament documents do not represent the earliest information about Jesus. The four canonical Gospels represent only a fraction of what was written about Jesus in early centuries. They represent only the Nicene orthodoxy as it emerged in the fourth century after many debates and theological controversies. For those reasons, some Christian scholars are beginning to recognize that the Qur'an, which comes later in history, contains a tradition about Jesus that may precede even the canonical tradition.

Similarities in the Qur'an and the New Testament about Jesus

Jesus is the son of Mary. The Qur'an often refers to him as *Ibn Maryam* (a total of twenty-two times, see 2:87; 2:253; and others). Some questions have been raised whether the Arabic name *'Isa* actually refers to Jesus, or to a different person. The Arabic word *'Isa* is probably just a phonetic variant on the Syriac *Yeshu'a*. Furthermore, *'Isa*'s identity as Jesus is assured because of his mother, Mary.

The Qur'an also accepts Jesus' virgin birth (see 3:45–47 and 19:16–36). It speaks about it in very strong terms. "How shall I have a son when no man hath touched me?" Mary said to the angel who announced to her the birth of a child (3:47; see also 19:20; 66:12). [Ed.: throughout this chapter, we have retained what appears to be the author's own translation of the Qur'an; where he follows Ali, we have conformed the translation to the eleventh edition, as we have done in other chapters.] Jesus is called *Kalimatuhu* (3:45, "His Word") and *Ruh minhu* (4:171, "a Spirit proceeding from Him"). Both titles are associated with his miraculous birth. In the Qur'an they bear no incarnational connotation. The Qur'an does not use *Kalimah* in the same sense as *Logos* in the Gospel of John. Similarly, *Ruh* (spirit) is distinct from *Hayat* (life). According to the Qur'an, Jesus was created miraculously through the intervention of the Spirit from God (generally interpreted as sending the angel Gabriel to Mary to give her the news of his miraculous birth). The Qur'an clearly rejects the idea of God's incarnating himself or begetting a son (see 2:116; 10:68; 17:111; 19:88–89; and others). The Qur'an never calls Jesus "the son of God."

The Qur'an gives Jesus many other titles of honor and respect. Some of these titles are similar to those he has in the New Testament. He is often called *al-Masih* ("The Christ"; this title occurs about eleven times, see 3:45; 4:157, 171, 172; and others). The Qur'an does not give this title to anyone other than Jesus. He is the only recipient of this title. The Qur'an, however, does not seem to give this title any eschatological meaning. It is an earthly title of Jesus. It is, perhaps, used in its most obvious meaning "The anointed person" or "The blessed person"; Jesus is also called *Mubarak* ("A blessed person"; see 19:31).

Jesus is, of course, a prominent messenger of God. So the Qur'an calls him *Rasul Allah* ("Messenger of Allah"; see 4:157, 171). He is also a "Servant of God" *('Abd;* see 43:59; 4:172). He is "honorable in this world and in the hereafter" (*wajihan fi al-dunya wa al-akhirah,* 3:45) and he is one of those "brought closer to God" *(min al-muqarrabin,* 3:45). He is "a sign" *(aya,* 19:21) and "a mercy" *(rahma,* 19:21) from God.

The Qur'an says that Jesus performed many miracles. The Qur'an uses the word *bi-idhni* ("by My permission"; this expression occurs four times in 5:110, with every type of miracle) to indicate that Jesus was only an agent and whatever he did was not by his own will or power but by the power and permission of God alone.

The message of Jesus, the Qur'an says, was that of commitment to God. He used to say, "Allah is my Lord and your Lord, Him therefore serve ye" (19:36). He taught righteousness and wisdom (3:49; 5:112–120). He was the messenger of truth and love.

The Qur'an mentions the difficulties that Jesus encountered in performing his mission and presenting his message. He was denied, rejected, accused, and abused (see 3:52–54; 4:156). He asked his followers to support him and assist him (3:52; 61:14). But after this the New Testament and the Qur'an part company. According to the New Testament Jesus was finally crucified and put to death. But the Qur'an rejects this assertion. "They killed him not, nor crucified him . . . " (4:157). According to the Qur'an neither the crucifixion of Jesus took place, nor his death at the hands of his enemies. The circumstances, however, created some confusion/illusion in people's minds about the end of his earthly life. The Qur'an removes this confusion by saying that God lifted Jesus toward him [ed.: 4:158]. "And those who differ therein are full of doubts, with no (certain) knowledge, but only conjecture to follow, for of a surety they killed him not" (4:157).

Part II: Circles of Scripture, Community, and Interpretation

Differences between the Qur'an and New Testament Concerning Jesus

Unlike the New Testament, the Qur'an emphasizes that Jesus came to affirm the unity of God. He did not teach the Trinity. He asked his followers to worship God alone, who is his Lord and their Lord (3:51; 19:36; 43:64). The Qur'an asks Christians to shun the doctrine of the Trinity. "[B]elieve in Allah and His Messengers. Say not, 'Trinity': desist: it will be better for you" (4:171). It also says, "They do blaspheme who say: Allah is one of three in a Trinity: for there is no god except One God . . . " (5:73). However, the Persons of the Trinity are not identified in the Qur'an. Whatever they may be, the concept itself is unacceptable and is contrary to the message of Jesus.

On the Day of Judgement, the Qur'an says, God will ask Jesus, "O Jesus the son of Mary! Didst thou say unto men, 'Worship me and my mother as gods in derogation of Allah?' He will say: 'Glory to Thee! Never could I say what I had no right (to say). Had I said such a thing, Thou wouldst indeed have known it. Thou knowest what is in my heart, though I know not what is in Thine. For Thou knowest in full all that is hidden'" (5:116). Based on this verse some Christian scholars have suggested that according to the Qur'an the Trinity consists of "Father, Mother, and Son" and not "Father, Son, and Holy Spirit."[2] Since the former is not a generally held Christian view of the Trinity, these scholars argue that either the Qur'an has mistaken the Trinity or it has criticized the wrong notion of the Trinity, but not the orthodox notion of the Trinity. Actually, in 5:116 there is no discussion of the Trinity. It discusses the false notion of the divinity of Jesus and Mary that was held by some Christians. From the qur'anic perspective, it does not make any difference whether the Trinity is "Father, Son, and Holy Spirit" or "Father, Mother, and Son." Every notion of the Trinity of God is unacceptable to the Qur'an, regardless of its interpretation.

The Qur'an also stresses the fact that Jesus never claimed himself to be "God," "Son of God," "Lord," "God incarnate," or co-equal or cosubstantial with God. In the Gospels, too, Jesus is not told to have made use of these titles for himself. More than seventy times he calls himself "son of man" and only twice "son of God," but according to new critical studies of the Gospels these are not most probably his own words.[3] Also, many critical

---

2. "The question how Muhammad had come to conceive of Maryam as one of the persons of the Trinity has often been asked" (Wensinck, "Maryam," 328).

3. "In Roman Catholic seminaries, for example, it is now common teaching that Jesus of Nazareth did not assert any of the divine or messianic claims the Gospels attribute to

New Testament scholars have pointed out that in Aramaic or Hebrew the expression "son of God" means only "the one who is blessed by God" and nothing else.[4]

The Qur'an does not say that Jesus denied the importance of Mosaic law or rejected it or asked his followers not to follow it. Jesus, according to the Qur'an, was very much like the Israelite prophets. He did not introduce any new law, but he was sent to confirm the previous laws that were given to Moses.

As mentioned earlier in this chapter, the Qur'an has denied that Jesus was killed or crucified. Along with this, all the concomitant notions of Original Sin, redemption and ransom do not find any place in qur'anic theology or in its discussion about Jesus.

Dialogue between Islam and Christianity

Dialogue between Muslims and Christians is very important. We have many issues to discuss that are at the core of our two traditions. Instead of shying away from discussion, we should talk about these issues in an atmosphere of friendship and frankness. After all, we are all members of one Abrahamic family that needs reconciliation. We come to dialogue at least to have a better understanding of each other.

May the Peace and Blessings of God be with us all in this important undertaking.

---

him and that he died without believing he was Christ or the Son of God, not to mention the founder of a new religion" (Sheehan, "Revolution in the Church") [ed.: this overstates the case, even at the time it was written]. According to Gardner-Smith, "Christology," 143, "Whether Jesus used it [the expression 'Son of God'] of Himself is doubtful." Joseph Fitzmeyer, a leading biblical scholar, in his *A Christological Catechism*, asks, Did Jesus claim to be God? He answers, "The Gospels have not so presented that claim. . . . It is impossible to imagine how such a statement would have been understood" (quoted by Murphy, "Who Do Men Say That I Am?", 39).

4. See Price, *Interpreting the New Testament*, 297. S. Johnson, "Son of God," 411 writes, "He [Jesus] is not often represented as speaking of 'the Son' in an absolute sense, and scholars often question the genuineness of the passages where he is said to do so."

PART II: CIRCLES OF SCRIPTURE, COMMUNITY, AND INTERPRETATION

Appendix

The following are the main quotations of the Holy Qur'an concerning Mary and Jesus [ed.: the headings are the Arabic names for the chapters of the Qur'an, following Ali's spelling]:

Al 'Imran

Behold! When the wife of Imran said: "O my Lord! I do dedicate unto Thee what is in my womb for Thy special service: So accept this of me: For Thou hearest and knowest all things." When she was delivered, she said: "O my Lord! Behold! I am delivered of a female child!"—And Allah knew best what she brought forth—"And no wise is the male like the female. I have named her Mary, and I commend her and her offspring to Thy protection from the Evil One, the Rejected." (3:35–36)

Right graciously did her Lord accept her; He made her grow in purity and beauty; to the care of Zakariya was she assigned. Every time that he entered (her) chamber to see her, he found her supplied with sustenance. He said: "O Mary! Whence (comes) this to you?" She said: "From Allah: for Allah provides sustenance to whom He pleases without measure." (3:37)

Behold! the angels said: "O Mary! Allah hath chosen thee and purified thee—chosen thee above the women of all nations. O Mary! worship Thy Lord devoutly: Prostrate thyself, and bow down (in prayer) with those who bow down." (3:42–43)

This is part of the tidings of the things unseen, which We reveal unto thee (O Prophet!) by inspiration: Thou was not with them when they cast lots with arrows, as to which of them should be charged with the care of Mary: Nor was thou with them when they disputed (the point). (3:44)

Maryam

Relate in the Book (the story of) Mary, when she withdrew from her family to a place in the East. She placed a screen (to screen herself) from them; then We sent to her Our spirit, and he appeared before her as a man in all respects. She said: "I seek refuge from thee to (Allah) Most Gracious: (come not near) if thou dost fear Allah." He said: "Nay, I am only a messenger from thy Lord, (to announce) to thee the gift of a righteous son." (19:16–19)

Al 'Imran

Behold! the angels said: "O Mary! Allah giveth thee glad tidings of a Word from Him: his name will be Christ Jesus. The son of Mary, held in honour in this world and the Hereafter and of (the company of) those nearest to Allah; He shall speak to the people in cradle and in maturity. And he shall be (of the company) of the righteous." (3:45–46)

She said: "O my Lord! How shall I have a son when no man hath touched me?" He said: "Even so: Allah createth what He willeth; when He hath decreed a Plan, He but saith to it, 'Be,' and it is!" (3:47)

"And Allah will teach him the Book and Wisdom, the Law and the Gospel, and (appoint him) a messenger to the Children of Israel (with this message): 'I have come to you, with a Sign from your Lord, in that I make for you out of clay, the figure of a bird, and breathe into it, and it becomes a bird by Allah's leave: And I heal those born blind, and the lepers, and I quicken the dead, by Allah's leave; and I declare to you what ye eat, and what ye store in your houses. Surely therein is a Sign for you if ye did believe; (I have come to you) to attest the Law which was before me. And to make lawful to you part of what was (before) forbidden to you; I have come to you with a Sign from your Lord. So fear Allah and obey me. It is Allah Who is my Lord and your Lord; then worship Him. This is a Way that is straight.'" (3:48–51)

Maryam

So she conceived him, and she retired with him to a remote place. And the pains of childbirth drove her to the trunk of a palm tree: She cried (in her anguish): "Ah! would that I had died before this! would that I had been a thing forgotten and out of sight!" (19:22–23)

But (a voice) cried to her from beneath the (palm tree): "Grieve not! for thy Lord hath provided a rivulet beneath thee; and shake towards thyself the trunk of the palm tree; it will let fall fresh ripe dates upon thee. So eat and drink and cool (thine) eye. And if thou dost see any human, say, 'I have vowed a fast to (Allah) Most Gracious, and this day will I enter into no talk with any human being.'" (19:24–26)

At length she brought the (babe) to her people, carrying him (in her arms). They said: "O Mary! Truly an amazing thing hast thou brought! O sister of Aaron! Thy father was not a man of evil, nor thy mother a woman unchaste!" But she pointed to the babe. They said: "How can we talk to one who is a child in the cradle?" (19:27–29)

He said: "I am indeed a servant of Allah: He hath given me revelation and made me a prophet; and He hath made me blessed wheresoever I be, and hath enjoined on me Prayer and Charity as long as I live: (He) hath made me kind to my mother, and not overbearing or miserable; so Peace is on me the day I was born, the day that I die, and the Day that I shall be raised up to life (again)"! Such (was) Jesus the son of Mary: (it is) a statement of truth, about which they (vainly) dispute. (19:30–34)

Al Baqarah

We gave Jesus, the son of Mary, clear (Signs) and strengthened him with the Holy Spirit. (2:87)

Al 'Imran

When Jesus found unbelief on their part he said: "Who will be my helpers to (the work of) Allah?" Said the Disciples: "We are Allah's helpers: We believe in Allah, and do thou bear witness that we are Muslims. Our Lord! we believe in what Thou hast revealed, and we follow the Messenger; then write us down among those who bear witness." And (the unbelievers) plotted and planned, and Allah too planned, and the best of planners is Allah. (3:52–54)

Behold! Allah said: "O Jesus! I will take thee and raise thee to Myself and clear thee (of the falsehoods) of those who blaspheme; I will make those who follow thee superior to those who reject faith, to the Day of Resurrection: Then shall ye all return unto me, and I will judge between you of the matters wherein ye dispute. As to those who reject faith, I will punish them with terrible agony in this world and in the Hereafter, nor will they have anyone to help. As to those who believe and work righteousness, Allah will pay them (in full) their reward: But Allah loveth not those who do wrong. This is what We rehearse unto thee of the Signs and the Message of Wisdom." (3:55–58)

The similitude of Jesus before Allah is as that of Adam; He created him from dust, then said to him: "Be": and he was. (3:59)

Al Ma'idah

Behold! the Disciples said: "O Jesus the son of Mary! Can thy Lord send down to us a Table set (with viands) from heaven?" Said Jesus: "Fear Allah, if ye have faith." They said: "We only wish to eat thereof and satisfy our hearts, and to know that thou hast indeed told us the truth; and that we ourselves may be witnesses to the miracle." (5:112–113)

Said Jesus, the son of Mary: "O Allah our Lord! Send us from heaven a Table set (with viands), that there may be for us—for the first and the last of us—a solemn festival and a Sign from Thee; and provide for our sustenance, for Thou art the best Sustainer (of our needs)." Allah said: "I will send it down unto you; but if any of you after that resisteth faith, I will punish him with a penalty such as I have not inflicted on anyone among all the peoples." (5:114–115)

We sent Jesus the son of Mary, confirming the Law that had come before him: We sent him the Gospel: therein was guidance and light, and confirmation of the Law that had come before him: A guidance and an admonition to those who fear Allah. Let the People of the Gospel judge by what Allah hath revealed therein. If any do fail to judge by (the light of) what Allah hath revealed, they are (no better than) those who rebel. (5:46–47)

Al Saff

And remember, Jesus, the son of Mary, said: "O Children of Israel! I am the messenger of Allah (sent) to you, confirming the Law (which came) before me, and giving Glad Tidings of a Messenger to come after me, whose name shall be Ahmad." But when he came to them with Clear Signs, they said, "This is evident sorcery!" (61:6)

Al Nisa'

(They have incurred divine displeasure): . . . that they uttered against Mary a grave false charge; that they said (in boast), "We killed Christ Jesus the son of Mary, the Messenger of Allah"—but they killed him not, nor crucified him, but so it was made to appear to them, and those who differ therein are full of doubts, with no (certain) knowledge, but only conjecture to follow, for of a surety they killed him not—nay, Allah raised him up unto Himself; and Allah is Exalted in Power, Wise. (4:155–158)

And there is none of the People of the Book but must believe in him before his death; and on the Day of Judgement he will be a witness against them. (4:159)

Al Zukhruf

He was no more than a servant: We granted Our favour to him, and We made him an example to the Children of Israel. (43:59)
And this shall be a Sign (for the coming of) the Hour (of Judgement). (43:61)

Al Tahrim

And Allah sets forth, as an example of those who believe . . . Mary the daughter of Imran, who guarded her chastity; and We breathed into (her body) of Our spirit; and she testified to the truth of the words of her Lord and of his Revelations, and was one of the Devout (Servants). (66:11–12)

Al Ma'idah

One day will Allah gather the Messengers together, and ask: "What was the response ye received (from men to your teaching)?" They will say: "We have no knowledge: it is Thou Who knowest in full all that is hidden." Then will Allah say: "O Jesus the son of Mary! Recount My favour to thee and to thy mother. Behold! I strengthened thee with the holy spirit, so that thou didst speak to the people in infancy and in maturity. Behold! I taught thee the Book and Wisdom, the Law and the Gospel. And behold! thou didst make out of clay, the figure of a bird, by My leave, and thou didst breathe into it, and it becometh a bird by My leave, and thou didst heal those born blind, and the lepers, by My leave. And behold! thou didst bring forth the dead by My leave. And behold! I did restrain the Children of Israel from (violence to) thee when thou didst show them the Clear Signs, and the unbelievers among them said: 'This is nothing but evident magic.' And behold! I inspired the Disciples to have faith in Me and Mine Messenger; they said, 'We have faith, and do thou bear witness that we bow to Allah as Muslims.' (5:109–111)
And behold! Allah will say: "O Jesus the son of Mary! Didst thou say unto men, 'Worship me and my mother as gods in derogation of Allah'?"

He will say: "Glory to Thee! Never could I say what I had no right (to say). Had I said such a thing, Thou wouldst indeed have known it. Thou knowest what is in my heart, though I know not what is in Thine. For Thou knowest in full all that is hidden. Never said I to them aught except what Thou didst command me to say, to wit, 'Worship Allah, my Lord and your Lord'; and I was a witness over them whilst I dwelt amongst them; when Thou didst take me Thou wast the Watcher over them, and Thou art a witness to all things. If Thou dost punish them, they are Thy servants: If Thou dost forgive them, Thou art the Exalted in power, the Wise." (5:116–118)

Allah will say: "This is a day on which the truthful will profit from their truth: theirs are Gardens, with rivers flowing beneath—their eternal home: Allah well-pleased with them, and they with Allah: That is the great Salvation. (The fulfillment of all desires)." (5:119)

Bibliography

Gardner-Smith, P. "Christology." In *Dictionary of the Bible*, rev. ed., 139–52. New York: Scribner's, 1963.

Johnson, S. E. "Son of God." In *The Interpreter's Dictionary of the Bible* 4:408–13. New York: Abingdon, 1962.

Murphy, Cullen. "Who Do Men Say That I Am?" *The Atlantic Monthly* (1986) 37–44.

Price, James L. *Interpreting the New Testament*. New York: Holt, Rinehart, and Winston, 1961.

Robinson, Neal. *Christ in Islam and Christianity*. Albany: SUNY Press, 1991.

Shafaat, Ahmad. *Missionary Christianity and Islam*, vol. 1. Montreal: NUR Media Services, 1982.

Sheehan, Thomas. "Revolution in the Church." *New York Review of Books* (June 14, 1984). http://www.nybooks.com/articles/archives/1984/jun/14/revolution-in-the-church/.

Wensinck, A. J. "Maryam." In *Shorter Encyclopaedia of Islam*, 327–30. Leiden: Brill, 1961.

6

People of the Book

Potential Uniting Themes and Barriers to Unifying Dialogue

Jamal A. Badawi

I BEGIN BY GREETING you with the common greeting of all of the prophets: May the peace, mercy, and blessings of God be with you all. And may God's peace and blessings be upon all the prophets in history.

    My goal in this chapter is to explore several themes that can serve to unite Muslims, Jews, and Christians, as well as potential barriers to unifying dialogue. The Qur'an uses the appellation "People of the Book" to refer to Jews, Christians, or both, depending on the textual and/or historical context of a specific verse(s); hence, the title of this chapter. After a brief introduction, I discuss several potentially uniting themes between and among the three ethical monotheistic religions: Judaism, Christianity, and Islam. Next, the chapter deals with what I see as some of the main barriers to positive and constructive dialogue. Due to their crucial contemporary significance, I include some key hermeneutical principles in interpreting the Qur'an in this section, providing a few specific examples to show the serious consequences of disregarding or insufficiently applying these principles. In concluding, I ask: Where do we go from here?

Introduction

Dialogue is a central theme in the Qur'an, which makes mention of dialogue before the creation of humans, such as the dialogue between God and the angels when he told them: "I am going to create a trustee on earth" (2:30).[1] Then came the dialogue between God and Satan after the creation of Adam and Eve (7:11–18), and the dialogue between God and Adam and Eve after the latter ate from the "forbidden tree" (7:20–25). Throughout the Qur'an, we see also dialogues between God and his messengers (23:26–29; 2:260; 20:9–48), between prophets and their peoples (19:41–48), and between various groups of people (2:249–251). Dialogue varies also by level: family, group, community, national, and global.

From another perspective, topics of dialogue vary in focus: social, economic, political, and interfaith. This chapter deals with the sub-area of interfaith dialogue; more specifically, dialogue between Muslims and the People of the Book as defined above. I am aware that the title of this conference focuses on "Muslims and Jews" and is sponsored by Jewish and Muslim organizations. However, from my perspective and in light of the subject matter covered in this chapter, I believe that it applies equally to Christians as well. Christianity is an integral and pivotal member of the three major Abrahamic religions.

Potential Uniting Themes

In this section I describe, from an Islamic perspective, twelve core uniting themes of the three Abrahamic religions.

---

1. The main translation of the Qur'an used in this chapter is Muhammad Asad's, available at http://www.islamicity.org/quransearch/?AspxAutoDetectCookieSupport=1. In a few cases, I have made modifications for greater clarity and accuracy.

Faith in the One Universal God ("Allah" in Arabic)[2]

The cornerstone of Islam is the belief in the One and Only God, the Sole Universal Creator, Sustainer, and Cherisher of the universe and all that exists. God is impartial toward his creation and provides for all, including those who reject faith in him. He cares for the well-being of all and gives them many opportunities to repent to him and to end the state of separateness suffered by those who reject him or are unmindful of him. No wonder that among his ninety-nine divine attributes, the most often repeated in the Qur'an is the attribute of mercy. Only Allah is the ultimate judge of any person's "theological correctness." As such, no human is entitled to oppress, mistreat, or deprive any other fellow human on the grounds of his or her perceived "theological incorrectness."

Unity and Universality of the Core Teachings of All Prophets

That core message is peace in submission to Allah; literally, "Islam." According to the Qur'an, a Muslim must accept, revere, and believe in all the prophets of God, without discrimination. They all comprise one brotherhood of faith, extending vertically to include all generations and horizontally to embrace all of humanity. The Qur'an instructs Muslims to tell other fellow believers in God, " . . . we [Muslims] make no distinction between any of His messengers [i.e., God's messengers]" (2:285). In another verse, we read: "[In matters of faith], He [God] has ordained for you [O Muhammad] that which He had enjoined upon Abraham, Moses and Jesus; steadfastly uphold the [true] faith and make no divisions therein . . ." (42:13).

Moral Behavior

Examples from the Qur'an include, "Indeed, God enjoins justice, the doing of good, and generosity towards relatives; and forbids lewdness, abominations and oppression. He exhorts you that you may take heed" (16:90). In disqualifying mere ritualism as an act of piety, the Qur'an states: "True piety does not consist in turning your faces towards the east or the west—but the truly pious is one who believes in God, and the Last Day and the angels,

---

2. The term Allah is the identical term used by Arab Christians to refer to God. It appears in the Arabic Bible and sounds strikingly similar to the Aramaic term for God, *Alaaha*.

and revelation, and the prophets; and gives wealth, in spite of love for it, to relatives, orphans, the needy, the wayfarer, those who ask [for help], for freeing slaves; and [who] is constant in prayer, and renders the purifying dues [*Zakah*]; [those who] fulfill their promises whenever they promise, and [those who] persevere in patience in poverty, illness and in time of peril: it is they that have proved themselves true, and it is they, they who are conscious of God" (2:177).

Sanctity of Human Life

The Qur'an affirms what God ordained for the children of Israel: " . . . if anyone slays a human being, unless it be [in punishment] for murder or for spreading corruption on earth, it shall be as though he had slain all mankind. Whereas, if anyone saves a life, it shall be as though he had saved the lives of all mankind . . . " (5:32). Also, "And do not take any human being's life which God has willed to be sacred except for just cause . . . " (17:33).

Human Dignity

The Qur'an affirms that God created the human in the "best of molds" (95:4), commanded the angels to bow down, in respect, to Adam, and appointed humans as his trustees on earth (2:30). He created everything on earth and in the heavens for the benefit of the human race (45:13). The Qur'an states categorically: "Indeed, We [God] have conferred dignity on the children of Adam, and borne them over land and sea, and provided for them sustenance out of the good things of life, and favored them far above most of Our creation" (17:70). It is noted that this verse is inclusive of all humans irrespective of their religions, their belief in God, or rejection of belief in him. Rejection of belief in God and/or disobedience to him will surely have consequences in the afterlife. However, it is up to God to determine these consequences. After all, the human is a free agent, and each person, individually, is held responsible before God for his/her beliefs and moral choices. A person can be held accountable in this life only if his/her moral choice infringes on the inalienable rights of others, as in the commission of crimes or acts of aggression. In other words, no human is entitled to dehumanize or punish another on the sole ground that the latter is following a different religion or no religion at all.

PART II: CIRCLES OF SCRIPTURE, COMMUNITY, AND INTERPRETATION

Universal Justice

The Arabic term for justice is *Adl*, which means "to be in a state of equilibrium, to be balanced." That balance is inherent in the cosmic order and ecology as much as it is inherent in spiritual and ethical values. The Qur'an warns against disturbing that balance. Within that broad context, we can examine the concept of justice as it relates to human relationships. Briefly, that concept has the following characteristics:

1. Justice is not mere "political correctness" or something to pursue for worldly gain. For the believer, it is a divine command: "Behold, God enjoins justice . . . " (16:90).

2. Justice is at the heart of prophetic teachings: "Indeed, [even aforetime] did We send forth Our apostles with all evidence of [this] truth; and through them We bestowed revelation from on high, and [thus gave you] a balance [wherewith to weigh right and wrong], so that people might behave with equity . . . " (57:25).

3. Justice is a universal concept that should be observed without nepotism: "O you who have attained to faith! Be ever steadfast in upholding equity, bearing witness to the truth for the sake of God, even though it be against your own selves or your parents and kinsfolk. Whether the person concerned be rich or poor, God's claim takes precedence over [the claims of] either of them. Do not, then, follow your own desires, lest you swerve from justice: for if you distort [the truth], behold, God is indeed aware of all that you do!" (4:135).

4. Doing justice applies to dealing with an enemy: "O you who have attained to faith! Be ever steadfast in your devotion to God, bearing witness to the truth in all equity; and never let hatred of any one lead you into the sin of deviating from justice. Be just: this is closest to being God-conscious and remain conscious of God: verily, God is aware of all that you do" (5:8).

The above concept of universal justice relates to peace in at least two ways. First, it is inconceivable to secure genuine lasting peace without justice. In fact, justice is a prerequisite to peace. To deprive others of their rights, lands, and legitimate property is a prescription for violence and radicalization, especially when sustained for a long time. Second, to harm, persecute, or fight against any person, group, or nation because of their religious convictions is one of the worst forms of injustice, which is condemned in the Qur'an (60:8).

Universal Human Family

Addressing the entire human race, the Qur'an states: "O humankind! Behold, We [God] have created you all out of a male and a female, and have made you into nations and tribes, so that you might come to know one another. Verily, the noblest of you in the sight of God is the one who is most deeply conscious of Him. Behold, God is all knowing, all aware" (49:13). It is notable that this verse does not address Muslims exclusively, but begins with the inclusive address "O humankind," an address that embraces all. It reminds humanity that they belong to one family, with the same set of parents. Humanity is like a bouquet of flowers, in which each flower is beautiful in its own right. However, the combination of all flowers and the rich diversity of their colors and shapes is more beautiful. This categorical and all-inclusive statement in the Qur'an about over-arching universal humanity is a profound basis for peace for and among all, if truly implemented by all.

Acceptance of Plurality and Diversity of Human Societies, including Diversity of Beliefs

The Qur'an is quite explicit in reminding all that if God willed, he would have made of all humankind one nation (5:48; 11:118). This value inculcates the attitude of being non-judgmental and accepting people as they are, that all human beings are entitled to choose, and all are answerable to their Creator. It is true that the Qur'an makes it a duty on Muslims to communicate the message of God to fellow humans and to be witnesses for God to humankind: "And who could be better of speech than he who calls [others] unto God, and does what is just and right, and says, 'Verily, I am of those who have surrendered themselves to God'?" (41:33; see also 2:143). The Qur'an mandates that such invitation should be with wisdom and in the most gracious way: "Invite [all humankind] to the path of your Lord with wisdom and goodly exhortation and argue with them in the most kindly manner" (16:125). However, the Qur'an strictly and repeatedly prohibits coercion in matters of faith. A few examples on this prohibition include: "There shall be no coercion in matters of faith" (2:256); "And so [O Prophet], exhort them; your task is only to exhort. You cannot compel them [to believe]" (88:21–22); "Had your Sustainer so willed, all those who live on earth would surely have attained to faith, all of them: do you, then, think that you could compel people to believe?" (10:99).

Inculcating Moderation and Shunning Extremism

The Qur'an shuns any form of extremism and calls for moderation: "And thus have We [God] willed you to be a community of the middle way, so that [with your lives] you might bear witness to the truth before all humankind, and that the Apostle might bear witness to it before you . . . " (2:143). The original qur'anic Arabic expression *Ummatan Wasatan* may be rendered as "moderate community." Muhammad Asad renders it as "community of the middle way," while Abdullah Yusuf Ali translates it as "an Ummat justly balanced," which is the preferred rendering by this author. The core concept of "just balance" applies to the cosmic order, ecology, and matters of beliefs, worship, and socio-econo-political life where a just balance must be maintained, for example, between the rights of the individual and society. Just balance is the opposite of extremism.

Universal Mercy

The essence of Islam and its Prophet's mission is summed up in the following verse: "And [thus, O Prophet], We have sent you as [an evidence of Our] grace towards all the worlds" (21:107). To remove any particularization of this mercy, the Prophet Muhammad (PBUH) explained that mercy is not being merciful to one's companion but merciful to all.[3] He also explained: "Have mercy on those who are dwellers of the earth and the One who is in heavens will have mercy on you."[4] It is obvious that Muslims are not the only dwellers of the earth. Hence, the command to be merciful applies to all. In fact, mercy applies as well to animals and other creatures of God. A logical fruit of this attitude of mercy is to love humankind as persons and fellow honored creatures of God, even if they hold differing beliefs or convictions.

---

3. Narrated by Al-Tabarani, quoted in Al-Ghazali, *Khuluq Al-Muslim*, 254, translated by the author. PBUH stands for "peace be upon him," a formula commonly used by Muslims to invoke God's peace and blessings upon Prophet Muhammad and other prophets whenever their names are mentioned.

4. Al-Azdi, *Sunan Abi Dawood*, vol. 4, Hadith no. 4941, page 285, translated by the author.

Peaceful Co-Existence

Peaceful co-existence, justice, and compassion are the foundation of the normative relationship between Muslims and people of other faith communities. The most pertinent text of the Qur'an is: "As for such [other communities] who do not fight against you on account of [your] faith, and neither drive you forth from your homelands, God does not forbid you to show them kindness and to behave towards them with full equity: for, verily, God loves those who act equitably" (60:8). The original qur'anic Arabic term for "kindness" is *Birr*, the same term used in the Qur'an and Hadith to describe one's relationship with his/her parents. Such relationship is more than showing them kindness, since it includes also love and respect.

Peaceful Dialogue, Especially with the People of the Book

All of the above themes apply to all people of diverse faith communities. In addition, the Qur'an accords Jews and Christians a special position as People of the Book. The very term "People of the Book" is a complimentary title as it acknowledges that, like Muslims, their religions are based on revealed books or scriptures. The Qur'an exhorts Muslims to engage in peaceful dialogue with Jews and Christians: "Say: 'O People of the Book! Come unto that tenet which we and you hold in common: that we shall worship none but God, and that we shall not ascribe divinity to aught beside Him, and that we shall not take human beings for our lords beside God.' And if they turn away, then say: 'Bear witness that it is we who have surrendered ourselves unto Him'" (3:64). The Qur'an encourages peaceful dialogue and invites all to build upon common ground. It instructs Muslims: "And do not argue with the People of the Book other than in a most kindly manner—unless it be such of them as are bent on evildoing. And say: 'We believe in that which has been bestowed from on high upon us, as well as that which has been bestowed upon you: or our God and your God is one and the same, and it is unto Him that We [all] surrender ourselves'" (29:46).

While the above twelve themes are presented and documented from an Islamic perspective, they are by no means exclusive to Islam. It is my conviction that they are shared, to some degree or the other, though not identically, by the People of the Book, many other faith communities, and many other decent persons. The challenge facing us all is to work hard to translate such noble common themes into action at all levels, individual, family, community, society, and the world at large. We can do that more effectively if we all tackle some of the potential barriers to mutual understanding. We turn to these barriers next.

Potential Barriers to Unifying Dialogue

At the risk of over-simplification of this profound issue, this section summarizes, briefly, some of the issues that may stand in the way of promoting genuine mutual understanding among various communities in our pluralistic world today, especially religious communities.

Confusing the Normative Teachings of Any Faith and the Actions of Some of the People Who Claim to Belong to That Faith

From an Islamic perspective, God's core and definitive teachings are perfect because God is perfect and free from error, ignorance, and bias. However, Muslims as people are by nature imperfect. The same applies to all other religious communities as well. On the level of cultural practices, there are some, if not many, "un-Islamic cultural practices" that violate authentic Islamic teachings. Islam and Muslims are not identical. The fact that some Muslims do wrong does not mean that normative Islam is to blame for their deviations and aberrations. Nor do these deviations justify stereotyping a whole community of faith that may number hundreds of millions and painting them with the same broad brush. Presumption of "guilt by association," or the implicit assumption that a Muslim, Jew, Christian, or any person is guilty until otherwise proven innocent, are forms of injustice especially in a democratic society. Stereotypical anti-Christian, anti-Jewish, anti-Semitism, anti-Arab, and anti-Islam views are forms of bigotry and/or racism. Such irrational hatred has nothing to do with objective criticism of specific ideas, actions, organizations, or states for that matter. They may have little or nothing to do with the true spirit of genuine religiosity.

Media Stereotypes and Images

In the media, criminals are generally not identified by their religious community, with the common exception of Muslims. Far too often the name of Islam is attached to negative and criminal acts, such as the use of terms like "Muslim terrorist" or "Islamic terrorist." There is a terrible double standard and irresponsible depiction in the media that borders on incitement of hate, even violence against innocent people who have nothing to do with such crimes and who are quite often the victims of these crimes themselves.

History

While understanding history is useful, being selective and partial in examining it, belittling positive relational legacies, or being frozen in negative historical legacies is not. I think that we need a more level-headed, objective, and honest assessment of both the positives and the negatives of our respective histories as peoples. For, after all, we are all humans; we have all committed mistakes, with differing degrees of gravity. Likewise, we have all contributed a great deal of good to human well-being. Rather than being enslaved by the negatives of history or over-romanticizing our own history, let us focus on how to avoid the negative aspects of our relationships and nurture the positive or potentially positive aspects, while keeping our eyes on the future.

Some Issues in Interpreting Our Sacred Texts

While general hermeneutical rules are broad enough to be common across more than one faith community, some hermeneutical issues are of greater relevance and importance to a particular faith community. For example, to Muslims, the Qur'an is not simply a book or a text. It is the verbatim word of God as dictated to Prophet Muhammad (PBUH) by Angel Gabriel. This excludes any human, including Prophet Muhammad (PBUH), from its authorship. In fact, while sound Hadith of the Prophet (PBUH) is a form of revelation, it is only revelation of meaning but the words are clearly demarcated as those of the Prophet. Consequently, no one, including the Prophet Muhammad himself (PBUH) is entitled to "copyedit" the word of God, whether by addition, deletion, or modification. What is encouraged, however, is to improve our interpretation of the Qur'an and its application to changing times, places, and circumstances while maintaining its integrity. Based on the acceptance of God as the real author of the Qur'an, it is his full right to make any statement of "theological truth." It is his domain also to approve or disapprove beliefs and actions by any of his servants, be they Muslims, Jews, Christians, or others, and also to forewarn all about the consequences of their choices in the life-to-come. In fact, some of the

Part II: Circles of Scripture, Community, and Interpretation

criticisms of some religious communities in the Qur'an have parallels in their own scriptures. For example, both the Qur'an and Hebrew scriptures criticize the breaking of the Sabbath by some of the Israelites. By exercising his domain as the Master of all, God still allows the human the freedom of belief, worship, and moral choices. People are free to agree or disagree with this foundational aspect of Islamic hermeneutics, but it needs to be declared honestly and clearly without any apology or hesitation. After all, promotion of serious mutual understanding requires, not only examination of the common potential uniting themes, but also understanding areas of differences and appreciation of where each community is coming from. This candidness may help members of faith communities to avoid misrepresenting the faith or scriptures of other faith communities.

There are cases, however, where errors of understanding may result from insufficient familiarity with pertinent information or hermeneutical rules. Following are three examples:

1. Problems with inaccurate, non-contextual translation of the original Arabic text of the Qur'an. For example, some claim wrongly that the Qur'an does not allow Muslims to befriend non-Muslims. The source of that misunderstanding involves the erroneous translation of the qur'anic Arabic term *Awliyaa'* into "friends" instead of "allies, protectors, overlords." Serious study of the verses on this issue and their historical context shows that the prohibition relates to a negative situation, such as not taking for your protectors those who mock your religion when you make the call for prayers. Additionally, this mistaken rendering is inconsistent with clear textual emphasis on peaceful and respectful co-existence (60:8–9) and the permissibility of some forms of interfaith marriage in Islamic family law.

2. Problems resulting from disregarding the occasion of revelation of some verses (*Asbaab al-Nozool*) and/or other historical context. For example 9:5 has been widely misunderstood to sanction the killing of the non-believers "wherever you find them." This verse was revealed in connection with the idolatrous Arabs in Arabia at the time of the Prophet (PBUH) who betrayed the peace treaty of Hudaybiyah and killed innocent people in cold blood, a war crime in modern terms. Understanding the historical context of the verse precludes its use to justify harming others because they are idolatrous or non-Muslims. It shows that fighting against them is allowed because of their aggression,

not their religion(s). If no similar aggression or "war crime" is committed by them, then they are entitled to the kind and just treatment mandated in 60:8–9 above.

3. Disregarding the "textual context" or other references in the Qur'an to the same topic or issue, or engaging in an exercise of "cherry picking" whatever fits one's agenda. This selectivity as well as a cut-and-paste approach to the Qur'an may be forms of "proof texting." This problem applies to the previous example of 9:5. It is inconceivable that the Qur'an protects the rights of minorities, affirms their freedom of belief and worship, teaches respect of their human dignity, and even allows some forms of interfaith marriage, but then says kill them wherever you find them ("them" may include your own beloved Jewish or Christian wife!). In fact, looking at the entire section where the "cherry picked" verse was quoted (verses 1–13) gives ample evidence that 9:5 applies only to those who committed the murders, as they exclude other idolatrous Arabs who did not betray their treaty in order to participate in the murders. Textual context requires also examining all of the situations in which the use of force to fight others is discussed in the entire Qur'an. For example, in 2:190–194 and 60:8–9 the permission to fight back is permissible only in legitimate self-defense or in resistance to severe oppression exemplified by being driven from one's land and home.[5]

Where Do We Go from Here?

In concluding, I lay out a few general principles that I believe should guide our way forward as we continue to engage one another on these incredibly important topics.

1. We have to maintain humility. We all have done wrong. Let's not exaggerate others' wrongs and trivialize our own.
2. We need to actively reach out to one another.
3. We need to develop mutual understanding and respect, building on the common ground that brings us together. Only then can we respectfully discuss differences.

---

5. The issues abbreviated in this section and similar hermeneutical issues are dealt with in greater detail in my article, "Muslim/Non-Muslim Relations."

4. We need to meaningfully connect the concepts of peace and justice. They both go together. It would be a travesty of justice to keep talking about theology without dealing with real problems on the ground, where many peoples are dispossessed, mistreated, and dehumanized. True peace must involve practical work towards those ideals of justice that we all find embedded in our own scriptures.

5. Finally, we need to work together in areas of common good such as alleviation of poverty and homelessness, better health care, elimination of all forms of hate and racism, and dealing with all forms of violence (family, communal, state, interstate, and global). We need to devise ways and means of breaking the vicious circle of violence and counter-violence. If we spent a fraction of the billions, hundreds of billions, almost trillions of dollars we spend on death and destruction to bring justice to the world, rather than on putting strategic economic interests above the lives of other people, I think we will all be in better shape. Protection of the environment and sustainability of valuable resources and enhancing family and community values are all areas we need to work on together. Let us move beyond theoretical, historical, and theological dialogues, useful as they may be. Let us start the practical dialogue of enhancing justice and equality as we emphasize our common humanity. We can and must leave this great legacy for our children and grandchildren.

Again, may God's peace, mercy, and blessings be with you all.

Bibliography

Al-Azdi, Abi Dawood Sulaiman, compiler. *Sunan Abi Dawood*. Beirut: Al-Maktabah Al-Asriyyah, n.d.
Al-Ghazali, Muhammad. *Khuluq Al-Muslim*. Kuwait: Dar Al-Bayan, 1970.
Badawi, Jamal. "Muslim/Non-Muslim Relations." http://www.fiqhcouncil.org/node/24.

PART III

The Past Is Never Dead

7

Historical Perspectives on Christian-Muslim Relations

Marilyn Robinson Waldman

WE ALL KNOW THAT comparative religion can be a tricky business, and the one story I know about Muslim-Christian interaction makes that point very well. It is a story about a famous Muslim folk hero who goes by many names but is here called Mulla Nasrudin:

> Nasrudin put on a Sufi robe and decided to make a pious journey. On his way he met a [Christian] priest and a[n Indian] yogi, and they decided to team up together. When they got to a village the others asked him to seek donations while they carried out their devotions. Nasrudin collected some money and bought halwa [ed.: an Indian sweet] with it.
>
> He suggested that they divide the food, but the others, who were not yet hungry enough, said that it should be postponed until night. They continued on their way; and when night fell Nasrudin asked for the first portion "because I was the means of getting the food." The others disagreed: the priest on the grounds that he represented a properly organized hierarchical body, and should therefore have preference; the yogi because, he said, he ate only once in three days and should therefore have more.
>
> Finally they decided to sleep. In the morning, the one who related the best dream should have first choice of the halwa.
>
> In the morning the priest said: "In my dreams I saw the founder of my religion, who made a sign of benediction, singling me out as especially blessed."

The others were impressed, but the Yogi said: "I dreamt that I visited Nirvana, and was utterly absorbed into nothing."

They turned to the Mulla. "I dreamt that I saw the Sufi teacher Khidr, who appears only to the most sanctified [and to whom Sufis owe complete obedience]."

"He said, 'Nasrudin, eat the halwa—now!' And, of course, I had to obey."[1]

This is not only a very good Mulla story, but it also suggests that there are many surprises in store for those who study the interaction of religious communities. The story also implicitly suggests some of the new perspectives that most Americans will need to adopt in order to make sense of the history of Muslim-Christian interaction. The way the world is right now, and especially the way American society is organized and the assumptions that it makes about religious affiliation, do not automatically provide adequate vantage points for thinking about the history of Muslim-Christian interaction around the world during the last 1,400 years. There are at least four unfamiliar facts that we will need to bear in mind.

The Significance of Eastern Christianity

The history of Muslim-Christian interaction involves eastern or orthodox forms of Christianity as much as western forms of Christianity, a fact that is usually ignored. Most people who have grown up in the United States would probably assume that the priest in the Mulla story is a Catholic priest, but he is much more likely to have belonged to some form of eastern Christianity. Yet most Americans do not ever learn enough about the history of Christianity as a global phenomenon to know what it was like in the areas where Islam arose (i.e., northwestern Arabia) and to which it quickly spread (i.e., westward to Egypt, North Africa, and Spain; northward into the "Middle East"; and eastward into Iran and Central Asia).

Furthermore, a knowledge of Christianity's current demography, in the world or in the United States, is not very helpful for putting ourselves back into northwestern Arabia and its environs at the beginning of the seventh century and in the centuries that followed. At the present time, large numbers of Christians live in the western hemisphere, and Christian identification is increasing rapidly in the rest of the world as well. Because of that fact, Harvey Cox has begun to predict that Christianity will become

---

1. Shah, *Pleasantries of the Incredible Mulla Nasrudin*, 75.

more of a "third-world" religion in the next millennium, and that one of the next few popes will be Latin American or African.

In the United States about 56 percent of all Christians are Protestant and about 33 percent are Roman Catholic. So Americans tend to forget, or never notice, that world-wide 56 percent of Christians are Roman Catholic and only 20 percent Protestant. I once asked a middle school class in north Columbus how many of the world's Christians are Roman Catholic, and they said "Oh, about 10 percent."

The current global expansion of Christianity, the numerical superiority of Roman Catholics worldwide, and the numerical superiority of Protestants in the United States, constitute a reality very different from that in which Islam arose. In the year 600, on the eve of the Prophet Muhammad's first encounter with God, there were relatively few Christians living west of Rome, because the Christian faith had not yet spread significantly westward from its eastern Mediterranean homelands. There were no Roman Catholics or Protestants per se, because the Protestant Reformation was 900 years away. The majority of Christians belonged, at least officially, to one Church, because the Great Schism had not yet been finalized; and many of its members were loyal to the Patriarch at Constantinople, not to the Bishop of Rome, even when he began to call himself the Pope. Most Christians lived in the Later Roman Empire, whose seventh-century capital was Constantinople, and many Christians practiced forms of Christianity unfamiliar to most Americans—Coptic, Nestorian, Monophysite, and so forth.

In Arabia, and in many other areas to which Islam spread, we are not entirely sure what Christianity was actually like, despite the efforts of many scholars. However, recent research on Syriac Christianity to the north of Arabia in the seventh century indicates that Christianity in that part of the world may have been much more similar to what is described in the Qur'an than has usually been thought. Many western scholars have argued that the Qur'an "got Christianity wrong," because it describes Christianity in a way different from our understanding; but those few scholars who work on the Christianity of Syriac-speakers to the north (Syriac being a Semitic language closely related to Arabic) have discovered that many things that characterize common Syriac Christian practice are similar to practices and ideas attributed to Christians in the Qur'an.

In Arabia, Christianity was presumably a minority religion when Islam arose; but in many of the areas to which Islam spread outside Arabia, Christianity was the majority religion. And many Christians in that part of the world used Syriac or Arabic in their worship, not Greek or Latin. So when we say Christian-Muslim interaction, we have to know what we mean by "Christian," and that is not always easy to do.

The Longevity of Muslim-Christian Interaction

Muslims and Christians have lived together and interacted with each other for a very long time, in fact since the emergence of Islam in northwest Arabia early in the seventh century of the Common Era. In many other parts of the world and at many other times, they have not been so foreign to each other as they tend to be in the United States. It is not the case that there was no polemic, that there was complete understanding; but it is the case that Muslims and Christians of this part of the world were probably better able to converse with each other than we are in the United States. For example, it would have been much easier for Muslim and Christian scholars in Damascus in the eighth century to have a theological discussion than it would be for us, because Muslims and Christians in the parts of the world in which interaction has primarily taken place often spoke "a common language," in either the figurative or literal sense of the term. There were Arab Christians in the environs of Muhammad's community, some of whom became Muslim. Figures who appear in the Christian Bible also appear in the Qur'an. Since the earliest Muslims viewed Islam as the natural and original religion, they believed that all messengers of God had brought essentially the same message, which culminated in Muhammad.

During the first 200 years of Muslim expansion and rule in the Middle East, Muslims only very gradually became a majority of the population in the areas they controlled, largely through the peaceful absorption of large numbers of Christians and a much smaller number of Jews. In fact, the transformation of this area from predominantly Christian to predominantly Muslim is one of the most understudied major cultural transformations in human history. In the course of it, many of these new Muslims or children of new Muslims became important figures in the development of Islamic thought and culture. Conversely, Islamic thought influenced the ongoing development of Christian thought as well. For example, it is thought that the attempt by an eighth-century Byzantine emperor to ban the use of icons was influenced by familiarity with Muslim prohibitions on the use of images in worship. Furthermore, the Muslim view of Jesus as messenger of God rather than son of God had precedents in certain early Christian views that had not become part of mainstream Christianity, and caused Arab Christians to redeem their notions of prophecy. We have Syriac Christian accounts of the rise of Islam that are earlier than the earliest surviving accounts written by Muslims in Arabic. Christian architects helped to build some of the first mosques (Muslim places of prayer). Raymond Lull, the famous fourteenth-century Christian-Majorcan scholar and writer, knew Arabic better than he knew Latin, and was influenced by Muslim Sufis (as well as the Jewish Maimonides). The earliest European universities may well have been influenced by Muslim schools in locales like Sicily. To this day, as in the past, many Arab Christians who use an Arabic translation of the Christian Bible and call God "Allah" are well aware of the Muslim understanding of that term even though they understand it differently.

A particularly important site of Muslim-Christian interaction was the Ottoman Empire, which expanded into southeastern Europe in the fifteenth and sixteenth centuries. Most of the Ottoman ruling class, at least in these early centuries, was composed not of Turks or of Muslims, but of Christian youths who were "drafted," converted to Islam, and trained in the Ottoman language and in Ottoman administrative and military skills.
It is this expansion, by the way, that produced today's Muslim communities of countries like [ed.: the former] Yugoslavia or Bulgaria or Albania. In the Ottoman Empire, Christian communities were quite various, and the different Christian communities came to be associated with different ethnicities or nationalities.

Furthermore, most Muslim-Christian relationships in the past have to be put under the heading of some kind of co-existence, rather than conflict. Where conflict has occurred, it has originated as much on the Christian side as on the Muslim side. Here again, the instances of Muslim-Christian conflict that Americans know best, the Crusades of the eleventh and twelfth centuries, and the era of European colonialism in the nineteenth and twentieth centuries, do not provide adequate models for understanding the whole sweep of Christian-Muslim interaction. In those cases, Europeans went to a predominantly Muslim part of the world and tried, unsuccessfully, to conquer it. Similarly, the major instances of Muslim expansion into Christian lands—the Middle East and North Africa in the seventh century, Spain in the eighth century, and the Later Roman, or Byzantine, Empire in the fifteenth century—are not adequate models either.

For despite obvious instances of conflict involving force, most Muslims and Christians have coexisted, sometimes uneasily, sometimes with very positive cultural results, as in Spain (both during the period of extensive Muslim control and in areas that first came under Christian domination). Even the Crusades, which we identify with violence and forced contact, probably promoted a great deal of interaction as well: we are just beginning to know about the influence of the Muslim east on medieval Europe's literature, art, education, and music; and it came about even in an instance where violence was the intended result of the contact.

One of the most unusual examples of Muslim-Christian encounter occurred in the Philippines in the sixteenth century. It illustrates the extent of the peaceful expansion of Islam through trade and commerce and preaching, but also the negative reaction of European Christians to it. After the Spanish made their conquests in the New World, some of them sailed across from Mexico to what became the Philippines. When the Spaniards reached what is now Manila, they were shocked to find Muslims from the south, who had come up from Java and Borneo, converting large numbers of locals to Islam. When the Spaniards encountered these Muslims, who were a mixture of Middle Eastern and Indian Ocean peoples, they referred to them as the Moros (their label to the present day); that is, they referred to them with the same name they had used in Spain—Moras, the Moors. One can imagine their shock, just having conquered the last Muslim stronghold of Granada in 1492, and thinking they had gotten Muslims under control, coming halfway around the world and finding them there.

It is important to remember that even before northern European Christians began their attempt to reconquer the Holy Land from Muslims, Spanish Christians had begun to reconquer the Iberian Peninsula from Muslims. Ironically, the conquest Americans tend to know more about, and make more of—the assault on the Holy Land—"failed," whereas the one Americans are very little interested in, the conquest of Spain, "succeeded."

The Spanish experience in the Philippines also suggests a different view of 1492, and a different perspective on the Quincentenary which celebrates it. It reminds us that Muslim peoples were still economically powerful at the time of the New World explorations. After all, Christopher Columbus was really seeking a route to the east when he stumbled on the Americas, a route that would allow Europeans to bypass Muslim and other middlemen in the Indian Ocean trade. The year 1492 was significant not only for Columbus' landing in the New World, but also for the fall of Granada and the subsequent expansion of Spaniards into the Indian Ocean itself. So the second point is, one cannot disentangle the history of Muslim and Christian communities in the world no matter how hard one tries.

Christians as Subject Communities

Unlike the United States, where Muslims are a small but increasingly visible minority living in a predominantly Christian environment, in most places where Muslims and Christians have lived together in the past, Muslims have predominated politically, and usually numerically, and Christians have been minority communities. Much less often have Muslims been minority communities in predominantly Christian lands. Usually where Muslims were minorities in Christian lands, they were the rulers anyway despite the numerical inferiority.

Following the pre-Islamic practice of the empires that they began to conquer in the mid-seventh century, Muslims tended to organize the population for social and political purposes along the lines of religious affiliation, classifying non-Muslim communities as *dhimmi*s (protected minorities). This system reached its height under the Ottomans, who extended their rule from Anatolia to Europe in the fifteenth and sixteenth centuries (conquering Constantinople in 1453) and to Arabic-speaking North Africa and Middle East in the sixteenth and seventeenth centuries. So the third point is, the American reality of Muslims living as minorities in Christian lands reverses the historical picture, in which Muslims have generally lived either as a majority ruling over a Christian minority, or even as a minority ruling over a Christian majority. The American situation is a novel one, both full of pitfalls but also full of opportunities.

Religion as Nationality

As a result of organizing people into religious communities, in the major areas of Christian-Muslim interaction, religious labels have also functioned differently than in the United States, more the way they function for Catholics and Protestants in Northern Ireland, as symbols of much broader cultural, social, and political identities. This same social organization that helped the various communities under Muslim rule coexist has unfortunately, as we have seen in recent years, also contributed to new kinds of conflict, most notably in places like Lebanon, which at the time of its creation by the French had one of the most complicated sets of religious communities in the region. Much Middle Eastern "religious" conflict in recent years can in fact be traced to the difficult transition from loosely held clusters of virtually self-governing religious communities to nation-states, with their expectations of equality before a single secular national law and the relegation of religious identity exclusively to the private sphere.

Another story well illustrates this pattern of using religion as a shorthand for cultural differences, and even as an indicator of ethnicity and nationality. It was told to me by Alford Carleton, who worked with the World Council of Churches in the British Mandate of Palestine during most of the interwar years. One day Mr. Carleton (a tall, thin, fair, blond patrician-looking person) found himself crossing the Bosporus in a ferry boat with a Turkish Muslim. The Turkish Muslim could not speak English and my friend, an American Presbyterian, could not speak Turkish. But they both spoke French, and in the conversation that ensued they became so friendly so fast that the Turkish Muslim said to the American Presbyterian, "nous musulmanes," "we Muslims." My friend feared the possible consequences of participating in this deception, so he said, "Excuse me, sir, I'm sorry to have to tell you I'm not a Muslim." And the Muslim said, "Well, then, what are you?" And my friend said, with some trepidation, "Well, I'm a Christian." And the Muslim looked at him in disbelief and said, "That's funny; you don't look a bit Armenian!" Being an heir to the Ottoman Empire, the Turk could imagine a pale, European-looking Muslim, but he couldn't imagine a generic Christian apart from a specific ethnic-religious community. Religion and nationality, religion and ethnicity, have a connection in the Middle East, and elsewhere, that they do not have in the United States, and not understanding that connection is an obstacle to understanding the Middle East. However, in this case, Middle Eastern tradition is not a very good resource for building intercommunal relations in America; in fact, one of the challenges for Americans—Muslims and Christians alike—is to understand religious communities in a different way from the way in which they have functioned historically in the areas in which Muslims and Christians have most come in contact with each other.

It is clear even from this brief and superficial sketch of a very complicated topic that Muslim-Christian interaction has come in a variety of forms. The image of the Crusades as the primary way that Christians and Muslims have related simply is not adequate to the task. Historical study shows that all things are possible, from tragic conflict to tolerance to mutually creative interaction. I know that it is traditional for Americans to repeat the line, "Those who do not know history are condemned to repeat it." But that is not the way I think about history. My line is, "Those who do not know history are closed off from the opportunities that it presents." I think the knowledge of history shows us that all things are possible for us. However, a note of caution: as I mentioned earlier, we are a moment in this long history; we are not separate from it. What we do in and with this volume will become part of the history of Muslim-Christian interaction. We may be trying to stand at a distance to look at it, but we are also part of it, and what we do will affect its course. This is the first time in human history that Muslims have been called upon to live as a permanent minority in a predominantly Christian land with a pluralistic value system. That is the challenge on the Muslim side. The challenge for the non-Muslim American is to question the long-held assumption that religious pluralism is captured in the phrase "Protestant, Catholic, Jew." The presence not only of Muslim-Americans, but also of Buddhist-Americans and Hindu-Americans, Bahai-Americans, Jain-Americans, and so forth, demands that non-Muslim-American citizens as well as Muslim-American citizens rethink the history of Muslim-Christian interaction, and, I hope, take the opportunity to contribute to it in perhaps the most creative way yet.

Bibliography

Shah, Idries. *The Pleasantries of the Incredible Mulla Nasrudin*. New York: Dutton, 1971.

8

Historical Perspectives on Jewish-Muslim Relations
Marilyn Robinson Waldman

THE MAIN PURPOSE OF this chapter is to show that Jewish-Muslim relationships have a history, and that Jews and Muslims in the United States are part of that history. To say that relationships have a history is to say that they have changed and are still changing. Indeed, Jews and Muslims have interacted with each other in many different places and situations for more than a millennium, and their historical experiences suggest that they are fully capable of adapting to the unprecedented circumstances in which they find themselves in the United States today. In fact, it is more important than ever to recognize the openness of history, and the variety of ways in which groups are capable of perceiving and relating to each other, regardless of any dark moments in their past.

Two personal experiences have taught me just how flexible and how complicated people's conceptions of religious identities can be. The first occurred after one of my lectures at a church in Columbus, when a woman came up and asked a question unprecedented in all my twenty years of teaching and lecturing: "Don't you consider the Muslims to be Gentiles?" I replied, "No, that never occurred to me." She protested, "But my mother brought me up to believe that the world is divided into two groups—Jews and Gentiles—and if you are not one, you are the other, and that makes Muslims, Gentiles."

The second experience arose from attending a lecture by an anthropologist who had worked in the Iranian town of Yazd, which has a very old Jewish community. The Jews of Yazd, like the woman at my lecture, have also divided the world into Goyim (Gentiles) and Galutim (peoples of the Diaspora). In their view, the Galutim include not only themselves, but also the Zoroastrians, the Armenian Christians, and the Sunni Muslims; the Gentiles consist simply of the Shi'i Muslims. To them, "Gentile" refers to any group that predominates or is in power; "Galutim," to anyone who is disenfranchised and out of power.

Jewish-Muslim relations have been as variable and complex as these two stories would suggest, and they have also been very extensive. In his editor's introduction to a volume of essays on Islamic-Judaic interactions, William Brinner makes the following observation:

> It is becoming increasingly clear that these two religious civilizations [Judaism and Islam] have interacted on a number of levels, from that of folklore and folk-religion to the realms of theological and philosophical speculation. It is also becoming more apparent that, for a variety of reasons, this interaction was probably more profound than that which existed between Islam and Christianity.[1]

If that is so, why has Jewish-Muslim interaction, not to mention Jewish-Christian interaction, received relatively little scholarly attention? First, until recently, these three religions have normally been studied by specialists in different fields, so opportunities to study their interaction have been limited and professionally unrewarding. Second, since most professional historians are themselves "western" and study "the west," they have generally defined Judaism and Christianity as "western" and Islam as "eastern." Thus, they have tended to overlook the fact that Judaism, Christianity, along with Islam, originated in "the east," and that all three continued to interact there long after some of the Jews and Christians had moved "west." Recent scholarship has begun to correct that oversight, and in this brief essay I summarize some of the major lessons it is teaching us about the history of Jewish-Muslim interaction.

Before attempting to learn those lessons, it is important to remember that Muslims and Jews have most often lived together in societies with very different social expectations from our own. The institutionalized equality of all human beings was virtually unknown anywhere in the world before modem times, so belonging to a religion other than that of the ruler often brought subordinate status of some sort. The assigning of lower status to non-dominant religions seems to have been a common pre-modern habit, not just in the Middle East, where Islam developed, but in Europe as well.

---

1. Brinner, "Introduction," ix.

Part III: The Past Is Never Dead

We have only to look to the Protestant Reformation for an example of the distribution of subject peoples into religious communities with different statuses: if a ruler became Catholic, the Protestants suffered, and if a ruler became Protestant, the Catholics suffered.

An amusing apocryphal story well illustrates the trials of subordinate religious communities in medieval Europe. A bishop decided that the Jews in his town had to go. In the face of protest from the Jewish community, the bishop agreed to let them stay if one of them could defeat him in a public non-verbal duel of wits. Naturally, no Jew was quick to volunteer, but finally a poor tailor named Mentl reluctantly agreed.

The bishop arrived dressed in magnificent regalia and accompanied by a large entourage; the tailor came alone in his work clothes. The bishop drew a large circle, and the tailor stomped furiously on the ground. The bishop began to look a little nervous, but continued. He held up three fingers and Mentl held up one. The bishop began to sweat and seemed very nervous as he took the bread and the wine from under his garments and swallowed them, at which point Mentl took an apple out of his pocket and bit into it. The bishop threw up his hands and said, "That's it. The Jews can stay."

That afternoon, the bishop's followers asked what had happened, and he answered, "I drew a circle to remind us God is everywhere, but the Jew stomped on the ground to remind us that God is not in Hell. I held up three fingers to remind us of the Trinity, but he held up one to remind us of the oneness of God that it represents. I took out the bread and the wine to remind us of the sacrifice of our Lord, but he took out an apple to remind us of the sin that made it all necessary."

Across town, Mentl's friends asked him what had happened. "Well, he made this big circle to show us he wanted us outside the city walls, but I stomped on the ground to say, 'No way.' He held up three fingers to say he would give us three days to clear out, but I held up one to tell him not one of us is moving. And then when he took out his lunch, I took out mine."

This type of structure—subordinate religious communities under the power of a dominant ruler and his religion—was characteristic of the Roman and Sasanian empires, the pre-Islamic rulers of the areas that first came under Muslim rule. In many of the areas into which Arab-Muslims began to migrate in the mid-seventh century of the Common Era (CE), religious communities were already functioning as separate bodies joined together primarily by their allegiance to a common ruler. Furthermore, rulers were already using the religious community as an important vehicle for social and political management, and for assigning social status, long before the emergence of the first Muslim empire.

The new Muslim rulers appear to have appropriated this social structure (though not right away) and institutionalized it in the form of *ahl al-dhimma*, or *dhimmi*s, protected scriptural communities who had a subordinate legal status but lived largely under their own rules. Since most of the Muslim-ruled lands probably did not become majority Muslim until about 875, two hundred and fifty years after the beginning of the conquest, the early Muslim community was itself a minority in the lands over which it ruled. The subject majority was composed of Jews, Christians, and Zoroastrians.

So the hegemony of the Muslims had ironic effects. It eventually resulted in the conversion of some Jews and of most Christians and Zoroastrians; but it protected from each other those who retained their religious affiliations, and even allowed them a degree of consolidation and renewal. The great scholar of Jewish-Muslim interaction, perhaps the greatest of our century, Shlomo Dov Goitein, once remarked that the establishment of Muslim hegemony revitalized and possibly saved medieval Judaism from extinction.

The relationships between Jews and Muslims living under this kind of socio-political structure have naturally not been ideal by today's American standards, which assume a very different structure. At best the structure in which the Muslims and Jews found themselves sometimes promoted, to be sure, tensions and unequal relationships. At worst, Jews experienced discrimination and persecution that violated Muslim ideals as well.

On the other hand, social mobility, intercommunal contact, and cultural freedom seem to have been far greater for a religious minority in the Muslim-ruled lands than in Christendom, and Jews benefited from that as much as any subject group. We have, for example, as many critiques of Islam by the Jewish scholar Maimonides (1135–1204 CE) as we have critiques of Judaism by any single Muslim scholar. So regardless of the imperfect political and social record, members of the two traditions have managed during the last fourteen centuries to influence each other in unpredictable and unexpected ways.

I want to illustrate that changeable pattern of mutual influence with brief sketches of four different situations: the community of Muhammad (622–632 CE), the early 'Abbasid empire (especially mid-eighth to mid-tenth centuries), al-Andalus ("Moorish Spain," especially the tenth to the thirteenth centuries), and the Ottoman Empire (fifteenth to twentieth centuries).

Part III: The Past Is Never Dead

The Community of Muhammad

It is all too well known that the prophet Muhammad's relationships with the Jews of Arabia were often tense and sometimes even violent. The conflicts between Muhammad and his followers (Muslims) on the one hand and the Jews on the other are referred to not only in the Qur'an (the revelations of God as spoken by Muhammad), but also in early Muslim historical sources. Yet the Qur'an also reveres such figures as Abraham and Moses as legitimate prophets, and prescribes for Muslims certain requirements (e.g., multiple daily prayer) and taboos (e.g., against eating pork) that were shared by Jews.

In fact, then, Muhammad's relations with Jews were ambivalent. At the beginning of his prophethood, Muhammad appears to have thought of himself as a reformer within the Jewish (and Christian) tradition. As such, he expected Jews (and Christians) to recognize him and follow his lead. Some probably did; others resisted and even worked against the success and survival of his fledgling community. As a result, Muhammad began to think of himself as the proclaimer of a pure and "generic" surrender to God (Islam) that Jews (and Christians) had turned into their own "name-brand" religions over time. However, even after making that shift in emphasis, Muhammad offered Jews and Christians, as peoples who each had a Book from God, protection in return for submission to the political hegemony of the Muslim community.

The history I have just sketched is clear enough, but unfortunately we do not yet have a clear enough picture of Arabian "Jews" to understand it very well. Certainly, we must be very careful about using the Qur'an to explain relations between Jews and Muslims in our own time. In fact, the Qur'an uses two relevant labels—"Yahud" and "Banu Isra'il"—so we cannot even know whether it is referring to a single people or group. Furthermore, individuals bearing those labels could belong to tribes of their own, or be mixed in the same tribe with members of other communities. Such individuals spoke Arabic, like the first Muslims, and may have been indistinguishable from other Arabic-speakers except in matters of personal habit and ritual practice. Finally, Muhammad's conflicts with them may have arisen more from their lack of support for the economic and political expansion of his community than from disagreements over faith and belief. Whatever the relationship between Arabian "Jews" and the first Muslims really was, many Jews outside of Arabia soon came under the rule of Muslims as dhimmis. When, by 640, Muslim rulers had gained control over all of what we now call the Middle East, their relationships with the Jews of that region were of a different nature.

The Early 'Abbasid Empire

From the origins of the 'Abbasid dynasty in 750 to the tenth century, Jewish-Muslim interaction was particularly intense and the impact of Jews on Muslims particularly strong. During this period some Jews were becoming Muslims; some of the Jews who became Muslims, or their descendants, also became scholars of Islam; and Jews who did not become Muslim could still play a role in the development of the ideas and institutions of the Muslims. Marshall Hodgson, one of the most creative American scholars of Islamic history and civilization, even invented a new adjective, "Islamicate," to describe the participation of so many non-Muslims in the civilization that was inspired by the spread of Muslim rule and the Islamic faith.

Eventually Muslims came to think and act more "Islamically," and to view themselves as having superseded Jewish understanding of material in the Qur'an that was common to both traditions. Nevertheless, Jewish lore filtered into Islamic lore, particularly by means of a genre called *qisas alanbiya'* (stories of the prophets), which reworked Jewish tradition to provide Islamic accounts of prophetic figures who are common to Jews and Muslims. Before long, all sorts of Muslims had absorbed and begun to use these shared materials. For example, the eleventh-century Persian author Bayhaqi, in the course of his narrative of Iranian history, illustrated the trait of compassion by recalling an occasion on which Moses took the time to return a lost lamb to its mother before continuing on his journey.[2] The story does not appear in the Torah or in the Qur'an, but does appear in Midrashic lore.

We also know that many Muslim scholars in the early 'Abbasid period specialized in the study of Jewish sectarianism. Since the Muslim taxation system made distinctions for various religious affiliations, Muslim rulers needed to know who could be considered Jews and who not. However, the 'Abbasids's Jewish subjects and their leaders often could not or would not tell or agree, so Muslim scholars made a point of finding out on their own. As a result, we know much of what we know about certain "Jewish" movements only through the accounts of Muslim authors. One of these movements, the 'Isawiyya, even recognized Muhammad as God's messenger to

---

2. Waldman, *Toward a Theory of Historical Narrative*, 179.

the Muslims. And in the end, some of what was viewed as heterodox or extremist by the majority of Jews found its way into the practices and ideas of certain Muslims.

In her chapter in this volume, Tamar Frank identifies religious law as a point of commonality between Muslims and Jews, expressed through Shari'a in one case and Halakha in the other. The work of other scholars shows just how extensive and close the parallels are. Of course, some of Talmudic law actually reflects life under Muslim rule, just as some of the Shari'a reflects interaction with Jews or even the contributions of converts with a Jewish heritage.

In fact, the degree to which members of these two traditions have used divinely inspired law to regulate daily behavior, and the extent to which they have defined such discipline as a major form of piety, may not have a counterpart in any other religious community. So perhaps something that Jews and Muslims take for granted should not be taken for granted, and could even provide an important and constructive topic of interfaith conversation.

Al-Andalus

The Iberian Peninsula provided a somewhat different environment for intercommunal relations. Especially during the period when Muslims ruled most of the peninsula (tenth to thirteenth centuries), Jews were much influenced by Arab-Muslim culture and much involved in Muslim rule itself. Although officially in conflict, the Christian rulers in the north and the Muslim rulers in the south were socially and politically intertwined, and Jews often played a mediating role.

For example, in the mid-tenth century Toda, the queen mother of Navarre, was the grandmother of its future king, Sancho. However, she was also the great-aunt of the famous Umayyad Muslim ruler of Cordova, 'Abd al-Rahman III. Toda's Christian grandson Sancho was too obese to ride a horse and thus to come to the throne, so Toda appealed to her Muslim great-nephew. The great-nephew, 'Abd al-Rahman III, sent Hasdai ben Shaprut, his Jewish personal physician, to treat Sancho, in exchange for some of Toda's lands. Hasdai ben Shaprut brought Sancho back with him to Cordova, where he put him on a vegetarian diet and reduced his torso sufficiently so that he could sit on a horse and, eventually, become king.

Hasdai ben Shaprut also became the first great patron of Hebrew letters, and in fact it is in the area of language and literature that Arab-Muslim culture had its greatest impact on Andalusian Jews. Arabic forms and metres influenced Hebrew secular poetry, and Arabic metres even came to be used in Hebrew religious poetry. The Jewish Andalusian style, developed by such famous poets as Ben Gabirol, Judah Halevi, and Avraham ben Ezra, spread to the Jewish communities of Babylonia, Egypt, North Africa, Palestine, Italy, Greece, Turkey, and Yemen. The Arabs' intense interest and skill in philology was one important source of inspiration for the revival of biblical Hebrew and the study of its grammar. Jewish writers frequently wrote in Judeo-Arabic (Arabic in Hebrew characters). Jewish philosophers like Maimonides were much influenced by reading philosophical texts written by Muslims in Arabic.

By the thirteenth century, al-Andalus, the territory under Muslim control, had begun to shrink very rapidly, and Muslims and Jews began to become minorities under Christian control. However, since at first the Christians treated them the way the Muslims had treated Jews and Christians, productive cooperation among the religious communities continued for some time. For example, Alfonso X of Castile (r. 1252–1284) styled himself "king of the three religions" and attempted to promote as much interaction as possible, especially through establishing a team of translators at Toledo. The Jews, knowing not only Hebrew and Arabic but also Castilian, now became natural intermediaries between Christians and Muslims. They also thus became central in the transmission to Europeans of Arabic folklore, literature, mathematics, science, and philosophy.

This period is in fact one of the few occasions in the history of the world in which Muslims and Jews lived as minorities under Christian domination in a relatively constructive way. However, that relationship did not survive the Christian domination of the peninsula. By the fifteenth century, Christian intolerance had begun to grow. The Jews were expelled in 1492; the Muslims, in 1609.

The Ottoman Empire

The Ottoman Empire regularized and routinized the structure of faith communities even further, not only in the Middle East, but in North Africa and Europe as well. In so doing, it left a problematic legacy to the more than thirty modern nations that were born out of its dissolution. The transition from empire to nations was also exacerbated by British and French Mandate administration in the early twentieth century. In the Ottoman

Empire, religious communities were joined together and kept in balance only by the administrative control of the Sultan, but otherwise left largely to regulate their own communal life. In the British and French Mandates, the religious communities were often set against each other, and their social and economic power reallocated. The borders drawn for the new nation-states often created further intercommunal tensions, and the demand for all citizens to be equal before the same law was difficult to meet. Even in today's Israel, citizenship is distinguished from nationality, which is based on religious affiliation, and quasi-autonomous legal systems are recognized for a number of religious communities. In fact, the tensions between Israelis and Arabs, or between Muslims and Jews, have been caused more by these relatively recent factors than by any age-old inevitable rivalries.

Conclusion

From this brief historical survey we can make two observations: 1. The United States is not the first place in which Jews and Muslims have lived as minorities in a culture dominated by another religion, but it *is* the first time they have lived together as minorities in a society that celebrates pluralism, and insists on the equality of all faith communities under a single legal system and a single national identity. 2. Just as Jewish-Muslim relations have adapted to other changes in the past, they should be able to adapt to this one. The history of Jewish-Muslim interaction provides us with enough resources to make the kind of creative adaptations so often required of Jews and Muslims in the past.

We can learn from history; we are not its prisoner. The situation in which we find ourselves is not characteristic of any period in the history of our interactions with each other, and we are free to make creative adaptations of our traditions to the present situation. However, since Jews have rarely lived as a majority or as the dominant culture anywhere, this situation is less unprecedented for them. Still, their challenge will be to learn to live with Muslims on new terms. The Islamic tradition, on the other hand, has developed from very different historical experiences, for Muslims have generally lived in cultures in which they have predominated, and much of the Islamic tradition is based on that kind of social assumption. So Muslims will be challenged to find not only new ways to live as neighbors with Jews, but authentic ways to live as a minority in a culture dominated by another tradition altogether.

Bibliography

Brinner, William M. "Introduction." In *Studies in Islamic and Judaic Traditions: Papers Presented at the Institute for Islamic-Judaic Studies*, edited by William M. Brinner and Stephen D. Ricks, ix–xi. Atlanta: Scholars, 1986.

Waldman, Marilyn Robinson. *Toward a Theory of Historical Narrative: A Case Study in Perso-Islamicate Historiography*. Columbus: Ohio State University Press, 1980.

9

A Historical Perspective on Jewish-Muslim Relations

Reuven Firestone

I SOMETIMES BEGIN MY talks by citing an Egyptian colleague of mine who retired recently after directing the Middle East Center at the University of Utah. His name is Professor Ibrahim Karawan, and he begins his first class in "Introduction to Middle East Politics" with the following statement (paraphrased): "I understand that many of you take this course because you want to understand better what is happening in the Middle East. Many of your student colleagues have told me that you take the course because you believe I can help simplify things for you so you can understand what is really going on there. But you must know that if you really want to understand, I must complexify things for you."

That is a wise statement. Life is not simple. Life is extremely complex, and don't let anybody tell you that it is not. Like much else in the world, the history of Jewish-Muslim relations is also complex, neither reflective simply of wonderful harmony as some would claim, nor only of violence and persecution as others would claim. In this chapter I will offer an overview of the more complex reality that is Jewish-Muslim relations.

From the Islamic perspective, Jewish-Muslim relations began even before the birth of Muhammad and the emergence of a religious movement that came to be known as Islam. The Qur'an itself refers to Abraham as a Muslim:

> Sura 2 (al-Baqara):127–128: And when Abraham and Ishmael were raising up the foundations of the House [they prayed]: Our Lord, Accept [this] from us, for You are the Hearer, the Knower.

A Historical Perspective on Jewish-Muslim Relations

> Our Lord, Make us *muslimin*[1] to You and our progeny a *muslim* people to You. Show us the ritual places and turn toward us, for You are the One who turns [in forgiveness], the Merciful.[2]

So according to the Qur'an, while Jews were indeed Jews, when they were responding properly to the divine will they were functioning as Muslims! They were submitting to God's will, obedient to the divine command. This is the definition of the word *muslim* according to the Qur'an.

And from the perspective of Judaism, Jewish-Muslim relations began with the birth of Ishmael, who represents for the sages of the Talmud the progenitor of the Muslim peoples, whom they refer to as Ishmael or Ishmaelites (Hebrew: *b'ney yishmael*).

But these are pre-historical references that are based on sacred scripture rather than on the writings of human historical witnesses. My task here is to give you a sense of Jewish-Muslim relations in history. I will do this by treating the issue of the so-called "Golden Age" of Jewish-Muslim relations.

There are two very different perspectives on this golden age these days, two polarized views of the relations between Muslims and Jews during the Middle Ages.

One perspective has it that everybody was happy during the Golden Age. The Muslims treated the Jews as virtual equals, giving them high status in a shared society even if not fully equal, and provided a political and social environment in which Jews could thrive. Under such extraordinary conditions, Jews produced their greatest works of science and literature, religious law, philosophy and theology. In Baghdad, Saadia Gaon developed the first formal Jewish theology, produced a poetic dictionary, and translated the Hebrew Bible into classical Arabic. In Fostat/Cairo, Moses Maimonides wrote an encyclopedic code of Jewish Law, the Mishneh Torah, and the most important Jewish philosophical work in history, *The Guide for the Perplexed*. Dozens of other Jewish intellectuals and scientists developed new insights in linguistics, optical science, astronomy, geography, literature, poetry, and Bible scholarship in Spain, North Africa, Yemen, the Land of Israel, and much of the Middle East. Jewish grand viziers ran the administrations of Muslim sultans, and the Andalusian rabbi and poet, Shmuel Hanagid, even functioned

---

1. Translations often render this word as "submitter" or "submissive." I keep it in lower case to designate not adherents of a religion called Islam, but "submitter-muslims," meaning anyone who surrenders one's full being to the majesty of God.

2. See also Qur'an 2:130–131; 3:67; 4:125; 37:103; etc., which associated Abraham with the word root for Muslim and Islam.

as the head general for a Muslim king's armies for sixteen years. Jews (and Christians) were encouraged to be fully engaged in a great and open civilization made up of Muslims, Christians, and Jews. As amazing as this appears, all of these great developments are documented. They really happened, and they all occurred under Muslim rule.

In contrast to this rosy picture, the other perspective cites harassment and violence, discrimination, oppressive taxation, public humiliation and ridicule, pogroms and forced conversion. It was forbidden by law in the Muslim world for Jews to build or enlarge synagogues or even to make repairs on them. Jews were forced to wear distinguishing clothing and even yellow badges in some locations, and were forbidden from riding noble animals like horses. They were forcibly converted en masse in Spain and North Africa. It has been documented that children were removed from their Jewish families and raised as Muslims, and Jewish quarters were pillaged, men were massacred and women raped in Morocco, Algeria, Yemen, and Iran. Every one of these negative portrayals is documented by Jewish, Christian, and/or Muslim sources. There is no doubt among reasoned historians that they occurred.

So what was it? Was there a "Golden Age" or was there not a "Golden Age"?

The answer is. . . . Well, I won't answer the question. Keep in mind what I said above, that life is complicated. If we want to truly understand, we need to be willing to consider the true complexity of history. We can return to the question shortly. But first, I will tell you another story.

Muslim rule on the margins of Europe was repulsed in the Middle Ages by Christian Crusades and other armies. Spain, which had been a Muslim land for centuries, was taken over by Christians and the Muslims and Jews all forcibly converted or forcibly expelled. When the Jews were forced out in 1492 they were welcomed into the expanding and self-confident Ottoman Empire, a great empire ruled by a Turkish Muslim sultan. But many Jews chose or had no choice but to flee to other places. Some were forcibly converted to Christianity, many of them observing Jewish religious life in secret as crypto-Jews. Many suffered horribly during this dark time. Some Jews who found safe locations wrote to their families and friends remaining in Spain to inform them of the good news. One famous letter often cited in this regard is that of a rabbi named Isaac Zarfati:

> I have heard of the afflictions, more bitter than death, that have befallen our brethren in Germany of the tyrannical laws, the

compulsory baptisms and the banishments, which are of daily occurrence. I am told that when they flee from one place a yet harder fate befalls them in another . . . on all sides I learn of anguish of soul and torment of body; of daily exactions levied by merciless oppressors. The clergy and the monks, false priests that they are, rise up against the unhappy people of God . . . for this reason they have made a law that every Jew found upon a Christian ship bound for the East shall be flung into the sea. Alas! How evil are [Jews], the people of God in Germany treated; how sad is their strength departed! They are driven hither and thither, and they are pursued even unto death. . . .

Brothers and teachers, friends and acquaintances! I, Isaac Zarfati, though I spring from French stock, yet I was born in Germany, and sat there at the feet of my esteemed teachers. I proclaim to you that Turkey is a land wherein nothing is lacking, and where, if you will, all shall yet be well with you. The way to the Holy Land lies open to you through Turkey. Is it not better for you to live under Muslims than under Christians? Here every man dwells at peace under his own vine and fig tree. Here you are allowed to wear the most precious garments. In Christendom, on the contrary, you dare not even venture to clothe your children in red or in blue, according to our taste, without exposing them to the insult or beaten black and blue, or kicked green and red, and therefore are you condemned to go about meanly clad in sad coloured raiment . . . and now, seeing on these things, O Israel, wherefore sleepest thou? Arise! And leave this accursed land forever![3]

This letter is real. It documents the sentiment that was prevalent during much of the medieval period. This may sound odd to us today, but medieval Jews wrote that Christianity is an evil, violent, merciless, and bloody religion. Christians not only persecuted and killed Jews and Muslims in local massacres and Crusades, they also persecuted and killed other Christians whom they defined as heretics. While Jews of course did not accept Islam as an adequate expression of monotheism, they were far more favorable toward Islam and Muslims than toward Christianity and Christians. Jews wrote that Islam was a civilized religion, while Christianity was not.

When we consider stereotypes, I'm sure you may be thinking exactly what I thought when I first ran across this fact. It is largely a reversal of the common Jewish perspective regarding Christianity and Islam today.

3. Lewis, *Jews of Islam*, 135–36. H. Graetz dates the letter approximately 1454.

Part III: The Past Is Never Dead

In the twelfth century, some 80 percent or more of the world's Jews lived in the Muslim world. Only 10 to 20 percent lived in the Christian world. By the nineteenth century, the numbers were reversed. The reversal reflected the dramatic change in the economic and intellectual developments in Europe—and the economic and intellectual decline of the Muslim world.

Nineteenth-century Europe had experienced the Reformation and Enlightenment for its Christian inhabitants—and only the partial emancipation of its Jews (there were no Muslims to speak of living in Europe at the time). In the nineteenth century, Jewish intellectuals became impatient with the lack of Jewish emancipation in Europe, and especially in Eastern Europe. They complained about it and wrote about it, citing letters like the one I just read to you in order to push European Christians to rectify the situation. Their message to the European Christians went something like this: "If you are truly enlightened and believe in the ideas of the modern European social philosophers that you so often cite, you may not limit your consideration of humanity only to Christians. You must also accept us Jews!"

So here was their message to their Christian European overlords: "We Jews lived in a Golden Age under the Muslims, those very people whom you currently dominate intellectually, politically, and economically. How can you, enlightened Europeans, abide being outdone in moral stature by the now weak and under-developed Ottoman Empire, which is barely surviving while Europe is developing so quickly and with such self-confidence?"

This was the position of some Jewish intellectuals who wanted to embarrass their Christian rulers into granting full and equal rights to European Jews. Other Jewish intellectuals used the story of a Golden Age under Ottoman Muslim enlightenment to encourage Jews to leave Europe, and especially Eastern Europe, to settle in Ottoman Palestine under the new Zionist movement. "Under the Muslims," they said, "we Jews lived without problems, and Zarfati's letter (among others) is proof. So come and build up the Jewish homeland! The Muslims will not impede us! They will only welcome us!"

To a certain extent, this encouragement worked. The Jewish community of Palestine expanded greatly, first under the Ottomans and then under the British mandate after World War I. The more that the Jewish community grew and developed, the more land it settled and the more active it became in local (meaning Palestinian) social, economic, and political affairs, the more threatening it became to the local Arab population. You know the story here. As the tensions grew, so did violence. Each side genuinely felt that it was in the right and its opponent was in the wrong. Each had its own narrative as to who had the right to live and become dominant in the land.

Each community needed support from outside of Palestine in order to push its own agenda. The Palestinian Arabs looked toward their Arab comrades—both Muslim and Christian—while the Palestinian Jews looked toward the West for support. Each side accused the other of unacceptable behaviors, and each tried to gain the support of its own hinterland of potential supporters. Lots of writings were used for this. We would probably call these writings propaganda today because both sides cited some true facts and figures but withheld others, and then interpreted and even distorted the data to push their own agendas.

Some Jews accused the Arabs of being violent and primitive in their violent opposition to Zionist immigration. They wrote that the source of the problems between Arabs and Jews was Arab intransience with not a little amount of anti-Semitism.

Some Arab intellectuals countered this narrative by citing the story of good relations between Jews and Muslims in the Middle Ages. After all, they claimed, the Jews themselves wrote that Jews and Arabs lived together in peace under Muslim rule while Jews were being relentlessly persecuted by Christians. They argued that modern Arab anger is directed only against those Jews who are engaged in what they considered illegal and immoral colonialism of Arab Palestine. It was not the Arabs, but the Jews who were destroying the old harmony through Zionism and its claim for Jewish settlement, which meant uprooting and delegitimizing the natural Muslim-Arab right to Palestine. In other words, there is no inherent Arab or Muslim antipathy toward Jews and Judaism. "We Arabs are enlightened and ethical," they said. "We enabled the Jewish Golden Age. It is the Jews who have caused the problems, and Arab antipathy toward Jews would end when Zionism abandons its colonialist quest." Thus the true story of relatively good relations mixed with a certain level of discrimination and occasional anti-Jewish violence was transformed into the myth of a virtually perfect "Golden Age."

This myth was then countered by Jewish intellectuals through a Jewish "counter-myth" to challenge the Arab propaganda. They developed their own propaganda, especially after 1967 when Jewish writers played down the good aspects of life under Muslim rule and cited only the instances of prejudice, violence, massacres, and expulsions, of which there were plenty enough to cite. It began among journalists and popular writers but was taken up also by historians and other scholars. This narrative also distorts the facts, but in the opposite direction. This Jewish position reflects the frustration of Israel in continuous wars with its Arab neighbors, and what it considers to be unreasonable Arab intransigence and hatred. It also reflects the shock of discovering the new anti-Semitic rhetoric coming out of the Arab-Muslim world in the last few decades.[4]

Now I will add one more piece to the mix to show you how complex the situation really is. Both Jews and Muslims have their deeply ingrained prejudices—about themselves and about others. This is a natural aspect of human identity and behavior. Virtually all human communities define themselves as "better," more civilized, or even more human than others. I sometimes lecture about this, and when I do I usually cite texts from our religious traditions that paint the other in starkly negative terms. The Bible and the Talmud, for example, contain plenty of negative rhetoric about non-Jews, including Arabs, from centuries before the emergence of the religion of Islam. Those references to Arabs are understood in later Jewish literatures as referring to Muslims. The Qur'an and the Hadith have a lot of negative things to say about Jews as well as other non-Muslim groups. And Christian civilization has a lot of negative things to say about Jews and Muslims as well as others. So there is plenty of nasty rhetoric to make everybody feel bad.

Much of it is just "there." It is what I call "latent." Anti-"other" feelings lie deep in all cultures and societies. They are probably a part of human nature. Much of the time they are just "there." They remain buried and dormant, embedded deeply within culture. When tension arises or conflict occurs between communities, or if there is a reduction in fortune in the community as a whole, those dormant feelings can be re-discovered. They will then seem natural and can subsequently become actualized into hatred and violence. The result is scapegoating. Today, with the deep tensions that have grown up around the Middle East because of the Israel-Palestinian conflict and Western invasions of Iraq and Afghanistan, and the tension that has accompanied the large recent Muslim immigration to the West (and especially Europe), the latent prejudice on both sides becomes easily activated and disseminated—in op-ed pieces in newspapers, in books and magazines, on radio talk-shows and television, and especially on the

---

4. For a full rendering of this analysis and an excellent comparison of the treatment of Jews under Christians and Muslims in the Middle Ages, see Cohen, *Under Crescent and Cross*.

internet. Nasty anti-Semitic material is readily available in Arabic, Farsi, Urdu, and other languages spoken and read by Muslims. And nasty Islamophobic material is readily available in English and European languages spoken and read by Jews and Christians. All of these current tensions deeply affect our views of Jewish-Muslim relations.

So how "golden" was the Golden Age? The real story of Jewish-Muslim relations has always been affected by historical context.

So now, after "complexifying" the topic somewhat, I will give you my opinion. The position of Jews in the Muslim world was better overall than in the Christian world, for a number of reasons that I will not pursue now because that would take us away from the thrust of this argument. In fact, the position of Jews under Islam was the best that was available in the pre-modern world, at least in the monotheistic world (the small Jewish communities that settled in India and China seem to have been essentially ignored though they never thrived). But the status of Jews in the medieval Muslim world was not what we would wish for today. In the modern world the position of Jews has often been far better, such as in the United States today. But in some times and places it has been far worse, such as in Germany and most of Europe in the 1930s and 1940s.

The truth of the matter is that Jews and Muslims have always had a lot in common wherever we've lived. We share similar theologies and spiritual practices, and we share a great deal of correspondence in culture, spirit, and civilization. We also have common interests as minorities striving for many of the same goals in the United States and in Europe. It would benefit both communities to learn more about one another and work toward pooling our resources, experiences, and talents so we can build a better world for ourselves and for the larger communities in which we live.

Bibliography

Cohen, Mark. *Under Crescent and Cross*. Princeton: Princeton University Press, 2008.
Lewis, Bernard. *The Jews of Islam*. Princeton: Princeton University Press, 1984.

10

Muslims and Jews in America

Sayyid M. Syeed

SHALOM ALEICHEM, GOOD AFTERNOON and shalom. I want to begin with a quotation from a Jewish scholar who is advocating why every Jew should know more about Islam. He writes:

> For the past few centuries, most Jews have lived among and under the rule of Christians (although earlier, during most of the Middle Ages, most Jews lived under the rule of Muslims). Jews entered modernity through the Christian world, and all of the great Jewish achievements and calamities of modernity were influenced one way or another by the profound underlying relationship between Jews and Christians that had been developing for centuries.

But he continues: "Although the ambivalences that have marked this foundational relationship continue to have a greater or lesser extent today and will undoubtedly influence the future, it has become clear that the religious civilization that is having the greatest impact on Jews in the 21st century is Islam, both in the Middle East and in the West."

The author is our great scholar, Dr. Reuven Firestone, who is with us for this conference. He concludes, "Responsible decision-making is impossible without understanding. For the sake of the future of the Jewish people and the future of the world as a whole, it is important to develop a firm, sober, realistic understanding of Islam and how Islam affects the outlooks and behaviors of Muslims as they act in the world."[1] How powerful these statements are.

Here in America, in a pluralist democracy, Muslims recognized early on that we have a special role to play, which our brothers and sisters in other parts of the world, for various reasons, will not be able to play. Here we are in a position to have dialogue, here we are in a position to have conversations, here we can have joint or separate events where we can discuss the most difficult questions about ourselves, our neighbors, and others. We know that this kind of dialogue is very critical; it is this dialogue that has shaped America into what it is today. As we can see from the African American experience, progress does not happen all of a sudden. African Americans came as slaves, they had no rights at all. It took hundreds of years of struggle to recognize the rights that African Americans have, like any other human being, and today, we are proud to say as Americans that we have a black man in the White House.

Many of you may be aware of the history of the Muslim Students Association of the US and Canada (MSA). When I came to Indiana University as a PhD student, I got involved with this movement and was elected as MSA's President. In this capacity I had the honor to transform it into the Islamic Society of North America (ISNA), with its headquarters in Indianapolis. I believed that this was a wonderful, historic opportunity to give a sense of direction and a sense of belonging to Muslims in America by giving them this gift of a well-knit, well-organized institution. ISNA is now the oldest and largest Islamic umbrella organization in North America. During my tenure as ISNA's Secretary-General, American Muslims must have built and expanded two to three thousand Islamic centers. Our priorities were to provide places of worship and to consolidate the Muslim community as a richly contributing, constructively involved American entity.

But things changed after 9/11. It became critical for Muslims to reach out. This was a new responsibility. So I relinquished my position as the Secretary-General of ISNA and moved to Washington, DC where my office is now right on Capitol Hill. This is a continuation of ISNA's work—more involved, not in our own community building because that we have already done, but in building a wider community, a community of understanding, a community of dialogue with Christians, Jews, and all the different faith groups in America, and directly educating our country's decision makers about this new entity called the Muslim Community of North America.

---

1. Firestone, *Introduction to Islam for Jews*, 4.

Part III: The Past Is Never Dead

In this capacity, new possibilities are opening up. Many of the controversies with which we have been brought up are vanishing. A new confidence is being built in the Muslim mind. But the problem is that there are many mountains of hatred, mountains of misinterpretation, and mountains of resentment, and these mountains cannot be removed by one person, one organization, one community. This has to be done by all of us together. It is amazing, I am impressed, I express my gratitude to God Almighty, our Creator, that in our own lifetime, we are seeing something that others had to wait for centuries to see. Only in the 1960s did Catholics admit that the Jews were not the "Christ-killers," that they did not deserve the treatment that historically Christians had given them. (By the way, for Muslims, Christ was never crucified.)

In 1990 there was a conference in Los Angeles about Jewish identity in America. I expected the papers would deal with some things that Jews have in common with Muslims—such as interfaith marriages and problems with youth—since both groups are minorities in America. But there was one paper that surprised me: "The American Jewish Experience and the Emergence of the Muslim Community in America" by Jonathan Sarna, a professor of the history of Judaism in America. The topic was the impact of the growing Muslim community on Jewish identity in America. I was puzzled. How are Muslims impacting the identity of the Jews in America?

So I read the paper. Sarna explained how Jews in America had been subjected to much discrimination, how they were despised and so on, but he also described how step-by-step they lived with it, how step-by-step through their struggle they opened up the concept of pluralism, and how step-by-step they suffered but also built a safe, secure, responsible, respectable role for themselves in America. Sarna wrote that Jews have built a ladder for going up in American society.

There is a new community in America—Muslims—who have certain advantages and strengths. Jews came from the ghettos of Europe; they had many disadvantages. But Muslims are part of a brain drain; many are coming here, directly to American universities to pursue their higher studies. They are scientists, doctors, and engineers, so they have a certain cushion. The ladder that the Jews created for upward movement in America is equally available to Muslims so they will go step-by-step on this ladder to the highest influence in America. After having analyzed how Jews were able to create an influence in America, Sarna says there's no reason to think that Muslims will not be able to do the same thing. And therefore, he concluded that the Jewish community should recognize this fact and constructively involve themselves with the Muslim community. He knew that many Jews will be obsessed with what is happening in the Middle East, but it is critical for them that they treat Muslims as American citizens and as American neighbors.

I was so fascinated that I wrote a letter to Jonathan Sarna and got his permission to publish his paper in the *American Journal of Islamic Social Sciences* (I was at that time Editor-in-Chief of the journal),[2] because I thought our Muslim intellectuals should understand that there is already a recognition of this reality in America. And what Sarna is telling Jews, I would like to say the same thing to Muslims.

Now, about Columbus, Ohio. I discovered Columbus several years ago when we put together the first of these local conferences. Later, Norman Hosansky and Mazhar Jalil published the edited volume *Muslims and Jews: Building a Hopeful Future*.[3] Many people did not know about these efforts, but I realized that this is the direction we would like to take our Muslim community. They had published about five hundred or six hundred copies, maybe one thousand copies of the book, but I said this is something that everybody should know. So I got their permission to publish about ten thousand copies and we sent them all over America. I knew that many people would not even read the book because the curtains of hatred are so thick, and they would be turned off by the very first page. But this is what we stand for. If this is our vision, we have to take our community along with us in that direction so that their future sufferings, and their future understanding of themselves and understanding of others, are corrected at the right time. We do not want another 9/11, we do not want another son or daughter growing up like Nidal Hasan, the shooter at Fort Hood, Texas. We want healthy minds in the American Muslim community who understand their context, who understand their religious duty to provide leadership not only in America but throughout the world.

When I moved to Washington, DC, I thought we had done wonderful job of working with Christian denominations of all kinds, Catholics and Protestants alike. But the problem was how to have interfaith dialogue with Jews? There is an elephant in the room. It is easy to talk as fellow monotheists, but the problem is, the discussion does not end there. The major question is about Palestine and Israel, so for the last ten or fifteen years we have worked on that as well. We have made a tremendous breakthrough in

---

2. Sarna, "American Jewish Experience."
3. Hosansky and Jalil, *Muslims and Jews*.

this country by gaining the support of mainstream Judaism on this issue. I will come back to that again.

When I went to Washington, I said that we have to build some bridges with the Jewish community. So I spent three or four months meeting with Jewish leaders I knew. You cannot imagine how difficult these things are. I will never forget the time I was invited to Chicago to be a keynote speaker for a meeting of the Religions for Peace organization. It was wonderful. After I finished everybody came, shook my hand, kissed me—Jews, Christians, and Muslims—and people were taking pictures while I was shaking hands and kissing and hugging others.

One very enthusiastic man was hugging me, but when someone else posed to take a picture, the man held up his hand and said, "No, no, please, because I will lose my job." I was shocked to hear that someone would lose his job for hugging me. I made enquiries about the man and found that he worked for one of the national Jewish organizations, and if he was seen in a picture with the Secretary-General of the Islamic Society of North America, he would lose his job. I said to myself that if this kind of mistrust continues, whether it is from the Jewish side or from the Muslim side, we are on a very dangerous path.

So I met with Jewish leaders in Washington and in New York City, and I told them that we have two alternatives. One is that we wait for the time when the problems in the Middle East are solved and then jointly celebrate the news and build relationships here. But that may not happen for long. Until then we will have to be ready to see Middle East problems not only causing destruction there but visiting us here in America. We could have suicide bombers and other violent expressions of extremism visiting us here. We will have to raise walls here, we will recreate the entire scenario that's happening in the Holy Land. If we continue to wait, that is what will happen here. The other alternative is that we build bridges of understanding, we create trust and confidence, we establish a fund of goodwill and use that goodwill to address the issues in the Middle East. There is a possibility that our success here in building that goodwill will help us to address and to resolve the tragic situations in those parts of the world. Every Jewish leader I talked to expressed his/her preference for the second alternative, but how can it be done?

I also told those Jewish leaders that we have trained our Muslim community, our community is mature, we understand where we are, we understand what the Qur'an expects from us, we understand the common legacy, the common heritage, the Abrahamic heritage that we share with Jews. Our community one and all condemns suicide bombing, our community one and all condemns terrorism, our community one and all recognizes the brotherhood and the sisterhood of Christianity, Islam, and Judaism. Muslims take these things for granted, these are fundamental in our understanding of interfaith dialogue. Then I asked them how far Jews are ready to go.

I was invited to the headquarters of the Union for Reform Judaism in New York City. I spent a whole day with URJ's then-president, Rabbi Eric Yoffie, analyzing the American Jewish community. I found out that Reform Judaism, representing 1.5 million Jews and nine hundred synagogues in this country, had already gone in a similar direction. So we decided that we should take a bold step and invite him to address our convention. This was something unique: a Jewish leader addressing the Islamic Society of North America. It was the first time that a top Jewish leader addressed the annual ISNA convention. Some people thought that a crazy Muslim would stand up and either shoot at him or shout at him, but nothing like that happened. Instead, he was given a standing ovation. It was amazing. We had a similar kind of warm response at the URJ convention in San Diego a few months later.

An important project developed from this. We brought together about fifteen synagogues and fifteen mosques and prepared a book titled *Children of Abraham* as a study guide.[4] It's amazing how this project has spread. We started with Reform Judaism, but other Jewish communities told us that they had the same opinion and wanted to cooperate in this great work. Many Conservative synagogues have also joined this effort.

There's no time to recount the various organizations and cities that are involved in this serious work and what kind of fruits are coming out of it. Walter Ruby will discuss the Twinning initiative of the Foundation for Ethnic Understanding, which includes condemning both Islamophobia and anti-Semitism. We were able to bring together imams and rabbis for a conference that I addressed in New York City, out of which came annual, successful Twinning events. These kinds of initiatives are changing the face of America and bringing down the invisible walls that have separated communities that have more in common than they knew.

4. *Children of Abraham.*

Part III: The Past Is Never Dead

Bibliography

Children of Abraham: Jews and Muslims in Conversation. Washington, DC: Commission on Interreligious Affairs of Reform Judaism at the Religious Action Center of Reform Judaism, n.d. http://www.isna.net/uploads/1/5/7/4/15744382/children_of_abraham.pdf.

Firestone, Reuven. *An Introduction to Islam for Jews.* Philadelphia: Jewish Publication Society, 2008.

Hosansky, Norman, and Mazhar Jalil, eds. *Muslims and Jews: Building a Hopeful Future.* Columbus: Islamic Foundation of Central Ohio, 2003.

Sarna, Jonathan D. "The American Jewish Experience and the Emergence of the Muslim Community in America." *American Journal of Islamic Social Sciences* 9 (1992) 370–82.

11

Jewish and Muslim Perspectives on Intermarriage and Gender Roles

Nancy Heiden, Fatima Agha Al-Hayani, Batya Steinlauf, and Asma Mobin-Uddin

Intermarriage: A Jewish Perspective
by Nancy Heiden

INTERFAITH MARRIAGE HAS BEEN an issue in the Jewish community since biblical times. Abraham, for example, sends his servant back to their hometown to find a suitable bride for Isaac, specifically, one from their own people. Moses is criticized by his brother and sister for having married outside the tribe. In the eighth century before the Common Era, the northern kingdom of Israel was defeated by the Assyrians and its inhabitants taken into exile. Many legends have circulated over the centuries as to the fate of these "lost tribes," but scholars now believe that they simply assimilated and were absorbed into the populations among whom they lived, losing their identity as Israelites.

When the Romans destroyed Judea in the first century of the Common Era and effectively dispersed its people throughout the Empire, the fundamental issue was one of survival of a people without a land. Throughout the Mediterranean region at first and then in other parts of Europe, many Jewish communities were established over the centuries and, by remaining close-knit and self-contained, continued to exist and even, in some areas, to flourish. The rise of anti-Semitism in Europe, while it often threatened entire Jewish communities with destruction, also created a situation in which Jews, for the most part, could not have married outside the community even had they wanted to. Annihilation through assimilation was not a possibility for the Jewish community throughout the Middle Ages and Renaissance.

This situation changed with the Enlightenment, when legal and social restrictions began to be lifted. A new world of possibilities opened up for Jews; they could now live where they wanted, study where they wanted, and take up any profession they wanted. They no longer had to wear the distinctive clothing or badges that had been a requirement in previous times. And, at least in some areas, they could marry outside their own community. At the same time, leaders within segments of the Jewish community sought to do away with certain customs and beliefs that they felt were not essential to the practice of true Judaism and which had only served to separate the community from its non-Jewish neighbors. These leaders believed that it was possible to retain one's religious identity, while doing away with those differences between Jew and Gentile which were superficial and unnecessary. At the same time, there were leaders in the more traditional community who believed that it was possible to live peacefully within the non-Jewish community and even interact with one's non-Jewish neighbors and colleagues, while still maintaining such unique laws and traditions as the Jewish dietary laws and strict observance of the Sabbath. In any case, regular contact between Jews and non-Jews increased dramatically in the nineteenth century and, for the first time in many centuries, intermarriage and assimilation became very real possibilities.

Despite the easing of restriction on Jews and a growing acceptance in Gentile society, particularly in the United States, intermarriage rates remained relatively low, less than 6 percent in the United States, up to 1960. It is only in the past forty years or so that intermarriage rates for Jews have soared—to 12 percent in 1964, 29 percent by 1971, and over 50 percent after 1985. To what can we attribute this dramatic increase? In *Mixed Blessings,* their book on interfaith marriage, Rachel Cowan and her late husband, Paul Cowan, suggest that there was a period of social liberalization in American society beginning in the 1950s, illustrated most dramatically by the rise of the Civil Rights Movement.[1] In this new, freer social atmosphere, Jews found more and more academic and professional opportunities to in-

---

1. Cowan and Cowan, *Mixed Blessings.*

teract with non-Jews, and this phenomenon led inevitably to higher rates of intermarriage. We might also note that the 1950s and 1960s saw the beginning of increased mobility of the American population, the flight of urban dwellers to the suburbs, and the breakup of traditional ethnic neighborhoods, all of which increased the possibility that Jewish young people would meet and socialize with their non-Jewish counterparts.

But is this increase in the rate of intermarriage solely a product of increased proximity? I believe that there is much more going on. On the one hand, there are internal changes within the Jewish community itself. Even among the more observant Jews who came to the United States in the large wave of immigration that took place around the turn of the [ed.: twentieth] century, there was a strong desire to fit in, to be good Americans, and to show their appreciation for their adopted country. There were strong pressures to give up traditional observances, whether it was financial necessity that forced parents to work on the Sabbath or it was the difficulty of finding rabbis willing to move to small communities in the Midwest. Children of immigrants often looked at their parents and saw them as outsiders to American society—unable to speak the language properly, dressed in strange clothing, insisting on practices that set them apart from their Gentile neighbors. On the other hand, the immigrant parents wanted a life for their children that was free of the oppression and fear that they had known in the old country. Fitting into American society, learning English, doing well in school, and getting good jobs were all ways to ensure one's security in this country. Although these parents often encouraged their children to "be American," it was with mixed feelings that they saw the alienation that developed within their own families.

Over the generations there has been a falling off of traditional Jewish practice, to the point where today there are many Jews, who, although they are proud of their heritage and their people, and who will clearly state their identity as Jews, would be hard pressed to express exactly what it is that makes them Jewish. They know little of Jewish practice, history, or theology; they may not affiliate with any Jewish institutions; they may not even observe Jewish holidays, other than perhaps lighting candles on Chanukah. With each generation the link that joins them to the Jewish people becomes weaker and weaker. It is not surprising that in such an environment, the children would question the importance of marrying within the Jewish community. And increasingly, the young people that these children meet are no more knowledgeable about their own religion and tradition. Many of these young interfaith couples thus arrive at the conclusion regarding their own families, "We'll raise them with no religion, and if the children want, they can decide for themselves later on." Growing up with no religious instruction at all, of course, makes it very hard to choose a religious identity later in life. When I meet with young people such as these, many express a great sense of loss or a Spiritual vacuum in their lives. They feel they are missing something important, but aren't sure what it is.

The other important factor in the increase in intermarriage, and one that affects even families where religious practice and identification is very strong, is the very nature of the liberal, open society in which we live. America is now a place where most children are taught in school as well as in their homes that it is bad to dislike someone merely for who they are. Most of us would agree that we do not want our children being taught that there are people whom they should hate or fear or shun, simply because they are not like us. Over the last twenty years or so, however, this desire has, in some circles, crystallized into the message, "We are all the same: black, white, red, yellow; Protestant, Catholic, Muslim, Jew. We should all accept one another, because no one is really different from anyone else." The late Beatle, John Lennon, has achieved near sainthood status with some younger people, at least partially due to his call for a kind of utopian universality, as expressed in the song "Imagine," in which he imagines a peaceful world without religion, the implication being that religious differences are a major source of all the hostility in the world. I was dismayed a few years ago when the music teacher at my daughter's school included a song in their winter concert, the lyrics of which went something like this: "A winter holiday, a winter holiday, some call it Christmas, some call it Chanukah, some call it Kwanzaa, but no matter what we call it, we are all in the same family." Has it come to this, then, that in order to live peacefully with our neighbors, we must smooth over all differences and deny our uniqueness? Can we not maintain our own beautiful and rich traditions, and at the same time learn about and respect other traditions? Are we being clannish and exclusive if we insist on the value of our beliefs and heritage, and seek to pass these values on to our children? This is the dilemma facing not only Jews, but all peoples who have communities, histories, traditions, and beliefs of their own.

We must search for a balance in our lives and in our traditions. On the one hand, we want to participate fully in this wonderful, diverse society we live in—we want to meet our neighbors, learn about them, and interact with them in a spirit of mutual understanding and respect. On the other hand, we believe that our people, the Jews, and our religion, Judaism, including all its beliefs and traditions and practices, are of value, not only to us but to the whole world. I beg to differ with John Lennon. I think that a world without religion would be a very dull place, a world stripped of a great deal of beauty and wisdom and truth. In the past there has been much oppression and violence committed in the name of religion, and it would be dishonest for us to pretend otherwise. But we here in America have a unique opportunity to try a great experiment, to prove that there can be another way, that the great religions of the world and the different cultural and ethnic groups that make up our diverse society can co-exist without blending into a huge, undifferentiated mass of popular culture.

How do we go about doing this? I certainly don't have all the answers, but I think we must start by unashamedly proclaiming our commitment to our own cultures, and to celebrate the wonder and beauty of these cultures, for ourselves, for our children, and even for our neighbors. The increased emphasis in our schools on multiculturalism and diversity is a step in the right direction. We must work from the assumption that it is possible to be involved in and proud of one's heritage, and that this is something of value that is to be passed down to our children as a treasure, while at the same time learning about, respecting, and appreciating the cultures of those around us. This is the great challenge faced by all of us today.

Intermarriage: A Muslim Perspective
by Fatima Agha Al-Hayani

Marriage has a central role in Muslim family law and philosophy. Not only is it considered an important safeguard to chastity, but every Muslim is encouraged to marry, unless physically or financially unable to lead a conjugal life. Al-Ghazali, a medieval Muslim thinker, looked at marriage as the state that provides comfort for the heart and strength in the worship of God. The institution of marriage in Islam, moreover, is considered the building block of a society in which the individual is made aware of his or her obligations and rights, and where family liaisons are strengthened. Such liaisons create strong family units which, in turn, create a strong society.

Muslim scholars consider marriage as a relationship that elevates human beings from a physical to a higher, personal level. Marriage also creates, or should create, a bond between husband and wife wherein each finds comfort and joy. Finally, marriage is considered a social institution—family obligations and rights are an intrinsic part of the rest of society. Thus, if these obligations become unmanageable, Islam commands society to take appropriate action to implement the law in order to maintain harmony and equity within the family. Furthermore, the religious brotherhood espoused by Muslims creates or must create a social system in which the mutual expectations of the family are not established only by familial relationships. Islam recognizes marriage as the true foundation of the family, which must rest on solid grounds in order to provide continuity, security, and intimacy. It is clear, then, that the institution of marriage in Islam involves not only the couple and their immediate family, but also society at large.

On another level, the institution of marriage is considered one of God's bounties to mankind. The Qur'an (30:21) says, "And among His Signs is this, that He created for you mates from among yourselves, that ye may dwell in tranquillity with them, and He has put love and mercy between your (hearts): verily in that are Signs for those who reflect" [ed.: Ali]. Love and tranquility are the foundations of mating and raising a family. This verse establishes the base upon which a marriage must be constructed. Further, the Prophet Muhammad said that marriage is part of worship and a person perfects his religion by marrying. In brief, marriage in Islam is regarded as a positive and fulfilling practice. If the relationship follows qur'anic proscription, it would bring about joy and peace, would strengthen the family, and would help create social interaction, which, in turn, would lead to a more cohesive society.

As for the choice of a spouse, most of the hadith encourage Muslims to choose those partners who have *din* or faith over any other attribute, such as beauty, family, lineage, or wealth. Those who have *din* follow the straight path, that of piety, compassion, equity, and a commitment to fairness and decency. Such behavior is deemed crucial when one is contemplating marriage to someone of the same faith. In an interfaith marriage, however, it becomes even more crucial given the differences and the difficulties that present themselves under these circumstances. To most Muslim scholars, intermarriage between Muslims and people of a revealed book, such as Christians and Jews, is acceptable, but not recommended.

About one hundred years after the advent of Islam, Muslims inhabited most of the known world. They lived among non-Muslims and married them. Because of this, Muslim scholars felt a need to study all ramifications of such unions. They wrote extensively about this subject trying to institute guidelines which would safeguard the family and society, but primarily the religion. The fear was that the non-Muslim spouse would instruct the children in his or her faith. All of the scholars agreed that the children must be reared as Muslims. Living in a Muslim society, which is a patriarchal society, would guarantee that the children would be considered Muslims regardless of the religion of the mother. Scholars ruled, therefore, that only men may marry someone who is a *dhimmi* or a believer in another monotheistic religion, such as Christianity or Judaism. What happens, however, when the social and legal structure changes, as in Western society? Then there is no guarantee that the child will be raised as a Muslim. Most scholars grant the rights of the non-Muslim wife to practice her own religion since, in Islam, there is no compulsion to convert. When it comes to children, however, the scholars have ruled that they must be raised as Muslims. This ruling causes most of the problems in an interfaith marriage.

When one lives in a secular society, or in a non-Muslim one, the rules as applied in a Muslim patriarchal state cannot be enforced. What must be done in the case of a pending interfaith marriage? The couple needs to discuss their differences, decide on the religious upbringing of any children, and come to an understanding concerning the importance of their faiths. Through such preparation, the couple can avoid friction between themselves and turmoil within the family. But promises made may be broken. It has been shown that, in many cases, the non-Muslim wife changes her mind concerning her Muslim husband's conditions that she had agreed to. The husband, in most cases, is not aware that American law most likely will grant the wife not only custody of the children in a divorce situation, but also the right to take them to her church.

It is not surprising, then, that scholars discouraged interfaith marriages in non-Muslim countries. Unfortunately, most imams do not advise young Muslim men about the legal Muslim position and the repercussions of such a union. Many are not even aware of the position of the scholars. The imams tend to perform the wedding ceremony without hesitation, wrongly assuming that Muslim men are aware of the possible problems that may occur and their duties towards the education of their children. It is quite possible that many imams, themselves, do not know the laws pertaining to custody in the non-Muslim state and, therefore, cannot explain them to the husband or wife.

There have been many cases where the wife in the marriage did change her mind, negated her promises, and took the children to the church or synagogue. Many children attend a church one week and a mosque the next week. They thus receive contradictory information about what to believe. They are pulled in two opposite directions. Sometimes, the wife will inculcate the children in her own religion in the home. Or she may decide to eat pork, which is prohibited in Islam. Can the husband prohibit her from doing any of these things? The answer is no. Even though the scholars gave the non-Muslim wife the right to practice her own religion, they did not give her the right to teach the children her religion. On the other hand, even by exercising her right to practice her own religion, she can directly or indirectly influence the children, even in a Muslim country. The problem is much greater in a non-Islamic society where the children have little contact with the mosque or with Islamic practice outside of the home.

Traditional practices, unique to one faith or the other, are another potential cause of conflict. A simple example is the Christmas tree. Although the tree has nothing to do with basic Christian belief, it has become a Christian symbol associated with the birth of Jesus. One can also cite practices that are followed during Easter and St. Valentine's Day that have been accepted by many Christians as part of Christian practice. Once the interfaith couple realize, however, that these practices are part of the tradition and not part of the religious faith, room exists for discussion and compromise.

When the husband insists that his wife wear a veil and she refuses to do so, this, too, can become a major issue. The Qur'an asks both males and females to dress modestly and walk in a dignified manner. There is no clear description, however, of what this entails. In Islam, the veil is only recommended, not required. Furthermore, no husband can force his wife to wear the veil against her wishes. The same rules that apply to prayer and fasting apply here. The woman must wear the veil only out of conviction, not because of outside pressure. There can be no compulsion in religion, according to the Qur'an. Most of the conflicts in an interfaith marriage, therefore, can be circumvented when both parties understand their respective religions and know the difference between tradition and symbolism and basic beliefs and laws.

There is no question that to maintain a marriage successfully under the best conditions demands a great deal of effort and compromise. The difficulty is compounded, however, when there are basic religious differences. Lack of planning, understanding, and compromise can seriously affect the relations between husband and wife, and the position of the children who may become torn between two warring parties. Islamic law and practice have taken into consideration the diversities in the world we live in and exhort Muslims to be kind, understanding, and compassionate with their mates. Under no circumstances can a Muslim permit friction and disharmony within the family. On the other hand, no Muslim can allow the children of the family to be inculcated in a religion other than Islam.

Gender Roles: A Jewish Perspective
by Batya Steinlauf

There are many different ways that the role of women is understood in Judaism. There are, in fact, as many different understandings as there are Jews. There are, however, three basic approaches as represented by the three modern movements within Judaism: Reform Judaism, a movement not bound by *halakha* (Jewish law); Orthodox Judaism, which understands Jewish law as not having changed since the original giving of the written and oral law by God at Sinai; and Conservative Judaism, which understands an evolving nature of Jewish law and recognizes a historical context to the fundamental texts. (I am an ordained rabbi in Conservative Judaism, and my rabbinate is not recognized as legitimate by Orthodox Jews.) While these movements represent the general viewpoints, there are many different subgroups within each movement that cover the entire spectrum of opinion and observance.

Reform Judaism does not consider Jewish law as binding and, as such, is free to make whatever changes its leadership deems appropriate and necessary for its members. Its ideology is particularly concerned with social justice. Reform Judaism is completely egalitarian, and the movement has, for example, ordained women as rabbis for over twenty years [ed.: the first in 1972].

Orthodox Judaism, on the other hand, is bound by both law and custom. Its fundamental understanding of the role of women is in the text of the Torah, as understood by the rabbis of late antiquity. In Genesis 18:9, the messengers of God inquire after Sarah, Abraham's wife. They are told that she is in the tent. In Psalms 45:14, the text states that "the glory of the daughters of the king is within" [ed.: this appears to be the author's translation]. These images have come to define the traditional role of Jewish women as central to the home. They are responsible for creating a home and raising children in accordance with the demands of Torah and *halakha*.

Modesty, particularly noticeable in terms of dress, is important. The parameters of modest dress, however, vary considerably within Orthodoxy. For some, modesty means no pants and clothing that covers the knees and elbows. For others, women are covered to a greater or lesser degree. Married women cover their hair to a greater or lesser extent depending on their affiliation within the Orthodox community, that is, for example, with a scarf or a hat covering part or all of her hair, with a wig, or with a wig and a hat. The concern that a woman's voice itself is immodest has made a comeback within certain groups, curtailing activities that had been acceptable for women, for example, singing Sabbath songs.

Women have a limited role in the synagogue. In an Orthodox synagogue, for example, men and women do not sit together. There is, even further, a physical divider between the men's and women's sections so that the men will be not be distracted from prayer. In some synagogues, this divider is so high that one cannot see over it when standing. In other synagogues, the women's section is in a balcony behind the main sanctuary, sometimes with a screen in front.

Despite the emphasis on women's place being in the home, there is a tradition of women conducting business so that their husbands are free to study Torah. Thus, in many Orthodox communities, it is acceptable for women to work and even become professionals, regardless of their husbands' occupations. Many women have high-powered careers in the community at large, but limit their roles within their religious and synagogue community.

The role of women within the synagogue is curtailed by a number of factors, including the traditional emphasis on modesty, the differing roles of men and women, an understanding of a woman's voice as inherently immodest, and the different levels of obligation with regard to ritual matters. According to Jewish law, an individual obligation to a commandment can only be fulfilled by an individual with an equal or higher level of obligation. Since women are exempt from time-bound, positive commandments, such as prayer, they cannot fulfill that obligation for others, by leading services, for example.

Orthodoxy is currently struggling with women's expanded role in society in two opposing ways. While some currents are moving to the right, seeking to limit a woman's role (for example, by increasing the emphasis on her head covering), other currents are moving to the left seeking a place for women as legal authorities. No movement in Judaism is monolithic.

Each group has a different understanding of the correct interpretation of the Torah and the tradition, and each group thinks that it is right.

Conservative Judaism is halakhic-based (bound by Jewish law) and text-based, but it also has a concept of historical context. Conservative Judaism balances the biblical images of women in the home, which we discussed earlier, with the images of Devorah, a Judge and military leader, and of Beruriah, a scholar of the Talmud and rabbinical text.

Within Conservative Judaism, the role of women in the synagogue is still being negotiated. In most Conservative communities, men and women sit and pray together in the service. But while the movement is moving toward egalitarianism, there is still no consensus on the role of women. In some synagogues women do all that men do, and even wear the ritual garments formerly reserved for men. In others, women still sit apart and are not allowed on the *bima*, the podium where the scrolls of the Torah are.

One of the most troubling issues facing halakhic Jews today is the issue of the *agunah,* or bound woman. A woman whose husband disappears before he has had a chance to give her a document of divorce and whose death is not proved is forbidden to remarry. This situation can create personal tragedy as well as profound injustice, as in the case where the husband refuses to grant a religious divorce even though the couple is divorced by a civil court. This can be an occasion for revenge or blackmail since only the husband can grant a Jewish divorce and he himself is not biblically forbidden to remarry. Both Orthodoxy and Conservative Judaism are struggling to find an acceptable solution to this problem.

For all Jews, as for each movement in Judaism, the struggle to find a balance between tradition and modernity is difficult and emotionally charged. How each Jew chooses to find this balance is often a lifelong process.

Gender Roles: A Muslim Perspective
by Asma Mobin-Uddin

We can define the role of Muslim women in America by doing three things: one, looking at the way the nature and essence of women has been defined and at her spiritual status in Islam; two, discussing Muslim women in relation to their families, to education, and to economic and political rights; and three, discussing the challenges facing both Muslim and Jewish women in America and how America can benefit from women in society.

Part III: The Past Is Never Dead

What is a woman and what is her nature? Genesis tells two stories of the creation of Eve, one of which is the well-known version that she was created from Adam's rib. Genesis teaches that Eve was tempted by the serpent, succumbed, tempted Adam, and therefore brought about the fall of mankind. This interpretation is repeated in the New Testament: "For Adam was formed first, then Eve. And Adam was not the one deceived; it was the woman who was deceived and became a sinner" (1 Tim 2:13–14) [ed.: NIV]. Debates in sixteenth-century France focused on whether women were human, while Freud questioned whether women were capable of morality.

What does the Qur'an teach? Here we must be very careful to distinguish between Islamic teachings based on the Qur'an and the interpretation of these teachings in modern Muslim countries based on their own cultural norms.

In the qur'anic story, both Adam and Eve sin, both are responsible, both seek forgiveness, and both are forgiven. There is no concept of original sin traced back to either Adam or Eve and there is no concept of women being responsible for bringing sin into the world. In Islam, both men and women are of the same essence, spiritually they stand as equals before God.

The position of women in Islam is an honored one. Motherhood is exalted and considered a sacred trust from God. Being kind to your mother and father is a way of serving God. A man asked the Prophet, "O Messenger of God, who is the most worthy of my kindness and good treatment?" The Prophet said, "Your mother." The man asked, "And who is next?" The Prophet said, "Your mother." "And who's next?" "Your mother." "And who's next?" Then the Prophet said, "Your father." [Ed.: This is a well-attested hadith: Bukhari volume 8, book 73, number 2; Muslim book 32, number 6180.]

The husband-wife relationship in Islam is one of intimacy surrounded by warmth and compassion. Not only is a woman's consent required before marriage, but a man is enjoined to be kind to his wife. The Qur'an teaches "O ye who believe! Ye are forbidden to inherit women against their will. Nor should ye treat them with harshness. . . . [O]n the contrary live with them on a footing of kindness and equity. If ye take a dislike to them it may be that ye dislike a thing, and Allah brings about through it a great deal of good" (4:19) [ed.: Ali].

In terms of education, the Prophet taught that seeking knowledge is obligatory for every Muslim, male and female, and that one should seek knowledge from the cradle to the grave. A wonderful example is Aisha, the wife of the Prophet, who was honored for her expertise in medicine and in

Islamic law. Leaders of her time, from all over the Muslim world, sought her advice on legal problems and religious questions.

In the economic field, Islam placed no obstacles in the way of women as long as their primary roles as wife and mother were not adversely affected. Khadijah, the Prophet's first wife, for example, was a successful business woman whose earning supported the Prophet. With the coming of Islam, women became separate legal entities. They had the right to own and manage their own money, their own businesses, their own property, whether or not they were married.

In terms of economic responsibilities, the roles of men and women differ. A husband must support his wife so that she is free to take care of the children. Put another way, Muslim women have the right not to work. A man may not put any pressure whatsoever on his wife to work. On the other hand, if she does work, her earnings are completely her own nor does she have any legal obligation to contribute to the support of the household or even of her own children. In an extreme case, a poor husband has to buy the groceries for his millionaire wife!

In the political arena, Muslim women have always had the right to voice an opinion, to be heard, and to be taken seriously. It is reported in the Qur'an and in history that women freely expressed themselves in the Prophet's presence and argued and participated in serious discussions with the Prophet and other Muslim leaders of the time. This was difficult for some of the early Muslims to accept, coming out of the very male-dominated society of the early Arabs.

In all areas, then, women played a major and active role: The first Muslim after the Prophet was his wife. The first martyr to Islam was a woman. Women pledged their allegiance directly to the Prophet and were accepted individually by him. Women were known to extend amnesty or political protection to others in their own names with the approval of the Prophet. The original manuscripts of the Qur'an were given to a woman for safekeeping after Caliph Umar died.

So what is the role of us Muslim women in contemporary America? It is not much different from the role Muslim women adopted in seventh-century Arabia: to make the society in which we live a better place. To do this we start with the family, the foundation of any society. We take our responsibilities within our families very seriously. We work hard to raise our children to be compassionate, kind, responsible, honest, tolerant, and productive adults, living our lives with integrity and faith. We promote what is good and take a stand against what is bad. And, together with our husbands, we build strong, loving marriages, which are a shelter and a comfort to both of us. If we succeed in these areas alone, we will have truly succeeded and America will greatly benefit.

What are the challenges facing Muslim, Jewish, and Christian women in America?

How do we follow the God-given values that guide our lives and define our purpose in life?

How do we follow our religious beliefs and practices in a society that is increasingly hostile to such beliefs and practices?

How do we instill in our children a love and respect for our own religious traditions and heritage and a respect for those of others?

How do we take pride in our womanhood in a society that has less and less respect for the role of a woman as mother, wife, and believer?

And specifically for Muslim and Jewish women:

How do we work our hectic schedules around religious obligations?

How do we help our families adhere to dietary laws?

How do we and our children observe modesty in dress?

Where do we find time to teach our children the language of our holy books?

How do we observe our religious holidays and ignore the religious holidays of the majority community?

How do we deal with the prejudice and bigotry that exist?

On the other hand, we, as Muslim and Jewish women, have a lot to offer contemporary American society:

We have a world view, rooted in belief in God and in faith, that puts us on sound moral ground and that guides our actions.

We recognize that the world does not revolve around the individual and his wants, but that we must live our lives in accordance with what God has prescribed for us.

We bring the values of self-respect, modesty, and purity to a society that often uses our bodies to sell everything from hamburgers to cars, to satisfy the prurient interests of the marketplace.

We have a commitment to build strong, stable families.

We have a compassion for all humanity based on our belief that one, loving God created all of us.

We are women of faith. We can and we must use our unique talents to fulfill our role in the service of God, to make America and the world a freer and more peaceful place.

Bibliography

Cowan, Paul, and Rachel Cowan. *Mixed Blessings: Overcoming the Stumbling Blocks in an Interfaith Marriage*. New York: Penguin, 1987.

12

The Moral Obligation of Muslim-Jewish Relations
Walter Ruby

SINCE 2007, IT HAS been my great good fortune to be present at the creation, if you will—and actively involved in the building—of what we're calling an international movement of Muslims and Jews committed to communication, reconciliation, and cooperation. When I first put forward the concept of a Muslim-Jewish global movement, I thought maybe it was a little bit *chutzpadik* (impertinent or brazen), a little bit over the top, but since then we have seen such a movement begin to come into fruition and is now very, very exciting. Our piece of this movement was started by Rabbi Marc Schneier, the president of the Foundation for Ethnic Understanding, and his partner Russell Simmons, who many of you know as a hip-hop impresario. They decided that something needed to be done on the issue of Muslim-Jewish relations. They had been working together on Black-Jewish relations for ten years or more, but I guess Russell was very interested in this because of the large number of Muslims within the African American community and really felt that this was the direction that the Foundation should be going.

When we started out, it was sort of *one* direction the Foundation could be going, but over time it has become *the* direction, partly because it has gotten so much better, there's so much more momentum and excitement around it than any of us could have imagined when we started.

The most recent success in this venture took place only last month, with our second annual "Weekend of Twinning of Mosques and Synagogues across North America and Europe." That's the official title; it keeps getting longer. The first year it was "across North America," and this second year I'll mention quickly that we added Europe, so next year it will probably be "the world" and we'll have to come up with a new name.

So, what was it? Basically, on the weekend of November 13–15, 2009, 118 mosques and synagogues did one-on-one "twinning" programs. Actually, that's not quite accurate; there were, in fact, 118 "twinnings," but not all of them were mosques and synagogues; we had some student groups as well. For example, we had Hillels and Muslim Student Association groups at places like the University of Southern California, Michigan, Wisconsin, NYU, Emory, and many others. That's becoming a growingly important part of what we're doing. But, the great majority are still mosques and synagogues, one-on-one. So, you have these events going on in 118 different places across North America and Europe, on the same weekend. We call that, again with some hyperbole, the largest single gathering of Jews and Muslims in the world, with thousands of Jews and Muslims doing joint programs together. This year it stretched from New Haven, to New York City, to New Jersey, Philadelphia, Baltimore, suburban Washington, to Washington, D.C. itself, and to a place like Morgantown, West Virginia—which is not so far from here and which I felt really great about, because it showed that we were able to get a smaller town involved as well as major cities and metropolitan areas. There were also twinnings in Charlotte, Atlanta, West Palm Beach, Dallas, Columbus of course, Detroit, Toronto, Chicago, Madison, Minneapolis, St. Louis, Denver, Seattle, San Francisco, Las Vegas (another new one), and Los Angeles. And then we had the European component; we had thirty "twinnings" in France, which I'll mention below. We had much fewer, just one or two each, in the United Kingdom, Holland, Belgium, Italy, Switzerland, Germany, and Russia.

The Weekend of Twinning is sponsored by the Foundation for Ethnic Understanding, and it has the endorsement and support—really vital support—of the Islamic Society of North America, without which we could never have done what we've managed to do, and a few other groups, such as the Muslim Public Affairs Council (MPAC), the Center for Muslim Jewish Engagement at USC, which has been terrific, the ASMA Society (American Society for Muslim Advancement), the Canadian Association of Jews and Muslims, and finally, the Judeo-Muslim Friendship Society of France. The theme of the Weekend of Twinning this year was called "Building a Common Agenda between Jews and Muslims"; in other words, identifying issues on which our two communities can work together. The first year we did "Confronting Islamophobia and Anti-Semitism Together," and that remains one of our key priorities, but we placed it in a broader context this year.

Before I continue, let me acknowledge that I have the feeling that I'm taking too much credit for what has been accomplished and that feeling was really enforced for me by learning that Congregation Tifereth Israel and the Islamic Foundation of Central Ohio have been doing this for twenty-five years. That is astounding! I feel like I'm learning at the feet of Dr. Mazhar Jalil, Dr. Norman Hosansky, and Rabbi Harold Berman. There are a lot of places locally where this is happening. Columbus is one of the most inspiring examples. There are places where it wasn't happening where we have been able to get it going. So the main thing for the Foundation for Ethnic Understanding is not to reinvent the wheel, but rather to create a sense of a growing international movement; and in the process to let Columbus know that things are also happening in Las Vegas, in Toronto, in Paris, and to begin to stitch all this together and make it into a movement. We're still in the early stages of this, I'll have to admit, but it is happening.

Very briefly, two important dynamics take place during the Weekend of Twinning. First of all, I should say that we act as facilitators, but we also say to the people organizing the "twinning" event in Columbus, or wherever else, "It's up to you folks to decide what you want to do. We don't tell you what your program should be." We have a few guidelines, but ultimately, it's up to the local community.

So what exactly happens during a twinning event? One thing that happens, obviously, is a celebration of the joy of mutual discovery. We hear all the time very powerful testimony from people who do this, about what happens when Muslims come to the synagogue and they have a chance to listen to a Jewish service, or when Jews go to the mosque and listen to a Muslim one. First of all, many of the Jews have obviously never been to a mosque before, or many of the Muslims have never been to a synagogue. So they go to the sanctuary of the "Other" for the very first time and there they experience incredible hospitality and warmth from the other side and then as the service commences they recognize so many commonalities with their own faith tradition. I'm not going to go into them now, but suffice to say that people are blown away by this set of experiences; they can't believe what they are seeing and feeling.

This year, the Torah portion of the week during the Weekend of Twinning was the Chaiyei Sarah and it focused on the very beginning of the relationship between our peoples; starting with our common forefather Abraham/Ibrahim, the story of Sarah and Hagar, Isaac and Ishmael, the estrangement between the two families, and then Isaac and Ishmael coming together to bury their father. In a number of twinnings in cities across America there were moving conversations about that story. We know that Ishmael and Isaac were estranged but came back together in order to bury their father. But was there a genuine reconciliation between them? And what does this say, the story of the two estranged sons coming back together to bury their father, what does that story say to Muslims and Jews today? We would like to believe that it's a symbol for our need to reconcile and come together.

This year we decided to take the Weekend of Twinning a little bit beyond where we'd been the first year. We decided that we would ask the participating congregations to consider what societal issue would they want to take on together and once they have determined that, what specific actions might they take? We put forward ideas which could be fruitful for Muslim-Jewish cooperation, like healing the environment, fighting poverty, immigration reform, and confronting Islamophobia and anti-Semitism together. We encouraged participants in the most recent Weekend of Twinning that they should begin this conversation, that they would hopefully appoint a joint committee, and that they would carry forward working on one of those issues.

We did this in part because we believe that taking on such a project will really draw the congregations closer; otherwise, there tends to be a pattern of Muslims and Jews coming together, having a beautiful ceremony, hugging and kissing, and then not seeing each other for a year. This new tack is one way to ensure that they continue working together. We also feel that Muslims and Jews contributing together for the betterment of society is an overwhelmingly powerful symbol that will impact positively our own two communities and society as a whole. We believe it could have transformative consequences on people of all backgrounds in our society to see Muslims and Jews working together.

In Buffalo, they did something wonderful which we hope will happen in other communities. During the Weekend of Twinning, they did an educational program, and then after the program, a group of Muslim and Jewish doctors and dentists stayed in place to offer free medical and dental screenings to participants in the event. We were very happy that this was reported in the *Buffalo News*. We see this concept of Muslim and Jewish doctors and dentists offering free screenings to people without health insurance as something we really hope can happen, not only during the Weekend of Twinning, but throughout the year. We are also talking about Jewish and Muslim lawyers doing programs together; meeting with people free of charge and offering seminars on issues like foreclosure, to really address the needs of people amidst the economic crisis in America today.

We have to confront the Israel-Palestine issue because it comes up again and again. How do we deal with it, how do we prevent it from overwhelming what we're trying to accomplish in terms of bringing together Muslims and Jews in America and in countries around the world? Our formula has been that at twinning events, we urge the rabbi and the imam, or the president of the participating mosque or synagogue, to open the session by acknowledging the Israel-Palestine conflict together, to talk about the terrible pain and suffering—the violence, death, and blighted hopes—that is caused to Palestinians and Israelis alike; and then to pray together for an early resolution to that conflict. Once that has been said—hopefully in a profound and meaningful way, so that it's clear that we're not hiding from the issue, that we're not brushing it under the rug—the people leading the twinning program should then say, "Let's not make the rest of our session about the Middle East conflict, because if we do that, we'll leave here more embittered than when we came together. Maybe after we've been working together for a year or two, and we really know each other, then maybe certain communities will have gotten to the point where they can talk about it. But right now, let's focus on what we can do together right here in Columbus, because we feel that Jews and Muslims working together in Columbus and all across America is a moral imperative; a great good, in and of itself. Therefore, we shouldn't take away from our ability to accomplish great things here in Columbus. Finally, if we can ultimately make that work, we will be in a position to role model to our brothers and sisters in the Middle East that Jews and Muslims can in fact work together fruitfully; that we don't have to be enemies until the end of time, there is an alternative to mutual fear and loathing." All of that is very, very important.

So how did this all begin? We started working with imams and rabbis back in 2007 when Dr. Sayyid Syeed of the Islamic Society of North America was our keynote speaker at the dinner we had together with Ronald Lauder, President of the World Jewish Congress. That was a significant moment, in purely political terms, because we saw the national director of the most mainstream American Muslim organization and the president of the World Jewish Congress both publicly endorsing Muslim-Jewish dialogue and cooperation. I think it sent a very important signal to both communities that the idea of Muslim-Jewish communication and cooperation is no longer a marginal left-wing cause, but this was something that the mainstream values. That was very significant in terms of validating this cause in both communities.

Now, that's obviously the good news. Yet as several people have noted at this conference, we shouldn't kid ourselves that all opposition to this effort has disappeared. There are powerful and influential people out there causing problems. I could mention a few names, people like Daniel Pipes, Steven Emerson, and David Horowitz, who I just heard from colleagues at USC really caused some serious damage out there by throwing around qur'anic verses out of context and saying "this proves that Muslims are all genocidal and we can't deal with them." These people are demonizing all Muslims, and trying to pull the two communities apart; yet they are hardly the only ones. There are also people in Congress doing that, as well as prominent voices on talk radio and Fox News, and so forth.

These people, in my opinion, use McCarthyistic smear tactics and guilt by association, essentially opposing treating American Muslims like full citizens who deserve all civil rights and human rights and to whom we Jews should reach out. And there are other people, including many in the Jewish community, who ridicule the efforts by our organization, by the Union for Reform Judaism, and others, to reach out to Muslims. They basically say that what we are doing is a lot of meaningless platitudes that ultimately doesn't amount to anything.

On that point, I once tried to interest a columnist at the *New York Times* to cover the first Weekend of Twinning, and he said to me, "Well, unless you are dealing directly with Israel and Palestine, it's all Kumbaya." I explained to the columnist in detail why we choose not to deal directly or fundamentally with the Israel and Palestine issue, but afterwards, the more I thought about our conversation, I understood that his comment about our work being Kumbaya was probably the most profoundly wrong statement I've ever heard in my life. The truth is that what we do is the opposite of Kumbaya; yes, we do this for humanitarian reasons, we do this for moral reasons, but we also do this because it is in the interests of both communities; it is a win-win for both communities.

How so? I think that, among other things, the Muslim community is to some extent vulnerable, even endangered if, God forbid, there would be anything again like 9/11. We saw that after 9/11, civil liberties were really limited for Muslims, and many bad things happened. In short, the Muslim community needs allies, it needs support, and certainly the Jewish community can be a very strong support for the vast majority of Muslims who want to be part of America. A good example of this was in my neck of the woods, in Long Island. In 2006, Congressman Peter King launched a demagogic attack on the Islamic Center of Long Island claiming it is an extremist mosque, when, in fact, it is one of the most outreach-oriented mosques in the country. Many important rabbis on Long Island immediately came to the defense of the mosque and Congressman King soon lowered his rhetoric on the issue, so I think that that was a very important statement.

But, some will say, "Okay, clearly there is something in this for the Muslims, but what is in it for the Jews?" I believe that for the Jews, it is really important to let young Muslims know that Jews believe Muslims are a part of society, full partners in American society, and they deserve the same respect and all of the rights accorded to all other American citizens. That message can be very important in preventing any kind of extremist thinking from growing among Muslims. I fear that the opposite approach—putting the entire Muslim community under suspicion—could conceivably have the opposite effect; moving some to say, "Well, if they hate us anyway, maybe we should go in that direction." We know from surveys that the vast majority of Muslim Americans are law abiding citizens who want to be full Americans while maintaining their Muslim identity, just like Jews and so many other groups.

One of the moments when I was most proud to work for Rabbi Marc Schneier came several months ago when he published an op-ed in the *Washington Post*, in which he said that, as a Jewish leader, he is sick and tired of hearing so many in our community repeating non-stop, "Why don't Muslim leaders ever speak out against terrorism? Why don't they say anything?" Well, Rabbi Schneier wrote, "That just ain't true." Every time anything bad happens, for example the Fort Hood attack or several months ago when some young Muslims were arrested for threatening to attack synagogues in the Bronx, every Muslim leader that we deal with stands up and speaks out in the strongest and the most unequivocal of terms to say, "We denounce all of this; we denounce terrorism, we denounce violence." So, Rabbi Schneier wrote in his op-ed, "Please stop repeating that Muslim leaders are not speaking out against terrorism because they *are* speaking out."

I am convinced that Jews and Muslims have a great deal to do together. For example, we can work together against Islamophobia and anti-Semitism, which can have a big impact. Clearly it's not news and it has little impact when the Anti-Defamation League denounces anti-Semitism. But it is news when a mosque and a synagogue do so together; denouncing anti-Semitism and Islamophobia as well. It is of great importance that the Jews are there for the Muslims when something ugly happens, and the Muslims are there for the Jews, and they hold a joint press conference to say clearly and unambiguously that neither is acceptable.

Last year we did a public service announcement. We brought six imams and six rabbis together to New York City to produce a public service announcement that then ran on CNN. It said if either Islamophobia or anti-Semitism raise their ugly heads, we must fight them together, and that bigotry against any Muslim or any Jew is an attack on all Muslims and all Jews. Again, this message is not only for the larger society; it's for our own communities as well, because so many in our own communities are just used to giving vent to some of this stuff or accepting it quietly, and we have to put a stop to that. American Jews have to acknowledge that Islamophobia is a real phenomenon, in the same way that Muslims must accept that anti-Semitism is real and directed against Jews. There are still some Muslims who say there is no such thing as anti-Semitism or anti-Semites, because Arabs are Semites as well. Yet we've already seen a big change on both sides in recent years, with more Jews acknowledging Islamophobia and more Muslims using the term anti-Semitism to refer to anti-Jewish bigotry, so that represents real progress.

Two days from now I'm going to be in Paris to take part at the Gala Dinner of the Judeo-Muslim Friendship Society, celebrating their success in "twinning" thirty mosques and thirty synagogues across France. Hopefully, this achievement will help to popularize twinning in other European countries, where it's just beginning to happen. It's a remarkable thing that this is happening in France, which is the country where perhaps the relations have been the worst between the two communities. There has been plenty of violence, and some Jews are saying that they're fearful for the future of the Jewish community, that there's violence coming from Muslims. There's a courageous gentleman by the name of Rabbi Serfaty who goes out on a bus all over France with various imams to engage both Muslim and Jewish young people where they live, and they've had a tremendous impact. When they heard about "twinning," they put in an appeal to the *Figaro* newspaper, and thirty mosques and thirty synagogues responded by holding one-on-one twinnings. We're at the very beginning of this in France and Europe and there remain very difficult problems to overcome, but we really feel a sense of hope and excitement.

In conclusion, we believe that Jews and Muslims have a moral obligation to come together as friends and allies and to work for the betterment of both faith communities and of American society as a whole. In the process, we believe that we will also have an impact on our brothers and sisters in Israel and Palestine, by demonstrating that if Muslims and Jews can learn to like and trust each other in the U.S., France, or elsewhere, they can accomplish that in Israel and Palestine as well. Despite one hundred years of conflict, they don't have to remain enemies forever; they don't have to sacrifice the next generation and the one after that to death and violence. It took one hundred years or more for Muslim-Jewish relations to reach this level of hostility, and it will take many years to reverse the damage. Yet let us resolve to commence this long and uplifting journey together, today, right now; because for the sake of our children and our children's children, we can do nothing else.

13

Christians as a Majority in the United States

Thomas Templeton Taylor

[Ed.: This chapter serves well as a demographic snapshot of American Christianity circa 1990. Chapter 14 will update this snapshot and expand on Taylor's thoughts about relations between American Christians and their religious neighbors.]

I WILL BEGIN BY examining some ambiguities in the idea of a Christian majority, and then will try to report on one way of organizing the bewildering array of Christian groups in America into a coherent pattern, using an important recent book by sociologists Wade Clark Roof and William McKinney. Toward the end, I will make some observations on contemporary Christianity, drawing on the work of sociologist Robert Wuthnow.

Statistical Measures of American Christianity

From the point of view of many American religious minorities, Christianity certainly appears to be the majority faith in the United States. In fact, one might even be reminded of a cartoon of more than a decade ago, with two large fish swimming through the seas and smaller fish scampering away lest they be eaten. In the caption, one large fish says to the other, "Big fish eat little fish. I like that." From outside the tradition, American Christianity must look like a big fish that enjoys swallowing or at least intimidating smaller fish; and in truth many Americans do indeed like it that way.

Part III: The Past Is Never Dead

Certainly more Americans identify with the term "Christian" than with any other religious term. And few would argue that the Judeo-Christian tradition has not played a crucial role in shaping American life and institutions. And yet, one hears so much about the secularization of American life and sees so much that is irreligious in American culture, that it is easy to wonder about any "Christian majority."

According to the Gallup religious preference polls, roughly 85 percent of Americans still claim a preference for Catholic or Protestant Christianity. Gallup polls since the 1950s indicate that the percentage of the population identifying themselves as Protestant has dropped, from 67 percent to 57 percent, but the percentage identifying with Catholicism has risen, from 25 percent to 28 percent. Meanwhile Jewish identification has dropped from 4 percent to 2 percent, while other faiths have risen from 1 percent to 4 percent.[1] George Gallup, Jr. himself says, "Over the last 54 years of scientific polling, religion in America has been remarkably stable, both in terms of religious beliefs and practices."[2] The point is well taken.

Much of the talk about the decline of American religion is based on careless, and sometimes downright mischievous, use of data. For example, the apparent decline of religious indicators since the 1950s is deceptive. Although church and synagogue membership peaked at 75 percent in 1947, since 1975 it has hovered between 68 percent and 71 percent, roughly the same as the 72 percent of the late 1930s. When Gallup asks Americans, "did you, yourself, happen to attend church or synagogue in the last seven days?", about 41 percent say "yes," as they have since the early 1970s. That number is indeed down from a peak of 49 percent in 1955, but it is the same as in 1939, and it is higher than the 37 percent of 1940.

So in areas like religious membership and attendance at religious activities, the last fifty years have been years of stability, not unchecked decline. In fact, religious belief in America continues to astound us, particularly when we compare ourselves with other western industrialized democracies. At least 94 percent of Americans believe in God or a Universal Spirit. Seven in ten believe the Bible to be the Word of God; four of those seven believe it to be without errors. Seventy percent believe in life after death, compared with 45 percent in Great Britain, 39 percent in West Germany,

---

1. Except where otherwise noted, the data in these paragraphs are drawn from the Gallup *Religion in America* reports of 1984 and 1987. More detailed data can be gleaned from Gallup's *Emerging Trends*.

2. Quoted in Jones, "Tracking America's Soul," 23.

and 25 percent in Denmark. Seven in ten believe in heaven, although only five-and-a-half in ten believe in hell. And 70 percent of Americans claim to believe that Jesus is God, a figure down slightly from the 74 percent of 1952.

Gallup likes to ask, do you know who gave the Sermon on the Mount, can you name all four of the Gospels, and where was Jesus born? In 1954, about 34 percent knew who gave the Sermon on the Mount and could name the four Gospels; by 1982 the figure had risen to about 44 percent. The percentage that knows Jesus' birthplace fell from 74 percent to a still high 70 percent.

Despite the evidence for stability, most Americans probably think of America as less religious than it once was, and that may be right. The anomaly is that in many ways this nation is more secular than it once was. Many sociologists cling to the secularization thesis, which argues that as a society becomes more modern it becomes more secular, religious beliefs become privatized, and religion becomes marginalized. While there is much room to argue against this thesis (in America, thinkers have been predicting this for at least two hundred years), it is not rooted solely in the biases of secular-minded, modern sociologists. Indeed, what has many Christians worried is that these sociologists may be on to something.[3]

Some figures will illustrate the point. Since the 1950s, the percentage of Americans claiming no religious preference has risen from 2 percent to 9 percent. In effect, the openly secular portion of the population has increased greatly. This, coupled with the identification of many religious people with the secular values of the broader culture, has meant that secularism has indeed grown in America, mostly at the expense of more liberal religious traditions. Consequently, secularism and deep religious commitment flourish side-by-side.

Just how religious is the religious majority? Gallup's 1987 report on religion provides one answer. When people were asked for their religious preference, their religious affiliation, whether they had attended a church/synagogue in the last week, and whether religion was very important in their lives, only 4 percent gave negative answers to all four questions: that is, they had no religious preference, held no membership in a religious body, had not attended a service in the last week, and said that religion was not very important in their lives. Twenty-eight percent said they were neither a member of a religious body nor had attended a church/synagogue in the

---

3. For a brief explanation of this thesis and some counters to it, see Robbins and Anthony, *In Gods We Trust*.

previous week. A full 72 percent claimed either religious membership or attendance at a church service in the last week.

That sounds high, but the percentage that claimed to be members of a religious body, had attended a service in the last week, and said religion was very important in their lives was only 31 percent, a large percentage, but a minority. If one accepts these figures, the proportion of the population that identifies itself as Christian is still an overwhelming 85 percent majority. But a much smaller percentage actively participate, and the difference between active and non-active can be very important.

Another reason for concern about Christianity has been the numerical decline of certain major Protestant families. Of the five major Protestant families, only Baptists have held their own in the last twenty-odd years of Gallup poll religious identification surveys; while Baptists fluctuated between 19 percent and 21 percent, the other four fell: Methodists from 14 percent to 9 percent, Lutherans from 7 percent to 5 percent, Presbyterians from 6 percent to 2 percent, and Episcopalians from 3 percent to 2 percent. Consequently, Southern Baptist identification alone is greater than that for all Methodist groups, and indeed outnumbers identification with Lutherans, Presbyterians, and Episcopalians combined.

This shift is a source of major concern to just about everyone except Southern Baptists. Of the major communities of faith from the early 1950s, only Baptists and Roman Catholics have held their percentage of the population; Catholics may have grown by a point or two. Now identification polls can exaggerate the strength of large bodies, but the others still have declined significantly, both as a percentage of the population and in real numbers. So if there is a Christian majority, it has been shaken and to some extent rearranged in the last quarter century.

The Restructuring of American Religion

Princeton sociologist Robert Wuthnow refers to these changes as the "restructuring of American religion."[4] American Christianity remains strong, but it is diverse, and it faces a stiff challenge from secularism and non-Christian faiths. The religious landscape has changed significantly, even if total religious commitment has not.

What does this landscape look like? It does not much resemble the picture we painted of it in the 1950s, when mainline American religion was

4. Wuthnow, *Restructuring of American Religion*.

often summarized in three words: Protestant, Catholic, Jew. Using those three categories today, one would find little variety or controversy. On a host of issues there appear to be few serious differences among them anymore.

But sociologists have learned that clumsy categories like Protestant and Catholic obscure a world of tremendous variety and diversity. What Martin Marty predicted of religion in the 1980s will be true of the 1990s: religion will be everywhere, but it will be nowhere in particular. Consequently, sociologists look for new ways of organizing the diversity of mainline American religion into a coherent pattern.

One useful, though imperfect, schematic has been provided by Roof and McKinney in their noted book, *American Mainline Religion: Its Changing Shape and Future.* They divide mainline religion into socioreligious groups, combining dozens of religious traditions into a half-dozen bodies. In descending order, ranked by size, they are: Catholics (25 percent), Moderate Protestants (24.2 percent), Conservative Protestants (15.8 percent), Black Protestants (9.1 percent), Liberal Protestants (8.7 percent), and Jews (2.3 percent). These groups differ in important and revealing ways.[5]

Of the five Christian groups, Catholics, conservative Protestants, and black Protestants rate much higher than liberal or moderate Protestants in church attendance, denominational commitment, and actual membership in a religious organization (as opposed to merely identifying with a faith). The one exception to this pattern is that actual church membership for those calling themselves Catholic is not particularly high. (One should note that Mormons and Jehovah's Witnesses "out-attend" all three of these groups.)[6]

In socio-economic terms, Catholics are as likely to be middle- or upper-class as the population as a whole, while conservative and black Protestants are less likely, and moderate and liberal Protestants are more likely to be middle- or upper-class. In educational attainment, Catholics again reflect the national average, while conservative and black Protestants lag behind it, and liberal and moderate Protestants are well ahead of it.[7]

These groups differ significantly in their growth or decline. Roof and McKinney's liberal Protestants—Episcopalians, the United Church of Christ, and Presbyterians—have been losing members for decades now. To a lesser degree, so have the moderate Protestants, the Methodists,

---

5. Roof and McKinney, *American Mainline Religion*, 82. Roof and McKinney's data rely heavily on the General Social Survey; see their appendix, 253–56.

6. Ibid., 83–84, 101.

7. Ibid., 112–13.

Lutherans, Disciples of Christ, and Northern Baptists. Meanwhile conservative Protestants have grown in number, if not in total percentage of the population. Why?

Conservative Protestants are clearly more active in converting others to Christianity than are liberal and moderate Protestants. Roof and McKinney also argue that the age-distribution and higher birth-rate among conservative Protestants, as compared with liberal and moderate Protestants, have and will continue to fuel these disparities in growth.

People who switch from one group to another or move outside the church altogether add an interesting dimension to the problem. Although liberal Protestants appear to gain some "switchers," these new members are typically less active than the switchers they replaced, while switchers to conservative Protestant groups tend to be as active as those they replace. In other words, the net effect of switching is to weaken liberal and moderate Protestant groups further and to strengthen conservative Protestant groups.

The greatest problem for liberal Protestants is their losses to the unaffiliated category. As Roof and McKinney put it: "the challenge to liberal Protestantism comes not so much from the conservative faiths as from the growing secular drift of many of their not-so-highly committed members." Liberal Protestants and Catholics show particularly high losses of those under age forty-five, but the group most adversely affected by switching is moderate Protestants.[8]

Roof and McKinney find significant variations among these five groups regarding civil liberties, racial integration, sexual mores, and women's rights. On interracial socializing and integrated neighborhoods, conservative Protestants stand out for their low scores. In willingness to grant civil liberties to groups with unpopular ideologies, liberal Protestants rate much higher and conservative Protestants rate much lower than their counterparts.

After looking at various social and political issues, Roof and McKinney divided the religious spectrum into five categories, from the most liberal to the most conservative. At the farthest left are Jews and the unaffiliated; next come liberal Protestants, with Catholics and moderate Protestants making up the center. Black Protestants are more conservative, and conservative Protestants are the most conservative of all.[9]

It is especially noteworthy that switchers reinforce these differences, they do not dilute them, because switchers tend to share the social and

8. Ibid., 170.
9. Ibid., 224.

moral values of those whom they are joining. The differences become sharper still if one focuses only on active participants in these traditions, factoring out the inactive, who tend to be closer to the middle of the spectrum than are their more active counterparts.

Roof and McKinney predict continued growth among black and conservative Protestants, continued decline among moderate and liberal Protestants, and sharpening divisions between the groups. Although they refrain from making predictions about Catholicism, sociologist Andrew Greeley argues that much of the alleged disaffection from Catholicism has been the result of the age-distribution of American Catholics—what looks like people leaving in droves—is actually young people leaving and slowly returning, a perfectly natural occurrence. Greeley concedes widespread lay disagreement with the Papacy, but suggests that American Catholics have reacted to this not so much by leaving the church as by giving less. In his words, "The laity voted not with their feet but with their checkbooks."[10] For the immediate future, things look good, because so many Catholics appear determined to remain loyal. Greeley puts it this way: "As I read the data and listen to the laity, I draw the following conclusion: There is nothing more the Vatican, the bishops or we priests can do to drive the laity out of the Church. We did everything we could—and often continue to do it—and still they won't go!"[11] He and his colleague Michael Hout believe that "[t]he negative impact of unpopular teachings about human sexuality has probably spent itself. We expect that a new epoch of declining attendance—should one arise—will come from a new source."[12] If all of these predictions come to pass, Christianity's share of the population should hold steady or decline slightly, and it will become more conservative.

Basic Cleavages within American Christianity

This brings us back to Robert Wuthnow, who suggests that the basic cleavage within American Christianity transcends these categories and denominational boundaries. The fundamental division, he says, is between evangelical and liberal Christianity. Wuthnow writes,

---

10. Greeley, "Why Catholics Stay in the Church," 179.
11. Ibid., 180.
12. Hout and Greeley, "The Center Doesn't Hold," 340.

the major divisions in American religion now revolve around an axis of liberalism and conservatism rather than denominational landmarks of the past. The new division parallels the ideological cleavage that runs through American politics. It divides religious practitioners from one another over questions of social welfare, defense spending, communism, and the so-called politics of abortion, sex education, gender equality, and prayer in public schools. But this division is not only political; it is deeply religious as well.[13]

If you ask Americans whether they are evangelicals, about 33 percent will say "yes."[14] If asked whether they are liberal or conservative Christians, they split, 43 percent liberal and 41 percent conservative. And the differences between the two groups intensify with exposure to one another.[15]

Wuthnow does not argue that evangelicalism or fundamentalism have experienced a revival, as some claim. But he does note that they are now better organized, and that because government has intruded more and more into the public sector, with little likelihood of backing out, there is little reason to believe that religious-political conflicts will diminish.

There are serious implications here for Muslims. Liberal Christians are more likely to tolerate or embrace those of other faiths, but they are less likely to share the strong moral and social values of traditional Islam. Conversely, conservative Christians may share Islam's strong social and moral values, but they are less likely to accept Islam as a legitimate alternative to Christianity, because conservatives are more likely than liberals to cling to the traditional Christian doctrine that salvation is attainable only through belief in a divine Jesus Christ. All other paths are thereby false paths. This makes evangelicals both more determined to convert others *and* less tolerant of other faiths. What liberals call proselytizing, conservatives call evangelism. One can grow up in evangelical churches without ever hearing the word "proselytize" much less knowing what it means.

Admittedly, our age has witnessed the weakening of many institutional divisions within Christianity. The various recent mergers involving Presbyterians, Methodists, or Lutheran groups come to mind immediately, as do the extensive dialogues conducted between Catholics, Episcopalians, and Lutherans. But much of the talk of merger and reconciliation may miss the point. Sinking ships can merge and still sink. The real gulf in Christendom

---

13. Wuthnow, *Struggle for America's Soul*, 178.
14. *Religion in America* (1987) 28.
15. Wuthnow, *Struggle for America's Soul*, 23.

today lies not between Catholics and Protestants, but between liberals and conservatives. And the conflict between those two will become more intense as the avowedly secular portion of our society continues to grow.

It should be clear now that there is not one Christian majority in America, but at least and perhaps several Christian pluralities of various strengths. Each has a claim on the American value system; each wishes decisively to influence American civil religion, that public mix of religious and political values which at the broadest level unites many Americans.

In times of conflict, cultural outsiders often suffer more than the chief combatants, but because none of these Christian groups can claim a true majority, they will need allies, and they know it. One has only to think of the enormous contribution of Jews and Mormons to recent American politics to see civil religion's potential for incorporating new faiths. As a nation, we face fundamental questions about the role of religion in the public sphere; the answers to these questions will be as important to Muslims as they are to Christians.

Bibliography

Emerging Trends. Washington, DC: Gallup Organization.
Greeley, Andrew M. "Why Catholics Stay in the Church." In *In Gods We Trust: New Patterns of Religious Pluralism in America.* 2nd ed., edited by Thomas Robbins and Dick Anthony, 177–83. New Brunswick, NJ: Transaction, 1990.
Hout, Michael, and Andrew M. Greeley. "The Center Doesn't Hold: Church Attendance in the United States, 1940–1984." *American Sociological Review* 52 (1987) 325–45.
Jones, Timothy K. "Tracking America's Soul." *Christianity Today* 33 (November 17, 1989) 22–25.
Religion in America: 1984. No. 222. Princeton: American Institute of Public Opinion, March 1984.
Religion in America: The Gallup Report. No. 259. Washington, DC: Gallup Organization, April 1987.
Robbins, Thomas, and Dick Anthony, eds. *In Gods We Trust: New Patterns of Religious Pluralism in America.* 2nd ed. New Brunswick, NJ: Transaction, 1990.
Roof, Wade Clark, and William McKinney. *American Mainline Religion: Its Changing Shape and Future.* New Brunswick, NJ: Rutgers University Press, 1987.
Wuthnow, Robert. *The Restructuring of American Religion: Society and Faith since World War II.* Princeton: Princeton University Press, 1988.
———. *The Struggle for America's Soul: Evangelicals, Liberals, and Secularism.* Grand Rapids: Eerdmans, 1989.

14

American Christians and Their Abrahamic Neighbors

Paul D. Numrich

IN CHAPTER 1, I surveyed relations among Christians, Jews, and Muslims in Central Ohio from the late 1800s to the present and discussed the three goals of what this volume calls the Abrahamic encounter: enhancing mutual understanding and relationships, disseminating accurate information about the three major Abrahamic traditions, and contributing to the general betterment of society. In the previous chapter, Thomas Taylor offered a demographic and theological snapshot of American Christianity on the eve of the twenty-first century, concluding that "there is not one Christian majority in America." The present chapter builds upon those chapters, updating Taylor's national snapshot and identifying various ways that American Christians engage their Abrahamic neighbors.

As to the latter topic, I draw upon my book *The Faith Next Door: American Christians and Their New Religious Neighbors*. There I present case studies from the Chicago area of Christian responses to increasing local religious diversity, arguing that those cases illuminate "dynamics at work across a multireligious America."[1] Indeed, similar dynamics are at work in Central Ohio.

Since, as Taylor suggests, there is not a single Christianity in America, there is also not a single Christian perspective on Jews, Muslims, or the

---

1. Numrich, *Faith Next Door*, 12.

Abrahamic encounter. I place myself on record in *The Faith Next Door* that I do not care what theological stance my fellow Christians adopt on the religions of the world, "as long as they exhibit what I call 'meek Christianity' in their dealings with the adherents of those religions. . . . Whatever perspective a Christian adopts regarding adherents of other religions, it should include meekness of spirit."[2] I will return to this expectation at the end of this chapter.

American Christianity Today

Taylor's chapter is titled "Christians as a Majority in the United States." This has not changed, nor is it likely to change in the near future despite steady decline in the total number of American Christians since Taylor wrote. Citing Gallup data from the 1980s, Taylor reported that about 85 percent of Americans identified their religious preference as either Protestant or Catholic Christianity. That figure dropped to 82 percent in 2000, 74 percent in 2010, and 70 percent in 2014.[3]

Taylor breaks out American Christianity by denomination or denominational affinities, focusing on Catholics and what he calls "the five major Protestant families." Only Catholics and Baptists reported steady numbers or slight increases between the 1950s and 1980s; in contrast, Methodists, Lutherans, Presbyterians, and Episcopalians all declined.

Some of those trends have continued in recent years, although it is more useful to parse out the "Protestant families." According to figures from the Association of Religion Data Archives (ARDA) for the decade 2000–2010,[4] the United Methodist Church declined by 4.7 percent, the major Lutheran denominations suffered even greater losses (Wisconsin Evangelical Lutheran Synod minus 5.5 percent, Lutheran Church—Missouri Synod minus 9.9 percent, Evangelical Lutheran Church in America minus 18.2 percent), the Presbyterian Church (USA) declined by 22.0 percent, and the Episcopal Church declined by 15.7 percent. Whereas Catho-

---

2. Ibid., 163, 165.

3. "Religion." The 2000, 2010, and 2014 data break out a third category not found in the 1980s data, "Christian (nonspecific)," which I have folded into the totals here. The Pew Research Center study, "America's Changing Religious Landscape," reported virtually the same decline in Christian identity, from 78.4 percent in 2007 to 70.6 percent in 2014.

4. http://www.thearda.com/rcms2010/r/u/rcms2010_99_us_name_2000_ON.asp.

PART III: THE PAST IS NEVER DEAD

lics had increased slightly between the 1950s and 1980s, they declined by 5.0 percent between 2000 and 2010. Some Baptist denominations grew (Southern Baptist Convention plus 0.1 percent, Baptist General Conference / Converge Worldwide plus 8.9 percent), but others declined (American Baptist Churches in the USA minus 11.7 percent, National Association of Free Will Baptists minus 14.4 percent).

Taylor does not mention the Pentecostal/Holiness denominations, whose numbers showed healthy growth overall between 2000 and 2010, such as International Pentecostal Holiness Church (plus 19.7 percent), Assemblies of God (plus 14.9 percent), and Church of God of Prophecy (plus 8.0 percent). Taylor parenthetically notes the strength of the Church of Jesus Christ of Latter-day Saints (the Mormons, though some would not classify it as a Christian denomination): it increased a remarkable 45.5 percent between 2000 and 2010.

Taylor discusses certain trends that pertain to the scope and influence of Christianity in American society. He cites Gallup data on what has been called religious literacy to show high cultural awareness of Christianity: the percentage of respondents who could name all four Gospels and knew who preached the Sermon on the Mount had increased significantly from the 1950s to the 1980s to about 44 percent, while those who could identify the town where Jesus was born remained quite high at 70 percent. But subsequent years have seen a steady decline in such cultural awareness, according to religion scholar Stephen Prothero, who calls America "A Nation of Religious Illiterates."[5] On average, his college students could not name at least three of the four Gospels and only 60 percent could correctly identify Bethlehem as Jesus's birthplace.[6]

Taylor also points to two significant and related trends that have continued since he wrote: secularization and the rise of what is now called the "nones." Taylor correctly notes scholarly skepticism about a simplistic straight-line secularization theory ("as a society becomes more modern it becomes more secular"),[7] but he also perceptively observes that secularization to any degree worries many American Christians. Taylor's conclusion that "secularism and deep religious commitment flourish side-by-side" in this country is still apt.

---

5. Prothero, *Religious Literacy*, chapter 1.
6. http://www.pewforum.org/files/2007/12/protheroquiz.pdf.
7. See P. Berger, *Desecularization of the World*.

Recent studies suggest that "nones" or "religiously unaffiliated" may comprise one-fifth of the American population. This category includes "more than 13 million self-described atheists and agnostics (nearly 6% of the U.S. public), as well as nearly 33 million people who say they have no particular religious affiliation."[8] This is an important distinction: most nones are personally religious or spiritual to some extent but not affiliated with a particular institution or group. The numbers are significant: "Today there is not a single demographic group of people in the U.S. that does not include Nones. . . . In many ways, Nones are the invisible minority in the U.S. today—invisible because their social characteristics are very similar to the majority."[9]

Another trend that has drawn attention is multiple or hybrid religious identities. More than one-third of the respondents to a recent survey indicated that they attend religious services in more than one venue, "and most of these (24% of the public overall) indicate that they sometimes attend religious services of a faith different from their own." The report observes further, "Though the U.S. is an overwhelmingly Christian country, significant minorities profess belief in a variety of Eastern or New Age beliefs."[10] Such developments also worry many American Christians; witness the article in *Christianity Today* a few years ago titled "Dangerous Meditations."[11]

Thus, Taylor's observation that the American Christian majority "has been shaken and to some extent rearranged in the last quarter century" still holds. However, whereas Taylor could claim that "the last fifty years have been years of stability, not unchecked decline," such a claim is difficult to support today. It is true, as Taylor argues, that "religious belief in America continues to astound us, particularly when we compare ourselves with other western industrialized democracies." A recent Pew report found that half of Americans rate religion "very important" to their lives, whereas the percentages ranged from a mere 12 to 22 percent in Spain, Germany, Great Britain, and France. Similarly, nearly half of American Christians self-identify by religion first and nationality second, whereas less than one-fourth of the Christians in the four European countries do likewise.[12] Such

---

8. "'Nones' on the Rise," 9.

9. Kosmin et al., "American Nones," 21, 22.

10. "Many Americans Mix Multiple Faiths," 1, 2. On "hybrid" religious identities, see Beal, *Religion in America*.

11. Groothuis, "Dangerous Meditations."

12. "American-Western European Values Gap."

a cross-national analysis reveals that Christianity's scope and influence in the United States have not declined as much as in Europe. Of course, it is quite possible that the downward trend in recent decades portends a more Western-Europe-like status for American Christianity in the future.

The complexity of the contemporary American religious landscape is captured in a 2015 Pew report: the American population is becoming less religious overall, due especially to the rise in "nones"; at the same time, "by some conventional measures, religiously affiliated Americans are, on average, even more devout than they were a few years ago."[13]

The demographics of Christianity in Ohio generally mirror the national picture, with a few notable exceptions. Writing in the book *Religion in Ohio* in 2004, Donald Huber, academic dean of Trinity Lutheran Seminary in Columbus, noted the statewide shifts in Christianity since 1890: Protestants declined from about 67 percent to 56 percent while Catholics increased from 28 percent to more than 40 percent. Catholics comprised the single largest Christian grouping in the state, followed by Methodists, Baptists, Lutherans, and Pentecostal/Holiness denominations, in that order.[14]

According to 2010 ARDA figures,[15] Central Ohio's Franklin County was roughly comparable to the state as a whole: 64 percent Protestants, 36 percent Catholics. Catholics increased by 4.5 percent between 2000 and 2010, though they had declined by approximately the same percentage nationwide. The growth in local Pentecostal/Holiness denominations was roughly comparable to their national growth: Assemblies of God (plus 17.9 percent), International Pentecostal Holiness Church (plus 14.8 percent), and Church of God of Prophecy (plus 7.5 percent). The local decline in certain denominations actually exceeded the national decline: United Methodist Church (minus 7.5 percent) and the Lutheran denominations (Lutheran Church—Missouri Synod minus 15.6 percent, Wisconsin Evangelical Lutheran Synod minus 18.1 percent, Evangelical Lutheran Church in America minus 38.5 percent). The local Baptist denominations varied, however: American Baptist Churches in the USA declined by 10.1 percent, slightly less than the national decline; Southern Baptist Convention declined dramatically by 18.8 percent whereas it showed a slight increase nationally; National Association of Free Will Baptists grew by 1.6 per-

---

13. "U.S. Public Becoming Less Religious."

14. Huber, "Introduction," 12, 13.

15. http://www.thearda.com/rcms2010/r/c/39/rcms2010_39049_county_name_2000_ON.asp.

cent whereas it declined by more than 14 percent nationally; and Baptist General Conference / Converge Worldwide increased by a staggering 98.5 percent compared to a modest 8.9 percent increase nationally. The Church of Jesus Christ of Latter-day Saint (Mormons) also increased locally—by 83.5 percent, nearly double the national increase.

Although we do not have local empirical data on the other national trends discussed above—the decline in religious literacy and the increases in secularization, "nones," and hybrid religious identities—it is safe to conjecture that they have impacted the Christian majority in Central Ohio.

A 2014 article in the *Columbus Dispatch* reported the opinions of several Christian leaders on the "nones." My seminary colleague Linda Mercadante, whose book *Belief without Borders* analyzes the "spiritual but not religious" or SBNR phenomenon, "finds that most SBNRs have left religion behind because they stopped agreeing with certain views or positions. She suggests that churches and other religious groups review and rebuild their faiths and then reach out to SBNRs." A Catholic theology professor opined that "Faith groups need to consider the words and images they use to deliver their messages," and should adopt an approach of "speaking to the human heart first." A United Methodist pastor anticipates a "drastic change" in the Christian church with the coming of the five hundredth anniversary of the Protestant Reformation in 2017, noting that "she is among people of faith who believe that a church rebirth will stem the nonreligious trend." Finally, Christina Butler, then-president of the Interfaith Association of Central Ohio (and a Catholic), reported that the IACO has been discussing the possibility of including a membership category of "people of conscience." "They're not self-identifying with a faith tradition," she explains, "but are still compassionate, caring people."[16]

In the previous chapter, Taylor spends considerable time discussing the insights of sociologists about the conservative-liberal continuum in contemporary American Christianity. His quote from sociologist Robert Wuthnow's 1989 book, *The Struggle for America's Soul*, is worth repeating here:

> the major divisions in American religion now revolve around an axis of liberalism and conservatism rather than denominational landmarks of the past. The new division parallels the ideological cleavage that runs through American politics. It divides religious practitioners from one another over questions of social welfare,

---

16. Viviano, "Theology Professor Advises Faiths"; also, see Mercadante, *Belief without Borders*.

defense spending, communism, and the so-called politics of abortion, sex education, gender equality, and prayer in public schools. But this division is not only political; it is deeply religious as well.[17]

The conservative-liberal divide in American Christianity has become increasingly salient in recent decades, and, as Wuthnow points out, the distinction does not always follow denominational lines or affinities. Thus, for instance, the Baptist family includes both liberal and conservative denominations, while both the United Methodist Church and the Evangelical Lutheran Church in America, though typically labeled "liberal," have been riven by internal factions on opposite ends of the continuum. We can generalize that recent growth within American Christianity has tended toward the conservative end of the spectrum, recognizing that membership in some conservative denominations is either flat or declining (such as the Southern Baptist Convention and the Lutheran Church—Missouri Synod, as seen above). The Pew Research Center's 2015 study, "America's Changing Religious Landscape," revealed growth in only two of seventeen Protestant subcategories, both conservative: nondenominational and Pentecostal. Although the percentage of the overall US population that identifies as evangelical Protestants declined slightly between 2007 and 2014, their absolute numbers probably increased, making evangelicals the majority (55 percent) of all US Protestants and the largest religious group in the country with 62.2 million adherents (Catholics are second with 50.9 million).[18]

I will return to the conservative-liberal divide in American Christianity at the end of this chapter to discuss the implications for interfaith relations.

Christian Engagement with Neighbors of Other Faiths

In another place, I argue that the majority of American Christians do not engage in the kind of active, serious, and appreciative interfaith encounter described in this volume, nor will they likely do so in the future.[19] In *The Faith Next Door*, I suggest a basic distinction between those Christians who engage adherents of other religions with truth claims primarily in mind and those Christians who emphasize other claims.

---

17. Wuthnow, *Struggle for America's Soul*, 178.
18. "America's Changing Religious Landscape." For an evangelical commentary on this study, see Zylstra, "Pew."
19. Numrich, "Plan B."

Truth-Claims Approach

The oft-cited typology of exclusivism/inclusivism/pluralism is helpful in understanding the truth-claims approach. Diana Eck summarizes what she calls the three "responses" to religious diversity in this way:

> First, there is the exclusivist response: Our own community, our tradition, our understanding of reality, our encounter with God, is the one and only truth, excluding all others. Second, there is the inclusivist response: There are, indeed, many communities, traditions, and truths, but our own way of seeing things is the culmination of the others, superior to the others, or at least wide enough to include the others under our universal canopy and in our own terms. A third response is that of the pluralist: Truth is not the exclusive or inclusive possession of any one tradition or community.[20]

The Faith Next Door offers case studies of each type from the Chicago area, such as a Missouri Synod Lutheran pastor's exclusivist stance on the falsehood of Islam, the inclusivist approach of clergy informed by the theology of the Second Vatican Council, and the pluralist celebration of the truths of other religions by Protestant congregations. Each of these types can be found among Central Ohio's Christians as well.

The exclusivist position as summarized by Eck—"Our own community, our tradition, our understanding of reality, our encounter with God, is the one and only truth, excluding all others"—can manifest in straightforward fashion, as in the preaching of well-known Pastor Rod Parsley of World Harvest Church in suburban Columbus: "Religion is an attempt by man to get to God. That is not what Christianity is. Christianity is not man's attempt to get to God. Christianity is the story of God condescending and coming to men in the flesh and blood form of his son Jesus Christ of Nazareth."[21] Although this sermon and other statements by Pastor Parsley focus on Islam, it is important to note the larger exclusivist theology underpinning them: no religion is true in that all religions are futile human attempts to attain God. A Barthian dichotomy of "religion" versus the revelation of God in Jesus Christ is clear here.[22]

---

20. Eck, *Encountering God*, 168. Eck notes that these types can be found in all religions. She advocates the third response in her Pluralism Project at Harvard University.

21. "True Face of Islam Part 1."

22. Whether Barth himself can be classified as an exclusivist is a matter of some debate; see Chestnutt, *Challenging the Stereotype*.

Part III: The Past Is Never Dead

As noted in chapter 1, exclusivism can be an elephant in the room of Abrahamic encounters. As our interviewee put it, this sometimes manifests as "evangelism under the table," whether through "offhanded remarks about one's own religious perspective being the best" or in "more deliberate and confrontational ways." The example given of the latter involved Messianic Jews challenging a fellow Christian's understanding of the Bible at a local gathering of Jews and Christians. One of the tenets of the Messianic movement is summarized in this way by the organization Messianic Literature Outreach: "To obtain salvation and restored fellowship with God, every person must repent of sin, believe, accept Yeshua [Jesus] the Messiah and confess him."[23] This, of course, conflicts with the Jewish belief that Jesus was not the Messiah.

In my experience, the majority of Christians who participate in what we have called the Abrahamic encounter adopt an inclusivist and/or a pluralist approach to Judaism and Islam. Although inclusivism is sometimes criticized as being imperialistic, condescending, and assimilationist,[24] Catholic theologian Paul Knitter has suggested that everyone is actually an inclusivist, and thus those involved in interreligious dialogue should simply agree "to be included by the inclusivism of our partners."[25]

In chapter 1, Jeri Milburn, a Muslim, invoked the standard Islamic inclusivist perspective on Judaism and Christianity, namely, that the three faiths share the same prophetic lineage, Islam being the latest iteration. This led her to conclude that Muslims must respect the adherents of the earlier iterations: "When you're Muslim you have to be Jewish and Christian too, in a sense." What she did not say in so many words is that Islam considers itself the fulfilment, even the corrective, of the other two faiths. In chapter 5 in this volume, Muzammil Siddiqi notes, for instance, Islam's rejection of key Christian doctrines about Jesus. To invoke Diana Eck's summary of inclusivism: "There are, indeed, many communities, traditions, and truths, but our own way of seeing things is the culmination of the others, superior to the others, or at least wide enough to include the others under our universal canopy and in our own terms."

Inclusivist Christians feel this way about Judaism and Islam. Regarding Judaism, they can draw upon the foundational notion of the New

---

23. "What We Believe."

24. E.g., Eck, *Encountering God*, 184–85. Eck also states her opinion that "most Christians are probably inclusivists" (178).

25. Knitter, *Introducing Theologies of Religions*, 219.

Covenant (or New Testament) in Jesus Christ that fulfills the Old Covenant (or Old Testament) with the Jews (e.g., Heb 8). Inclusivist Christians can incorporate Islam into a Christian understanding of the divine presence and activity in the world since, in the words of Vatican II's *Nostra Aetate*, Muslims also "adore the one God" and "value the moral life and worship God especially through prayer, almsgiving and fasting." In the Wesleyan tradition, all human beings are touched by the Holy Spirit, as Philip Meadows summarizes: "So the doctrine of prevenient grace has the effect of immediately including all people in God's plan of salvation, not as those standing outside and waiting to get in, but already indwelled by the transforming presence of the Spirit, simply by virtue of being human."[26]

I do not often hear Christian inclusivism invoked in Abrahamic encounters, perhaps for fear of sounding imperialistic, condescending, and assimilationist. As we have seen in this volume, the social position of being the majority religion can have subtle effects. I more often hear Christian pluralism invoked, which maintains that (again citing Diana Eck), "Truth is not the exclusive or inclusive possession of any one tradition or community."

First Community Church in Columbus offers an example of a pluralist approach that extends well beyond the Abrahamic family of faiths. A perusal of the church's Website garnered the following educational offerings, in addition to numerous specifically Christian topics: Buddhism and the Practice of Mindfulness, Dharma and Karma: A Closer Examination, Forum on Eastern Religions, The Sikh Faith: A Practitioner's Perspectives, Understanding Aspects of Judaism, and Using the Head, Heart and Belly in Spiritual Exploration (based on the Diamond Approach of Sandra Maitri, a form of enneagram analysis).[27] First Community Church's statement of beliefs includes the following point reflective of a pluralist Christian perspective: "Strive to follow the path of Jesus Christ, while recognizing other athways to the Divine."[28] A similar pluralist sentiment is expressed in the title of the 2012 dialogue program mentioned in chapter 1, "Three Paths Up the Mountain: An Interreligious Encounter with Abraham," and is also implied by R. Marston Speight in chapter 4 in this volume: "we consider both Islam and Christianity as drawing upon a common store of . . . inspiration."

I find it intriguing that the issue of truth claims is referenced in parts II and III of this volume more often than one might expect given the reticence

---

26. Meadows, "Candidates for Heaven," 102.
27. http://fcchurch.com/.
28. http://fcchurch.com/beliefs-and-mission/.

to dwell on differences expressed in chapter 1 by several participants in the Central Ohio Abrahamic encounter. It does not take long for a focus on commonalities to uncover significant differences in truth claims. Speight understands this in his chapter on Mary. He recognizes "all of the stark and apparently irreducible divergence that exists between Islam and Christianity" even as he lifts up "the Scriptural figure of Mary that draws Muslims and Christians together," through whom perhaps "we shall together learn to deal more adequately with our religious disagreements."

Muzammil Siddiqi begins his chapter by saying that "Jesus is the common link between Islam and Christianity," yet he discusses both similarities and differences between the qur'anic and New Testament portrayals of Jesus. And he concludes with a straightforward appeal for dialogue in the face of fundamental differences: "Dialogue between Muslims and Christians is very important. We have many issues to discuss that are at the core of our two traditions. Instead of shying away from discussion, we should talk about these issues in an atmosphere of friendship and frankness."

In chapter 3, "On Scripture and Its Exegesis," Reuven Firestone also recognizes the power of truth claims. In monotheistic terms, "There is only one God, and God has affirmed for us that there is only one true religion—our religion," and further that there can be "only one true Scripture." Firestone unpacks the Jewish and Islamic views of the Abraham-Isaac-Ishmael stories as seen through the "particularist lenses" of each tradition, and he also mentions a couple of particularist Christian perspectives. In thought-provoking turns at the end of his chapter, Firestone advocates that "We must overcome the need to figure out 'who was right,' and move on to more important issues," yet he concedes that "Jews and Muslims act on what is believed to be God's demands upon them." Firestone correctly argues that these divine demands are filtered through "human perceptions and understandings of God" and thus cannot rise to the status of absolute truth, but they nonetheless function as truth claims in Abrahamic encounters. Firestone perceptively alludes to how truth claims can become relationship deal-breakers: "As we learn to respect the religiosity and spirituality of each other's traditions at the same time that we affirm the depth and meaning of our own, we need no longer suffer the affront nor the anger when we note the differences between us."

Truth claims can polarize a conversation given the implication that they stand against falsehood. The chapters in the present volume suggest that truth claims need not descend into unhealthy confrontation nor must they necessarily shut down relationships. Indeed, it may be that deep, mutual understanding cannot develop until truth claims are displayed on the dialogue table. As Catherine Cornille argues, bracketing out the truth claims of participants' religious traditions—what she labels "mission or evangelization"—"tends to deprive dialogue of its energy and zeal. In so far as its ultimate goal is the advancement of truth, dialogue may be regarded as a form of mutual or reciprocal witnessing."[29] If dialogue involves representing the wholeness of one's faith tradition with integrity, then the tradition's understanding of truth must be voiced. In my experience, many dialogue partners want to know what Christianity has to say about the deepest questions of human existence and the nature of ultimate truth.

Other-Claims Approach

Not all Christians "lead" with truth claims in engaging adherents of other faiths. Interestingly, the distinction between emphasizing truth claims or other kinds of claims may manifest in the same event or even in the same person. For instance, as we saw in chapter 1, Rev. Timothy Ahrens of First Congregational Church invests heavily in social justice initiatives but he did not hesitate to argue "nose-to-nose" publicly with his good friend, the imam of Noor Islamic Cultural Center, over the correct interpretation of a story from the biblical book of Genesis.

Even groups that place a premium on the truth of Christianity may at times choose to focus their attention on other issues, such as neighbor needs or mutual interests. In *The Faith Next Door*, I give examples of African American pastors who worked with leaders of the Nation of Islam to address pressing social problems in their communities, a fundamentalist pastor whose exclusivist theological views did not preclude him from advocating a non-Christian group's First Amendment rights, Greek Orthodox Christians and Turkish Muslims who sought reconciliation after centuries of conflict in their homelands, and Christians who addressed the practical needs of non-Christian immigrants and refugees.[30]

We have seen several examples of prioritizing other issues over truth claims in the Central Ohio Abrahamic encounter. Recall what Rev. Ahrens said about the importance of the relationships that arise from crises like the vandalism of a local mosque: "A call comes to a cell phone, not to an empty

29. Cornille, "Conditions for Inter-Religious Dialogue," 23–24.
30. See Numrich, *Faith Next Door*, 156–63.

line somewhere in a building that has been destroyed: 'What do you need? We're here for you.'" In the BREAD (Building Responsibility Equality And Dignity) organization, their respective theologies may motivate the participants to come together but social activism defines their work. The same can be said of We Believe Ohio, SAIL (Safe Alliances of Interfaith Leaders), and the Columbus Faith Coalition Against Violence. Moreover, some of the most delicate "elephants in the room" stem, not primarily from doctrinal differences, but from political factors such as the Middle East conflict or post-9/11 tensions. Indeed, hypothetically, the three main goals of the Abrahamic encounter can be pursued without any reference to truth claims: enhanced mutual understanding and relationships, dissemination of accurate information about these traditions, and general betterment of society.

One of the most remarkable Christian initiatives in this regard is the work of World Relief Columbus (WRC), the local branch of World Relief, the international humanitarian arm of the National Association of Evangelicals.[31] WRC partners with several local churches and nearly three hundred volunteers to meet the practical needs of refugees who come to Central Ohio from across the globe. From its inception in 2012 through fiscal year 2015, WRC served nearly seven hundred refugees from fifteen nationalities, including significant numbers of Muslims from Iraq and Somalia. Funded through federal and state grants, WRC provides assistance with housing, finances, employment, and health care. WRC also works closely with HIAS (Hebrew Immigrant Aid Society, a Jewish organization) and CRIS (Community Refugee and Immigration Services, an affiliate of Church World Service and Episcopal Migrations Ministries) in both delivery of services and advocacy.

World Relief's mission and vision statements read: "Empowering the local Church to serve the most vulnerable" and "In community with the local Church, World Relief envisions the most vulnerable people transformed economically, socially, and spiritually." The local church connection is central to the organization's work, says WRC's Director Kay Lipovsky. Volunteers are screened and trained to provide hands-on assistance ranging from English-as-a-second-language, to computer literacy, to citizenship requirements, to women's health issues. This is so important because World Relief's funding for each refugee individual or family runs out after ninety or 120 days (depending on the grant), after which they "pass the baton," to

---

31. http://worldreliefcolumbus.org/; http://worldrelief.org/.

use Lipovsky's phrase, to a church group or individual volunteers who can extend support for another six months to a year.

Lipovsky calls this "relational evangelism," what others have called "friendship evangelism" or "friendship ministry."[32] Staff and volunteers are careful not to violate the protocols against proselytization of the government grants, but if a client initiates the conversation, one is free to share one's evangelical motivations for doing this work. The Great Commission of Matthew 28 is certainly at the heart of this, "but before you go and make disciples," Lipovsky explained to us, "you have to feed the vulnerable, you have to meet some needs before people can hear the Gospel. I think seeing how God is working through somebody is very impactful for refugee populations."

"As a faith-based organization," she continued, "we want to show the love of Christ. We want to be able to come alongside people, and when they ask us why, we tell them why—to show God's love to you and to know he's providing for you." It is important to note that there are no strings attached to this loving service. It does not matter whether a client wishes to accept Christ or even to discuss the truth claims of the Christian faith. As Lipovsky put it, they are given "unconditional love and service with no expectation, [so that] God is glorified in all that we do." One of her touchstone New Testament passages is 1 John 3:17–18 (NIV): "If anyone has material possessions and sees a brother or sister in need but has no pity on them, how can the love of God be in that person? Dear children, let us not love with words or speech but with actions and in truth."

Meek Christians

I noted at the outset of this chapter that I do not care what theological stance my fellow Christians adopt on other religions. All of the approaches described in the previous sections—and many more—have legitimate theological roots in the long and complex Christian tradition. One of my seminary students once suggested that Christian engagement with adherents of other faiths ranges from wanting to convert them to merely wanting to converse with them. Wherever my students or other Christians place themselves on such a continuum, I demand only that they exhibit what I call "meekness of spirit."[33]

---

32. See Numrich, *Faith Next Door*, chapter 2 on immigrants evangelizing fellow immigrants and chapter 3 on World Relief and its partner churches in the Chicago area.

33. The following draws upon ibid., 163–65.

Meekness is not an American cultural value, but it is a scriptural mandate for Christians. The Greek word, which carries a meaning of meekness, gentleness, and humility, appears sixteen times in eleven different New Testament books. The Gospel of Matthew uses the word to characterize Jesus as a gentle (*praus*) master (11:29) and a humble (*praus*) king (21:5), and depicts Jesus blessing the meek (*praeis*) in the Sermon on the Mount (5:5). In various epistles the word functions as a mark of proper Christian attitudes and behavior, as in "put on affection, compassion, kindness, humility, gentleness [*prautēta*], patience, putting up with one another and forgiving one another" (Col 3:12) and "live in a manner worthy of the calling with which you were called: with all humility and gentleness [*prautētos*], with patience, putting up with one another in love" (Eph 4:1–2).[34] 1 Peter 3:15–16 links meekness and reverence when witnessing to one's Christian faith: "... revere in your hearts the Lord Christ, and always be ready to answer anyone who demands from you an accounting of the hope that is yours. Yet [do so] out of humility [*prautētos*] and reverence . . . ."[35] The usual translation for "reverence" (*phobou*) in this passage is "respect." Respect is a fine virtue in and of itself, and it is certainly preferable to disrespect. But for Christians, reverence carries much stronger weight: to revere Christ is to render reverent testimony before others.

The Apostle Paul does not use the Greek word for meekness in the famous Love Chapter of 1 Corinthians 13 but his sentiments there are perfectly compatible with meek Christian character. Christian meekness is not weakness but a different kind of strength that flows from divine love. Thus, "Love is patient and kind; love is not jealous or boastful; it is not arrogant or rude. Love does not insist on its own way; it is not irritable or resentful; it does not rejoice at wrong, but rejoices in the right" (1 Cor 13:4–6, RSV).[36] Consider one example of how meek love might have transformed an encounter reported in chapter 1.

Recall Jeri Milburn's meeting with some Christians from a local church. The senior pastor began by saying, "I don't understand the point of this. You're going to try to convert us and we're going to try to convert you."

---

34. The translation and Greek words here come from the Society of Biblical Literature's online Greek New Testament, http://sblgnt.com/download/.

35. Michaels, *1 Peter*, 183. The other appearances of "meekness" in the New Testament are 1 Cor 4:21; 2 Cor 10:1; Gal 5:23; Gal 6:1; 1 Tim 6:11; 2 Tim 2:25; Titus 3:2; Jas 1:21; Jas 3:13; and 1 Pet 3:4.

36. I prefer the RSV's rendering of the word "right" rather than "truth" in verse 6. For my rationale, see Numrich, "Christian Sensitivity," 74–75.

He quickly squashed the idea of an ongoing relationship with Milburn's mosque "if the Muslims would not convert to Christianity."

I would contend that this pastor violated both the letter and the spirit of 1 Corinthians 13. He was impatient and unkind, arrogant and rude, insisted on his own way, became irritable, and perhaps even rejoiced at what he perceived as wrong. I do not fault him for his desire to convert Muslims, but rather for his un-meek, unloving approach to this Muslim and her mosque. Note the difference between this pastor and the relational evangelism carried out by World Relief and its partner churches and volunteers described earlier.

Returning now to the conservative-liberal divide in contemporary American Christianity discussed earlier, Thomas Taylor suggested in the previous chapter that this dichotomy carries "serious implications" for adherents of other faiths, especially Muslims: liberal Christians tend to be more tolerant and conservative Christians less tolerant of the truth claims of other faiths, whereas conservative Christians are more likely than liberal Christians to agree with "the strong moral and social values of traditional Islam."

We can question the validity of these characterizations, and thus also their implications. For instance, how intolerant of other truth claims are conservative Christians? One study found that 47 percent of white evangelical Protestants believed that "many religions can lead to eternal life," far fewer than either white Catholics (84 percent) or white mainline Protestants (82 percent) but perhaps far higher than readers of this chapter might have guessed.[37] Robert Wuthnow's extensive survey yielded these conclusions about the proselytizing tendencies of Christian exclusivists:

> Although they thought their non-Christian friends were destined for eternal punishment, few of them were actively engaged in trying to convert their friends. Especially when these friends belonged to another faith, they seemed to be forbidden fruit. Here, it appears that most Christian exclusivists either do not know Muslims, Hindus, or Buddhists or, if they do, they prefer not to talk to them about Christianity. They apparently have enough people who do not attend church to keep them busy.[38]

Wuthnow argues that Christian exclusivists approach adherents of other religions with a mixture of "cautious or restrained tolerance" and "serious misgivings about these other religions." "Their tolerance," explains

---

37. "Many Americans Say."
38. Wuthnow, *America and the Challenges of Religious Diversity*, 223.

Wuthnow, "is rooted both in their understanding of the right to religious freedom and in their implicit norms of civility, nonjudgmentalism, and trying to approach people on a one-to-one basis rather than as members of a social category."[39] Although "tolerance" has its detractors today, I contend that it is far preferable to "intolerance." Moreover, the kind of tolerance described by Wuthnow has positive social and civic benefits.

Whether or not Taylor's characterizations ring true is of far less concern to me than the attitudes adopted by both liberal and conservative Christians toward their Abrahamic neighbors. I do not ask my fellow Christians whether they are liberal or conservative—after all, those labels are useful only to a point. I ask only whether they are meek Christians.

In an article titled "Christian Sensitivity in Interreligious Relations," I quoted Qur'an 57:27 in which Allah speaks in the majestic plural: " . . . We sent Jesus, son of Mary: We gave him the Gospel and put compassion and mercy into the hearts of his followers." My comment: "Many Muslims would like to ask us whether we, the followers of Jesus today, have compassion and mercy in our hearts toward them."[40] Jews and others also have a right to ask Christians the same question.

Bibliography

"America's Changing Religious Landscape." Pew Research Center (May 12, 2015). http://www.pewforum.org/2015/05/12/americas-changing-religious-landscape/.

"The American-Western European Values Gap: American Exceptionalism Subsides." Pew Research Center (November 17, 2011, updated February 29, 2012). http://www.pewglobal.org/2011/11/17/the-american-western-european-values-gap/.

Beal, Timothy. *Religion in America: A Very Short Introduction.* New York: Oxford University Press, 2008.

Berger, Peter L., ed. *The Desecularization of the World: Resurgent Religion and World Politics.* Grand Rapids: Eerdmans, 1999.

Chestnutt, Glenn A. *Challenging the Stereotype: The Theology of Karl Barth as a Resource for Inter-religious Encounter in a European Context.* Bern: Peter Lang, 2010.

Cornille, Catherine. "Conditions for Inter-Religious Dialogue." In *The Wiley-Blackwell Companion to Inter-Religious Dialogue,* edited by Catherine Cornille, 20–33. Malden, MA: Wiley, 2013.

Eck, Diana L. *Encountering God: A Spiritual Journey from Bozeman to Banaras.* Boston: Beacon, 1993.

Groothuis, Douglas. "Dangerous Meditations." *Christianity Today* 48 (November 1, 2004) 78.

39. Ibid., 183.

40. Numrich, "Christian Sensitivity," 52, 53. The translation is from Haleem, *Qur'an,* 361.

Haleem, M.A.S. Abdel. *The Qur'an.* New York: Oxford World's Classics, 2005.
Huber, Donald L. "Introduction: More Than Two Centuries of Religion in Ohio." In *Religion in Ohio: Profiles of Faith Communities*, edited by Tarunjit Singh Butalia and Dianne P. Small, 1-14. Athens, OH: Ohio University Press, 2004.
Knitter, Paul F. *Introducing Theologies of Religions.* Maryknoll, NY: Orbis, 2002.
Kosmin, Barry A., et al. "American Nones: The Profile of the No Religion Population." Hartford, CT: Program on Public Values, Trinity College, 2009.
"Many Americans Mix Multiple Faiths." Washington, DC: Pew Research Center's Forum on Religion & Public Life, 2012.
"Many Americans Say Other Faiths Can Lead to Eternal Life." Pew Research Center (December 18, 2008). http://www.pewforum.org/2008/12/18/many-americans-say-other-faiths-can-lead-to-eternal-life/#3.
Meadows, Philip R. "'Candidates for Heaven': Wesleyan Resources for a Theology of Religions." *Wesleyan Theological Journal* 35 (Spring 2000) 99-129.
Mercadante, Linda. *Belief without Borders: Inside the Minds of the Spiritual but Not Religious.* New York: Oxford University Press, 2014.
Michaels, J. Ramsey. *1 Peter.* Word Biblical Commentary 49. Waco, TX: Word, 1988.
"'Nones' on the Rise: One-in-Five Adults Have No Religious Affiliation." Washington, DC: Pew Research Center's Forum on Religion & Public Life, 2012.
Numrich, Paul D. "Christian Sensitivity in Interreligious Relations." *The Asbury Journal* 67 (Fall 2012) 51-83.
———. *The Faith Next Door: American Christians and Their New Religious Neighbors.* New York: Oxford University Press, 2009.
———. "Plan B in the Pluralist-Dialogue Approach to Religious Diversity in America." *Journal of Ecumenical Studies* 43 (2008) 453-75.
Prothero, Stephen. *Religious Literacy: What Every American Needs to Know—and Doesn't.* New York: HarperCollins, 2007.
"Religion." http://www.gallup.com/poll/1690/religion.aspx.
"The True Face of Islam Part 1." https://www.youtube.com/watch?v=Fz_H7LP1ahY.
"U.S. Public Becoming Less Religious." Pew Research Center (November 3, 2015). http://www.pewforum.org/2015/11/03/u-s-public-becoming-less-religious/?utm_source=Pew+Research+Center&utm_campaign=3c0f246dbe-Religion_Weekly_Nov_5_2015&utm_medium=email&utm_term=0_3e953b9b70-3c0f246dbe-399950629.
Viviano, JoAnne. "Theology Professor Advises Faiths on Reaching 'Spiritual but Not Religious.'" *Columbus Dispatch* (January 10, 2014). http://www.dispatch.com/content/stories/faith_and_values/2014/01/10/faiths-advised-on-how-to-reach-the-spiritual-but-not-religious.html.
"What We Believe." Messianic Literature Outreach. http://www.messianicliterature.org/index.php?route=information/information&information_id=6.
Wuthnow, Robert. *America and the Challenges of Religious Diversity.* Princeton: Princeton University Press, 2005.
———. *The Struggle for America's Soul: Evangelicals, Liberals, and Secularism.* Grand Rapids: Eerdmans, 1989.
Zylstra, Sarah Eekhoff. "Pew: Evangelicals Stay Strong as Christianity Crumbles in America." *Christianity Today* (May 11, 2015). http://www.christianitytoday.com/gleanings/2015/may/pew-evangelicals-stay-strong-us-religious-landscape-study.html?paging=off.

www.ingramcontent.com/pod-product-compliance
Lightning Source LLC
Chambersburg PA
CBHW060609230426
43670CB00011B/2037